Disrupted Childhoods: Children of Women in Prison

The Rutgers Series in Childhood Studies

The Rutgers Series in Childhood Studies is dedicated to increasing our understanding of children and childhoods, past and present, throughout the world. Children's voices and experiences are central. Authors come from a variety of fields, including anthropology, criminal justice, history, literature, psychology, religion, and sociology. The books in this series are intended for students, scholars, practitioners, and those who formulate policies that affect children's everyday lives and futures.

Edited by Myra Bluebond-Langner, Distinguished Professor of Anthropology, Rutgers University and True Colours Chair in Palliative Care for Children and Young People, University College London, Institute of Child Health.

Advisory Board

Perri Klass, New York University

Jill Korbin, Case Western Reserve University

Bambi Schiefflin, New York University

Enid Schildkraut, American Museum of Natural History and Museum for
    African Art

Disrupted Childhoods: Children of Women in Prison

JANE A. SIEGEL

RUTGERS UNIVERSITY PRESS

NEW BRUNSWICK, NEW JERSEY, AND LONDON

LIBRARY OF CONGRESS CATALOGING-IN-PUBLICATION DATA

Siegel, Jane A., 1949–
    Disrupted childhoods : children of women in prison / Jane A. Siegel.
       p. cm. — (The Rutgers series in childhood studies)
    Includes bibliographical references and index.
    ISBN 978-0-8135-5010-7 (hbk. : alk. paper) — ISBN 978-0-8135-5011-4
(pbk. : alk. paper)
    1. Children of women prisoners—United States.   2. Prisoners' families—
United States.   I. Title.
    HV8886.U5S54   2011
    362.82′950973—dc22   2010035283

A British Cataloging-in-Publication record for this book is available
from the British Library.

Visit our Web site: http://rutgerspress.rutgers.edu

Manufactured in the United States of America

For George, with love and gratitude

CONTENTS

ACKNOWLEDGMENTS

A book like this is never the work of just one person, and so there are several people I would like to thank for their assistance. Most important, this book would not have been possible without the generous participation of the children and their mothers and guardians, who graciously allowed me into their homes and spoke openly about their experiences. Virtually all the adults who took part in the research documented in this book were motivated by their desire to help children whose parents are incarcerated, hoping that by sharing their stories, they would bring attention to the children's plight. I hope that this study will in some small measure contribute to that goal. I especially appreciate the children's and adolescents' willingness to share with me the complex feelings they have about their situations and to allow me into their homes and lives. I will be forever grateful to all who spoke with me and hope that I have adequately conveyed the difficulties that parental incarceration visits upon children. May all the families find ways to reconnect that are good for everyone in their families, and may the children's futures be bright.

The Rutgers University Research Council and the Center for Children and Childhood Studies provided financial support for the project, without which the research would not have been feasible. The Center's founder, Myra Bluebond-Langner, has been an invaluable mentor and friend from the very start of the project, suggesting that I utilize the methodology of ethnographic researchers to tackle this issue, providing advice as the research progressed, and accepting my manuscript for publication in the Childhood Studies Series she edits for Rutgers University Press. I am grateful as well to my editors at the press, Adi Hovav and Marlie Wasserman, and thank them for their patience and guidance as the book made its slow journey to completion. I also greatly appreciate Bobbe Needham's sensitive and first-rate editing of the manuscript. Thanks also to the anonymous reviewers, whose suggestions helped improve the book.

Doing research with children of incarcerated parents poses the challenge of identifying and reaching them. I would not have been able to do so without the assistance of the public defender's office and the prison authorities in the locations where the study was carried out. I am especially grateful to Ellen Greenlee and Charlotte Blackwell, who both care deeply about prisoners' families and supported the project from its earliest days, enlisting their respective staff members to assist me in recruiting mothers for the study. Maria Maldonado, Pat Mandracchia, and the many attorneys who worked with them were always cooperative, taking time from their very hectic schedules in court to introduce me to women who might be eligible to participate. Tom Innes cheerfully accepted my early morning calls nearly every day for several months to help me with recruitment of women in jail, and has subsequently become a wonderful supporter of my work, for which I am very appreciative. I also thank Officers Mims and Moran, who made me feel welcome during my frequent visits to the jail and helped the hours spent waiting around there pass much more pleasantly. Bill Hauck made it easy for me to recruit women at the prison and to conduct interviews.

Several undergraduate and graduate students helped me by transcribing hundreds of hours of taped conversations that were frequently very challenging to decipher. Sincere thanks to Brian Epifano, Daisy Magnus-Aryitey, Shakirah Morgan, Chanelle Ridgeway, Nicole Sanchez, Caitlin Sperraza, and Diana Walton, who spent many hours listening intently to try to catch every word the children and their mothers and guardians spoke, sometimes amidst giggles and tears and sometimes as mumbled phrases. Nicole Logan and Brenna Staley not only transcribed interviews but also helped out in numerous ways that I continue to appreciate even after their graduation. I am also very grateful to Diane Marano, Ines Meier, and Dana Simone, who provided first-rate assistance with additional research required to complete the book.

My friends and colleagues have provided unwavering support and encouragement throughout the long process of writing and revising this book. I am especially grateful to Michelle Meloy, Wanda Foglia, and Janet Golden for the time they spent reading drafts of the book and the extremely helpful comments they provided. Thanks to Julie Cohen for helping me figure out how to find the time to write, and to Linda Williams, Vicki Banyard, and Veronica Herrera for trying to help me stay on track through our writing group. A very special thanks to Helen Pettengill, Sandy Rosenberg, Sinclair Brown, and Sophia Demas, my dear friends and long-time Scrabble group, who provided sympathetic listening, good times, and lots of laughter over the years I worked on this book.

The members of my family have been incredibly supportive of my work, and I thank them for their patience and understanding. Talking with children who encounter so many challenges in their lives deepened my appreciation for the loving and secure environment that my mother and father provided me during my childhood. I regret that my father is not alive to accept my appreciation, but as it is, my mother alone will have to accept my gratitude for all that they gave me. I am especially grateful as well to my sister, who has always stood by my side, and to her family. My stepsons and daughters-in-law have been a consistent source of encouragement and have tolerated without complaint the demands of my work, and their children have been a never-ending source of delight. Finally, my most heartfelt thanks go to my husband, George Manos, who has accepted all manner of disruption to our life with his characteristic good-naturedness. Among the many ways he contributed to this project, I particularly appreciate his very helpful comments on drafts of the book, which provided a much needed perspective from outside the field of criminology. His love, unwavering support, and belief in this work truly have been my mainstay throughout this process.

INTRODUCTION

Journeying into the Worlds of Prisoners' Children

"Although you're far, you're always near.
You'll always be my mommy dear.
For what you did will never change.
There is no reason to be ashamed.
The love for you is in my heart
although we're very far apart.
My love for you is very clear.
I'll see you soon my mommy dear."

Valencia was eleven years old when she wrote this poem to her mother, who was locked in a prison some three hundred miles away. After her mother was incarcerated, Valencia and her older sister went to live with her grandparents in a public housing project in another state. There they joined their teenaged brother, who had been raised by their grandparents and had never lived with Valencia and her mother. Valencia's new family also included her grandparents' infant great-grandson, who had been living with them since his birth. Her grandparents, living on a fixed income supplemented by food stamps, struggled to make ends meet, especially with Valencia, her sister, and the baby now in the household.

Valencia yearned to see her mother, but a six-hundred-mile roundtrip that would require a hotel stay was simply out of the question for the family. They could not afford the risk that their old, less than reliable car would survive the trip. If it broke down, they would not be able to repair it and they certainly could not afford to buy another one. And so Valencia and her mother remained exiled from each other. Three years would pass before Valencia would see her mother again, and many other poems would flow from her pen during those years, all expressing her longing to be with her mother.

Maintaining her connection with her mother while separated by hundreds of miles was just one of the issues Valencia would face during her mother's incarceration. The lines "For what you did will never change/There is no reason to be ashamed" suggest others. Valencia had to grapple with the fact that her mother "did" something that resulted in her imprisonment, meaning something that was at a minimum impermissible in the law's eyes. She also recognized that her mother's crime was irreversible and that there was no way to change what had happened. Valencia's admonition that there was no reason to feel ashamed reflects recognition that others would view her mother's actions and her incarceration as stigmatizing experiences. Valencia, however, chose to continue seeing her mother through a lens imbued with love and pride, rejecting the stigma that might otherwise have clung to her. In addition to dealing with those challenges, Valencia also had to adapt to a new household and cope with the constraints imposed when families are poor. What's more, she had to navigate this rough terrain without the support and assistance that her mother would have been able to provide during a time of turmoil had she been there. Managing all this upheaval and the difficult emotional aspects of her mother's incarceration was a tall order for an eleven-year-old. The unwavering devotion to her mother and belief in the enduring nature of their relationship that her poem reflects shone through the darkest days and helped sustain Valencia as she found ways to adjust to her circumstances.

Valencia is one of a group of children whose mothers were involved in the criminal justice system whom I interviewed in an effort to understand what parental incarceration meant to children's lives. I tell many of their stories in the pages that follow. They are emblematic, in several respects, of the situation many prisoners' children face: a parent's incarceration is a disruption to a child's world that can bring separation from all that was familiar, including friends, school, and community. It can also bring the challenges of integration into a new household, financial strain, and sorrow. Valencia and others you meet in this book are just a few of the growing number of children in the United States who have experienced parental incarceration. They represent the collateral consequences of the nation's historic experiment in mass incarceration that has touched the lives of millions of adults and their children. Although we do not know exactly how many children are affected by their parent's incarceration, we do have some estimates of the numbers and can identify the underlying reasons why this population has grown so much in recent years and is likely to remain a public issue for years to come.

Children of Incarcerated Parents, by the Numbers

In his classic work *The Sociological Imagination*, C. Wright Mills (1959) wrote that the analysis of social problems should recognize the importance of the intersection of personal biography with history, or the larger social forces at work during a given time. As Mills explained, personal troubles like those experienced by families affected by incarceration are inextricably tied to public issues, such as a society's punishment policies. Understanding the forces that brought us a moment in time in which we in the United States incarcerate so many people is important if we are to fully appreciate how this phenomenon engenders personal troubles for most of the individuals affected by incarceration.

The United States now has the highest incarceration rate in the world (Walmsley 2009). How did we attain this dubious distinction? Starting in the early 1980s, as crime rates increased and conservative politics came to the fore, demands to get tough on crime led to major changes in the nation's sentencing and correctional policies. Legislatures imposed mandatory prison sentences for certain crimes, such as drug- and gun-related offenses, and adopted sentencing guidelines to restrain judicial discretion. Where offenders in the past might have been sentenced to probation, the new laws required that they serve time in prison. Penalties for drug offenses became harsher as President Ronald Reagan declared a "war on drugs." Taken together, these measures resulted in larger numbers of convicted offenders being sentenced to prison. Other changes in criminal justice policy instituted during the same period ensured that people already in prison would remain there longer than had been the case in the past. Most states adopted stringent "truth in sentencing" laws requiring that people sentenced to prison for violent offenses serve on average at least 85 percent of their sentence in prison before becoming eligible for release. Many states eliminated parole, which meant that prisoners could no longer be granted discretionary early release from prison based on a parole board's assessment of the prisoner's readiness to return to the community. Those jurisdictions that did retain parole adopted less tolerant policies about how to deal with parolees who broke the rules governing their release, resulting in increasing numbers of parolees being returned to prison for violations of their parole conditions.

The result of these policy changes over the last three decades has been the largest increase in the nation's prison population since the start of the last century, affecting the lives of millions. From 1980 to 2008, the number of people serving long-term sentences in federal and state prison quintupled, while the number of inmates in local jails more than quadrupled, as can be seen in the accompanying graph showing the growth of the number of people incarcerated in the United States (see fig. I.1). By 2009, nearly 2.3 million people were imprisoned in the nation's jails and prisons, a figure far above that of any other country in the world.

Prisoners are disproportionately young compared to the general population, with half of adult prisoners under the age of 35, so it is not surprising that a majority of them are parents to minor children. However, no one has ever counted the number of children with a parent in prison, so we must rely on estimates if we wish to know how many there are. Based on the 2004 Survey of

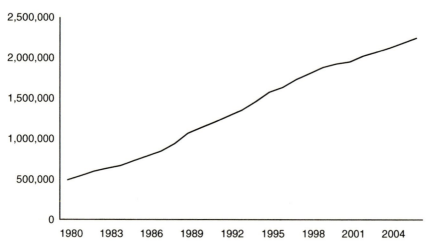

FIGURE I.I Number of prison and jail inmates, United States, 1980–2006

Inmates in State and Federal Correctional Facilities, the U.S. Department of Justice estimated that 1.7 million children under the age of 18 had a parent in prison in 2007, an increase of 761,000 children since 1991 (Glaze and Maruschak 2008). The California-based Center for Children of Incarcerated Parents maintains that an even greater number of children have an incarcerated parent, estimating that the parents of nearly 2.8 million children were in prison or jail in 2005 (Center for Children of Incarcerated Parents 2006), which would mean that they represented 3.8 percent of the nation's population of minor children at that time.

Some groups of children are more likely than others to be touched by parental incarceration. For instance, due to the overrepresentation of minorities in the prison population, 6.7 percent of African American children have a parent who is incarcerated, a rate that is seven and a half times greater than that for white children, and Hispanic children experience parental incarceration at nearly three times the rate that white children do (Glaze and Maruschak 2008).[1] Although women make up only a small segment of the prison population, children whose mothers are in prison, compared to children whose fathers are incarcerated, are likely to feel their absence more acutely and experience more disruption: while 64.2 percent of mothers in prison report they were living with their children before they went to prison, only 46.5 percent of incarcerated fathers did so.[2] Furthermore, men are far more likely to be able to rely on their children's mothers to care for the children during their incarceration than women can on the children's fathers: 88 percent of fathers in prison report that their children are being cared for by their child's mother, while only 37 percent of inmate mothers say their child is being cared for by the child's father. Instead, like Valencia, most children of women in prison are cared for by grandparents, other relatives, or friends. Foster care placement is relatively infrequent for children, but the rate at which children of incarcerated women are placed in foster homes is nearly five times greater than the rate for children whose fathers are in prison (10.9 percent vs. 2.2 percent) (Glaze and Maruschak 2008). In short, when Mom goes to prison, the potential for disruption to a child's family structure and living situation is greater than when Dad is incarcerated (Davies et al. 2008), and there is even evidence of long-term consequences: mothers who are incarcerated are two and a half times more likely than fathers in prison to report that their adult children have also been imprisoned (Dallaire 2007).

Clearly, the nation's imprisonment binge of the last three decades shows how history impinges on individuals' biographies. In this instance, public policy has had the perhaps unforeseen consequence of creating a sizeable population of children left behind when their parents are imprisoned. Any negative effects associated with parental incarceration thus are liable to affect numerous children, especially when we consider that the figures just cited represent only children whose parents are in prison at a given moment in time. Millions more have had a parent in prison at some point in their lives, and little is known about how enduring any negative consequences are once their parents leave prison, or what happens to children after their parents return home.[3] If children whose parents are or have been incarcerated are adversely affected by the experience, then policy makers must consider whether the perceived benefits of mass incarceration outweigh all the costs, both direct and indirect, associated with it.

Consequences of Parental Incarceration

As Valencia's story demonstrates, children face many challenges when a parent is imprisoned. Reflecting for even a short while on the issues that might arise for such a child illuminates the potential magnitude of the consequences of parental incarceration. The separation alone can result in deleterious consequences for a child, just as separation for other reasons might. Unlike children who live apart from their parents due to causes such as divorce, military service, or illness, however, children whose parents are in prison must cope with the additional element of stigma associated with imprisonment. They may even feel the need to keep the parent's imprisonment secret throughout the duration of the parent's time in prison, which may impede the child's ability to adjust to the parent's absence.[4] While all members of prisoners' families must find the means to survive the separation, the situation has an added dimension for their children because their fate will now be determined by other adults. With whom will the children live? Who will care for them? Will they be separated from their siblings? Put in foster care? Forced to leave their neighborhoods, friends, and schools behind? How will they maintain contact with their parent in prison? How do they fare while separated from their parent? The answers to these questions surely have the potential to alter the course of a child's life not just materially but also psychologically and emotionally.

Findings from research about prisoners' children conducted both in the United States and abroad are not encouraging.[5] Generally, researchers report that children are adversely affected by parental incarceration in a number of ways. An early wave of research found that parents or caregivers reported that children exhibited a number of emotional reactions to parental incarceration, such as sadness, withdrawal, fearfulness, difficulty relating to both peers and adults, and feelings of anger and shame. More recent research assessing children themselves has found evidence that those who have experienced parental incarceration are at greater risk of depression and of attention deficit hyperactivity disorder (ADHD) and conduct disorders than are their peers, even after taking into account other factors that might explain these differences. Many parents and guardians also report having observed behavioral changes in children that they attribute to the effect of parental incarceration, including "disturbed behavior" (Shaw 1987, 41), behavioral regression, difficulty in relationships with peers and adults, overactivity, developmental delays, disobedience and disruptiveness, and other unspecified behavioral problems. Reports of academic difficulties are common, including declines in school grades or performance, behavioral problems, suspensions, and school dropout, although some evidence indicates that prisoners' children performed poorly in school even before their parent went to jail (Stanton 1980).[6]

Perhaps the biggest concern about the effects of parental incarceration is that children will follow in their parent's footsteps by engaging in aggressive or antisocial behavior that ultimately could lead to their own imprisonment. The idea that prisoners' children are at risk of what has been termed "intergenerational incarceration" fits with many people's beliefs about the children, even if evidence is lacking. Those familiar with the research on children of incarcerated parents refer with dismay to the "six times more likely" phenomenon, because in recent years newspaper articles, Web sites, and even the U.S. Congress—in legislation authorizing funds for mentoring programs for prisoners' children—have claimed that prisoners' children are four, five, or even six times more likely than are other children to be imprisoned. However, attempts to locate the original source for such claims and exhaustive searches of the research literature predating these assertions have found no studies that have established whether such elevated risk exists and, if so, exactly how great it is. The "six times more likely" figure seems to have become a popular myth, although its origins remain unclear. Its staying power probably arises from its conformity to stereotypes about prisoners' children.

While the risk that prisoners' children will follow in their parent's footsteps may be overstated, we can still point to the reasons why people worry about such an outcome. For instance, many—but decidedly not most—prisoners are themselves children of an incarcerated parent (American Correctional Association 1990; James 2004; Poehlmann 2005b). Furthermore, the notion that children of criminals—as distinct from prisoners—might themselves become criminals, whether through heredity, learned behavior, or some other mechanism, has been of interest since criminologists first began systematic investigations of the causes of crime. Over time, a considerable amount of evidence has shown that parental criminality does indeed increase the likelihood of deviance in their children, making it difficult to disentangle the effect of a parent's incarceration from that of the parent's criminal behavior.[7]

Evidence that prisoners' children are at increased risk of antisocial and criminal behavior is accumulating, although it is not strong enough to conclude that parental incarceration itself is the cause of such behavior (Murray et al. 2009). There is ample evidence that the adults involved in prisoners' children's lives have noticed children engaging in more antisocial behavior during a parent's imprisonment. Parents—both in prison and out—as well as caregivers and teachers of prisoners' children report that the children engage in more fights and become aggressive during their parent's absence.[8] Research also shows that children of prisoners are at higher risk of arrest and conviction than are their peers, although only a minority of these children have in fact been arrested.[9] Furthermore, at least some of the risk prisoners' children face apparently can be explained by other aspects of the children's lives that are known risk factors for delinquency (Hanlon et al. 2005; Murray and Farrington 2005).

Despite the reports of negative outcomes revealed by research, some of the most recent studies of prisoners' children show that not all children are affected equally by parental incarceration: researchers have identified subgroups of children who differ significantly in some of these areas from children whose parents are not in prison. These subgroups include children who were exposed to many negative elements in their family environment before their parent went to prison. There is growing recognition of the need to address the issues confronting children of incarcerated parents before a parent is imprisoned (e.g., Johnston 2006). Some evidence also indicates that psychological, cognitive, and behavioral problems among the children while their parent is in prison are related to the environment where the children live during that time, because they encounter unfavorable conditions there as well. Nevertheless, whether attributable to the direct effect of the parent's absence, the family environment before the parent's imprisonment, or the child's circumstances during incarceration, the research makes clear that the millions of children whose parents are or have been incarcerated are at risk of adverse outcomes.

While the research on parental incarceration has provided much needed data about prisoners' children, gaps in two significant areas remain. First, the absence of children's voices from nearly all the research is striking. Although some research has utilized data obtained from children, few have featured the words of the children themselves.[10] As a result, what we think we know about children whose parents are incarcerated has been largely filtered through their parents or other adults involved in their lives. While adult reports are certainly an important source of information about children, a significant body of research across diverse fields has shown that children's accounts can bring fresh perspective and insight to an array of subjects. Second, parental incarceration generally has been viewed as a discrete event, decontextualized from the rest of a child's life. The growing evidence showing that the children of incarcerated parents most at risk of the problems reported to be so prevalent were also exposed to a variety of other risk factors before their parent's incarceration and that their home environments during parental incarceration also exert an important influence on them (Hagen, Myers, and Mackintosh 2005; Hanlon et al. 2005) underscores the need to examine parental incarceration through a broader lens.

Doing Research with Children of Incarcerated Parents

The research to date has painted a bleak and troubling picture of how prisoners' children fare, and the sheer number of children facing such poor prospects underscores the magnitude of this social problem. Nevertheless, the absence of children's perspectives on parental incarceration and of additional information about their lives that would provide a context for understanding the meaning of a parent's imprisonment left me wanting to know more about the worlds of prisoners' children. I decided, therefore, to embark on an investigation that would provide a window into children's lives before a parent is incarcerated as well as during the incarceration. To do so, I decided to talk to children and their families not only during the parent's incarceration but also before it occurred in order to put that event in context with the rest of the children's lives. In undertaking this research, I also sought to understand how children were functioning before their mother was incarcerated, how the process affected them, and how they fared after their mother was incarcerated. In addition, I hoped to learn how children with parents sentenced to probation fared compared to those with parents sentenced to prison. A final objective of the study was to give voice to the children by capturing their own words. I chose to focus on female offenders' children because of the evidence that children whose mothers are in prison can be expected to be directly affected by the incarceration.[11] Furthermore, there is reason (which I discuss in detail in the next section) to believe that children of female offenders may face elevated risk while their mothers are at home.

Over the course of more than three years, I interviewed a total of 159 children, mothers, and guardians, utilizing semi-structured interviews. I interviewed some of the children not long after their mothers were arrested, while others had been separated from them for years due to their mothers' incarceration. I invited children to speak freely, offering their own words and thoughts about their experiences, by asking open-ended questions about their family life, friends, school, activities, and interests as well as their understanding of and reaction to their parent's situation. The conversations I had with these children and their families, along with my observations of their homes, yielded a more nuanced picture of the role of parental incarceration in children's lives than has previous research and provided an opportunity for the children to tell their own stories.

To find out about life before incarceration and compare children whose mothers were on probation with those who were in prison, I needed to recruit children for participation before their mother's sentencing and ask them to agree to be interviewed both before and after the sentencing. That approach yielded information about children's responses to incarceration in the short term, but to learn about how they fared over a longer term during their mother's incarceration required recruiting children whose mothers had been in prison for some period of time. Therefore, two samples of children and their mothers participated in the research: one in which the mothers had been arrested but not yet sentenced when I first interviewed the children, and one in which the mothers had been incarcerated for at least a year. In both cases, children were identified through their mothers. For the first sample of children, I recruited women in an urban court at their arraignment or in the city's jail, where they were being held before trial. I recruited the second sample at a state prison. To protect the confidentiality of participants, I refer to the first sample as the city sample and the second as the state sample throughout this book. Both the city and the state are in the northeastern United States. I have changed all names to further protect the confidentiality of the individuals who participated in the research. In a few instances, I have altered particulars of individual histories where it seemed that they might make identification of the individuals possible because of unique aspects of the case (e.g., a crime that received attention in the media, unique words appearing on a tattoo).

A detailed explanation of the procedures used to recruit and interview the children and their families appears in Appendix A; what follows is a brief description of the people who participated. Between November 2001 and January 2005, I interviewed 67 children (33 males, 34 females), 74 mothers, and 18 guardians.[12] Among the children, 35 had mothers who were awaiting trial and were not in jail, while 15 had mothers who were being held in jail between their arrest and the outcome of their case. The remaining 17 children had mothers who had been in prison at least one year. I interviewed children and mothers in the city sample prior to the mother's trial date, and reinterviewed a sample of those children after the mother's sentencing. I conducted only one interview with participants in the state sample. On average, the children were about twelve years old, although they ranged in age from eight to eighteen, as intended. Like their mothers, the children were predominantly African American (73.1 percent). The rest were white (25.4 percent) or biracial (1.5 percent), reflecting the racial composition of the criminal justice populations from which I recruited the mothers. Most children were in elementary or middle school; among the twelve youths who were at least fifteen years old, however, nearly half (42 percent) had stopped attending school.

The average age of the mothers was 34.1 years old. Thirty-five were awaiting trial and were not in jail at the time of the initial interview, twenty-two were in pretrial detention in jail, and seventeen were in state prison.[13] Of the guardians I interviewed, twelve were caring for children whose mothers were in state prison, five were caring for children whose mothers were in pretrial detention, and one was a woman with whom a child actually lived, although her mother was not in either jail or prison. The mothers generally had fairly extensive criminal histories, having been arrested an average of 7.3 times and imprisoned 1.4 times. Their current charges were most often for drug offenses or assaults. (Appendix B contains more detailed information on the demographic characteristics of the children and their mothers.)

Theoretical Approach to Studying Prisoners' Children

My decision to adopt a research strategy that placed incarceration in context with the rest of a child's life is consistent with the life-course perspective, a theoretical approach to the examination of various social and individual conditions that is utilized in sociology, psychology, and criminology (Elder 1998; Heinz and Marshall 2003; Sampson and Laub 1993). The life-course perspective enables us to examine a particular phenomenon, like incarceration, not just as a snapshot of a particular moment in a person's life, but rather as one of many photos mounted in an album featuring the other events of a person's life. According to the life-course perspective, individual lives follow certain trajectories, heading toward particular outcomes. Certain key events, known as turning points, may intervene and deflect a person from the pathway toward which he or she seemed to be headed. Using this wide-angled lens enables us to place specific events in context with the rest of an individual's life experiences, thereby providing a way to understand the meaning of particular events for a person and allowing us to discriminate between a turning point and a way station on a pathway. The life-course perspective also stresses the notion of linked lives, a concept important to examining a phenomenon like parental incarceration, where children's lives are tied to their parent's life (Elder 1994).

In adopting this method to learn about children's lives, I was mindful of the different levels of environmental influences that affect children. Individual characteristics that shape a child's developmental trajectory are embedded in a family context that likewise influences the way a child develops. The family in turn is situated in a community formed by social forces and the interactions among them, as C. Wright Mills (1959) has explained. Such external forces also affect the family's life and the individuals within the family. These levels of influence surround a child like concentric circles of influence corresponding to what psychologist Urie Bronfenbrenner (1979) in his ecological systems theory dubbed the microsystems, mesosystems, exosystems, and macrosystems. For instance, imagine observing Valencia's behavior during her mother's incarceration and finding that she was doing poorly in school. We might conclude that her below average academic performance is attributable to her mother's incarceration. Doing so, however, would mean ignoring all the other events that occurred in her family, at school, and in her community before her mother went to prison. After all, Valencia was living with a mother who must have done something that resulted in her arrest and imprisonment. How did her mother's behavior affect Valencia? What was Valencia's life like up to the moment of her mother's arrest? Why wasn't her father taking care of her while her mother was in prison? Who were her friends? What was her neighborhood like? Her school? How did her neighborhood and the children in it affect the learning environment in school? Viewing parental incarceration in isolation from these other influential forces may lead us to a false conclusion about its relative impact. That is not to minimize the significance of the loss to a child when a parent goes to prison. However, we must also pay attention to the other aspects of children's lives that shape their trajectories if we are to properly understand parental incarceration's impact on children (Graue and Walsh 1998).

The Worlds of Prisoners' Children

Although researchers (e.g., Murray and Farrington 2005; Poehlmann 2005a; Wilbur et al. 2007) have begun to consider other facets of prisoners' children's lives that might account for problems they may have, very little is written that illuminates the worlds of these children. We know almost nothing about the children prior to their parent's incarceration that would enable us to gauge whether behavior observed after a parent's imprisonment represents a marked change in them or simply a continuation or worsening of a child's behavior or emotional state when the parent was still home. Putting a parent's incarceration in context with the rest of the child's life and identifying other issues that would put children at risk of poor outcomes will help us understand whether parental incarceration represents an abrupt and uniquely different type of experience for the children or whether it is yet another potentially harmful event with which children must cope.

Living with a Parent in Trouble with the Law

If we are to put a parent's incarceration in context with the rest of the child's life, we need to know what that life looks like. Children's lives are shaped by a multitude of factors, such as the nature of their family's relationships; their economic situation; their parent's emphasis on education, religion, civic engagement, or culture and the arts; their neighborhood and schools; and their friends. As this list indicates, parents are a key determinant of the nature of the forces that help mold a child, because children's lives are inextricably interwoven with those of their parents. Since we have scant information about prisoners' children's lives prior to their parent's incarceration, we can look to the pre-incarceration background of prisoners to infer what some aspects of their lives might be like.

When we examine the personal histories of incarcerated women, several characteristics are particularly striking. In the prison population, as in society at large, women's economic circumstances before imprisonment are worse than men's, with most reporting income levels that put their families below the poverty line.[14] A history of drug and alcohol use and abuse is common among incarcerated women, and a significant proportion of women prisoners are incarcerated for drug or drug-related offenses.[15] In fact, the war on drugs has sometimes been referred to as a war on women. Women in prison also are more likely to report that they have been victims of violence than are women in the general population and have victimization rates that are far higher than those for male prisoners (McClellan, Farabee, and Crouch 1997).[16] They also report high rates of mental illness or of mental health problems.[17] Many of these problems occur together. For instance, most prisoners who have mental health problems also reportedly abuse or are dependent on drugs, alcohol, or both, and many have experienced physical or sexual abuse (James and Glaze 2006). Of course, not all people who go to prison fit the profile of a typical prisoner, but the odds that they possess some of these characteristics are greater than they would be for a member of the general population. Their children, in turn, are more likely than are other youth to be exposed to these circumstances. Certainly, most of the children I met in the course of my research came from low-income families and had mothers with histories of abusing drugs or alcohol. Several mothers also suffered from depression and other mental health problems and were involved in abusive relationships.

Why do parental attributes like these matter to prisoners' children? The answer is simple. Each of these phenomena can put children in jeopardy of negative outcomes because they are associated with undesirable behaviors (e.g., delinquency, drug use) and psychological conditions (e.g., depression) as well as academic difficulties. In fact, the increased likelihood of such outcomes is so notable that we commonly refer to these conditions as risk factors. Most children I met during the course of my research came from families where one or more of these risk factors were present. To understand why exposure to these conditions is so troubling, we need look to only a couple of them: poverty and substance abuse.

Poverty jeopardizes children in several ways (for reviews, see Bradley and Corwyn 2002; Brooks-Gunn and Duncan 1997). Poor children do not fare as well as other children in domains such as health, cognitive ability, and academic achievement and are more likely to have emotional or behavioral problems, although evidence suggests that the most serious consequences of poverty for children are manifested in poor health and academic achievement (Duncan and Brooks-Gunn 1997; Duncan et al. 1998).[18] Simply coping with the everyday challenges of survival when money is scarce can create stressful environments for families living in poverty (for reviews, see Bradley and Corwyn 2002; Seccombe 2000), which in turn can produce harmful effects on children.[19] Poor people often live in neighborhoods of concentrated poverty, and these communities have high rates of both crime (Pratt and Cullen 2005) and reports of child maltreatment (Coulton et al. 2007). Children who live in these areas therefore are at increased risk of victimization both within and outside their homes and of witnessing violence in the community.

Nearly all the families who participated in my research were low income. For instance, a majority (74 percent) of the thirty-seven women who were not incarcerated when they were interviewed at home were receiving state aid of some kind (Temporary Assistance for Needy Families, food stamps). Most mothers who were at home awaiting trial were not employed, and few had any history of stable, long-term employment. In fact, several had never worked at all at any legal occupation, instead supporting themselves through prostitution, shoplifting, or drug sales. Their lack of employment experience is probably tied to their educational background, which trapped them in low-wage jobs when they were working at all.[20] In fact, six in ten of the mothers I interviewed had not completed high school. The mothers' lack of education not only locked them and their children into poverty but also had the potential to affect their children's development directly. Parents with less education have less knowledge about child development and appropriate parenting practices and may be more at risk of maltreating their children (Duncan and Brooks-Gunn 1997; W. E. Hawkins and Duncan 1985). Women with low educational achievement also have higher rates of births out of wedlock and of pregnancies at younger ages than better educated women have (Rank 2001), which can result in a family environment in which the parent is not well prepared to care for her child and the stresses of single parenthood can adversely affect the home environment. To the extent that prisoners' children disproportionately have poorly educated parents or parents who had children when they were teenagers, the quality of their home environment may be less than optimal for their development.[21] Teen mother-hood was even more common than high school dropout among the women I interviewed: 71 percent had their first child before they turned 20. Furthermore, the women who had been teen moms were even more likely to have dropped out of school, so their children faced a double threat. Some of the mothers spoke retrospectively of the difficulties they encountered as a result of having children while they were still so young. Beverly, who had her first of seven chil-dren when she was fifteen, said: "I didn't even know what was going on. I was scared. . . . I had a baby to take care of but I didn't even know how. . . . I caught myself with my older daughter, like, regretting I had her."

Living with parents who abuse drugs or alcohol is associated with problem-atic outcomes similar to those related to poverty. An extensive body of research about children of such parents shows that they are vulnerable to several behav-ioral, psychological, and cognitive difficulties in life.[22] In addition, the family environments of many substance abusers are characterized by negative condi-tions, including inadequate supervision of children, increased levels of vio-lence, emotional and psychological neglect, and parent-child relationships lacking warmth, all of which are known risk factors for a variety of adverse outcomes for children.[23] Furthermore, unique features of some drug addicts' lifestyles may contribute to home environments detrimental to children. Drug-addicted parents may expose their children to drug use and possibly to drug dealing, and may be so consumed by their need for drugs that they neglect their parental responsibilities.[24]

Many of the children I met during my research had lived with mothers who did indeed put their own need for drugs before other responsibilities. Tremelle, for instance, was an eleven-year-old whose mother, Denisha, abused both drugs and alcohol. Her problem was so severe that she was unable to care for her children, who therefore lived with their grandmother. As Denisha told me: "My addiction told me I didn't have time for my kids, they were in the way. . . . When my kids would ask me something normal like to take them to the play-ground, that was, like, so abnormal to me. But if you asked me to go to the bar, or to the drug dealer, I was fine. My life was chaos." One of the saddest illustra-tions of Denisha's all-consuming need occurred one Christmas Day. Tremelle, her brother, and their grandmother went off to church for Christmas services. When they returned, they discovered that Denisha, evidently in a frenzy for drug money, had come into the house and stolen all the children's Christmas presents from under the tree. Children's toys, apparently, bring good money in the underground economy where stolen goods are sold, especially at Christmastime. Anyone who has experienced the almost unbearable but delicious anticipation of opening gifts on Christmas can surely imagine how crushing it would have been for Tremelle and her brother to find that their presents had vanished. Knowing that their mother's addiction had brought her so low made their disappointment even greater.

Children who live in families where they are exposed to violence or have a parent with mental health problems face risks similar to those confronting poor children or those whose parents abuse drugs or alcohol.[25] Add to the mix other problems like parents involved in crime, and the cause for concern becomes clear, because these are the realities with which many prisoners' children live before their parents go to prison. All too often, unfortunately, several of these factors occur together, exposing children to multiple risks, as was the case for Beverly's children, for example. Overwhelmed as a teenage mother, Beverly dropped out of school after tenth grade. She had begun drinking when she was fourteen and a few years later became hooked on crack cocaine, although she had succeeded in leaving that habit behind a few years before we met. Her life had been difficult, characterized by involvement not just with drugs and alcohol but also with a series of abusive partners. Her latest relationship had left her terrified, but she also was depressed and anxious, crying frequently, drinking from early in the morning, and taking antianxiety medication. Because of the chaos in her life, she had never been able to take care of her children, so they lived with other relatives or with foster families. Beverly saw them mostly on weekends. As was true for Denisha's children, Beverly's children's lives had been disrupted long before their mother was imprisoned.

Given the number of risk factors potentially present in a prisoner's world, if ever a group of children could be considered at risk, it surely is this group. Of course, being vulnerable to increased risk does not mean that children are destined to negative outcomes. Children can be remarkably resilient, and many will succeed despite the odds against them. Nevertheless, there are strong theoretical reasons for concern. Families coping with only one or two of these problems can experience strain, affecting the quality of the entire family environment and the nature of the parent-child relationship, all of which can adversely affect children. Seen in this context, parental incarceration can be understood as another point on a trajectory that has already been mined with potential risks for the child. In other words, parental incarceration affects children who are likely to be most vulnerable to its ill effects, because they have already had to cope with so many adverse circumstances.

Parental Incarceration in the Mix

Although not all prisoners' children come from such high-risk environments, the life of a typical female prisoner is liable to bring with it numerous circumstances that may jeopardize her children even before she goes to prison. A child thus is subject to influences from within and outside his or her family both before and during the time a parent is in prison (see fig. I.2). In figure I.2, factors

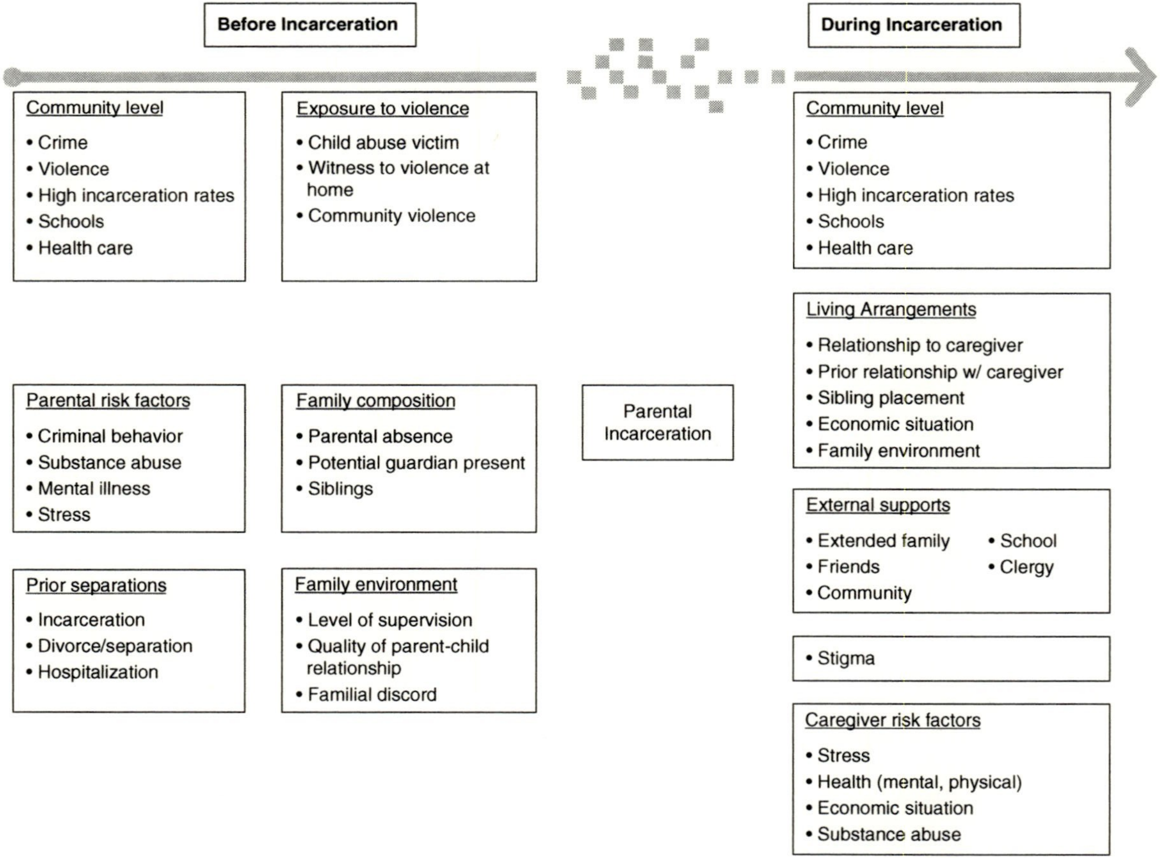

Before Incarceration
During Incarceration
Community level
• Crime
• Violence
• High incarceration rates
• Schools
• Health care
Exposure to violence
• Child abuse victim
• Witness to violence at home
• Community violence
Parental risk factors
• Criminal behavior
• Substance abuse
• Mental illness
• Stress
Family composition
• Parental absence
• Potential guardian present
• Siblings
Prior separations
• Incarceration
• Divorce/separation
• Hospitalization
Family environment
• Level of supervision
• Quality of parent-child relationship
• Familial discord
Parental Incarceration
Community level
• Crime
• Violence
• High incarceration rates
• Schools
• Health care
Living Arrangements
• Relationship to caregiver
• Prior relationship w/ caregiver
• Sibling placement
• Economic situation
• Family environment
External supports
• Extended family
• Friends
• Community
• School
• Clergy
• Stigma
Caregiver risk factors
• Stress
• Health (mental, physical)
• Economic situation
• Substance abuse

FIGURE 1.2 Risk and protective factors before and during parental incarceration

on the left are influences that can affect a child before a parent's incarceration, based on what is known about prisoners in addition to circumstances any child might encounter, like separation from a parent for reasons other than imprisonment. These influences include the parent's behavior as well as the family's composition and the environment within the family, such as the level of supervision the family provides and the quality of the parent-child relationship. Due to the parent's low income, the child has a higher likelihood than others of residing in communities characterized by high crime rates, exposure to violence, inadequate schools, and other adverse conditions associated with poor neighborhoods. The co-occurrence of several of these preincarceration factors in a child's life could cumulatively put that child at risk of poor outcomes. As one group of researchers has pointed out, children of incarcerated mothers "also live with poverty, violence exposure, drug use in the home, and an unstable home environment. These stressful life events accumulate over time and, especially when chronic, can create negative effects that are disproportionate in nature" (Hagen et al. 2005, 212).

Parental incarceration may disrupt the child's environment, as suggested by the broken arrow at the top of figure I.2, but other elements of the child's preincarceration universe, such as divorce, parental substance abuse, or parental absence (e.g., an absent father), also have the potential to disrupt the child's life. Most of the children I met in the course of my research had at least one parent who had substance-abuse problems and were living without their fathers. Denisha's and Beverly's children aptly illustrate the instability and disruption that can accompany these hazards.

Children whose parents are in trouble with the law are not uniformly at risk; for instance, before their mother's incarceration, they may find themselves in situations that have a positive influence on them. Consider children like Tremelle, whose mothers are unable to provide adequate care for them. As a consequence of having a mother who is overwhelmed by her addiction, these children may be cared for by another adult who can counterbalance the potential perils that would otherwise present themselves. Tremelle's grandmother provided her with a more stable household with more supervision and involvement than Denisha, so subjugated to drugs, could have managed at that time.

What occurs in children's lives while the parent serves time—shown on the right side of figure I.2—also influences the children's development, as well as how they respond to and cope with their parent's imprisonment. Just as before their parent's incarceration, children encounter community and family circumstances that can represent either risk or protective factors. Some children's living situations might actually improve during the parent's absence, and they may benefit from increased stability and supervision. Conversely, some guardians may be so stressed from the added responsibility of caring for the children that the home environment becomes an unwelcome one. The amount of emotional support children receive from individuals within and outside their family affects how they adapt to their new situation and handle the stigma associated with parental incarceration.

A major consideration in how children fare during a parent's imprisonment is their relationship with the parent both before and during the incarceration. Like Tremelle, some children will have experienced periods of separation from the parent, perhaps because the parent is running the streets, or because of earlier incarceration, or because—as is the case especially with fathers— the parent is absent from the family and has little relationship with the child. Such a parent's incarceration is likely far less consequential to the children than would be the case if they had spent their entire life with the parent, as Valencia had before her mother was incarcerated. Similarly, the child's prior relationship with the person caring for him or her can make a difference in a child's adjustment to the loss of the parent. Some children will be cared for by someone—most often a grandmother—with whom the child already has a strong relationship or who was already caring for the child before the parent's absence. Children in that situation will have an easier task of adjustment than children who are placed in foster care or with a relative with whom the child had little prior relationship.

An additional important determinant of children's adaptation to a separation from their parent is the quality of the relationship they can maintain with the parent during the time they are apart. The difficulty of keeping in contact with an absent parent may not be unique to prisoners' children, but it does pose challenges that other situations do not. Children are locked out of prisons as surely as their parents are locked in. They cannot simply pick up the phone to call Mom or Dad just to say hello, share some news, or seek advice, because prisoners cannot receive phone calls. Instant messaging, text messages, e-mails— none of these are options for communication between a child and a parent in prison. Visitation is strictly controlled by the prison, and children are dependent on adults willing to take them to visit, which can mean that children rarely see their parent. As many as half to three-quarters of parents in prison report that their children have never visited them (Bloom and Steinhart 1993; A. Smith et al. 2004). Some evidence also shows that children are more likely to visit their fathers in prison than their mothers, because the mothers caring for the children while the father is incarcerated make an effort to bring them to the prison. Most children whose mothers are in prison are being cared for by a relative other than their father, and sometimes that relative believes the incarcerated woman is a bad mother and will not make an effort to bring the child to visit (Koban 1983).

A child's age and sex are also likely to be important in determining how he or she adapts to the separation and is influenced in the longer term. A ten-year-old child who has lived with his mother his entire life will experience her incarceration differently than will his six-month-old sister.[26] The reunification that may occur after a parent's release can be especially challenging for children who have spent years with another parental figure, growing as attached to that person as they would have to their parent, particularly if the children and parents have had little contact during the incarceration. As with a child's age, the effects of parental incarceration are liable to vary by a child's sex. Girls and boys have been found to react differently to parental incarceration or to have different expectations placed upon them during their parent's absence. In England, for instance, Roger Shaw found that it was a "common occurrence" for the oldest son of male prisoners to assume the role of head of the family (1987, 35). Research focusing on jailed mothers and their children found that girls were asked to take on domestic responsibilities but boys were not (Stanton 1980). For sons and daughters, adopting such roles can be a difficult task and, once assumed, difficult to relinquish upon the parent's return. In addition to responsibilities that differ by sex, some research has found that girls have more difficulty in school than boys (Friedman and Esselstyn 1965; Gabel and Shindledecker 1993a) but that boys react in more overtly negative ways, such as aggression and delinquency, than do girls to their parent's incarceration (Fritsch and Burkhead 1981; Sack, Seidler, and Thomas 1976).

Clearly, the nature and extent of a child's reaction to a parent's incarceration are conditioned by these many factors. For some, the imprisonment of a parent may represent yet another disruption in a life characterized by disorder. For most children, however, parental incarceration can be a turning point in their lives, knocking them off balance and profoundly disrupting the life they were living before. Because children are resilient and many are able to rebound from childhood adversity, negative outcomes are far from inevitable for children whose parents are incarcerated. Nevertheless, that some youth are more susceptible to the damaging effects of an experience like having a parent in prison and react in ways that can have long-term consequences makes this a pressing social issue, particularly in light of the number of children touched by parental incarceration. Research can play a vital role in illuminating how parental incarceration affects children and what needs children have while a parent is in prison.

This book opens a door into the worlds of prisoners' children that I observed, from shortly after a mother's arrest through her incarceration, giving voice to the children by using their own words to describe their experiences and feelings.

Part 1 focuses on children during the period following a mother's arrest but before the conclusion of her criminal case, providing a look into the worlds of offenders' children before incarceration disrupts them; chapter 1 examines the home and family, and chapter 2 deals with the children's lives beyond the family. One of the most disturbing phenomena I encountered in the course of my research was the pervasiveness of violence in the children's lives, an issue that chapter 3 addresses.

The chapters in part 2 show how the steps in the criminal justice process affect these children. Chapter 4 examines the earliest phase, which includes arrest, an often protracted court case, and, for some, the pretrial detention in jail of the mother. A portrait of the children's lives during their mother's incarceration is presented in chapter 5, showing that the children, in a sense, do time along with their mothers. By contrast, children whose convicted mothers remain home on probation are generally unaware that their mothers are even involved with the justice system. This chapter also considers children's experiences after a mother is released from prison, showing that her homecoming is not necessarily a panacea for the problems that they have experienced while she was away and that new issues may arise when she returns.

The concluding chapter argues that incarceration does indeed create numerous difficulties for children and their mothers but that the experience of having a parent in prison must also be situated within the broader context of the children's lives both before and after the parent is incarcerated if we are to understand fully the reasons why such children may be considered at risk.

PART ONE

1

Living with Mom—Most of the Time

I was high, sitting on the toilet, nodding out. John [her boyfriend] came in and told me to move. I couldn't, so we started fighting. I picked up a frying pan and a glass. I hit him with both of them, anything else I could find. I stomped him in the mouth. John called the cops and told them I had a knife. They came and they was looking for a weapon. The cops said, "She's fucked up," and took me out of the house in my bra. I was fighting them, telling them, "Take him, take him," but they handcuffed me.

—Shaquilla, twenty-eight-year-old mother of two[1]

Ronald, Shaquilla's eleven-year-old son, had witnessed this episode between his mother and her boyfriend four years earlier. The event is emblematic of the trauma that many children whose parents are involved in the justice system experience. Shaquilla's removal from the house would have been a shocking event for a child to witness, but to view the arrest in isolation from what preceded it is to ignore the reality of such children's lives. Which aspect of this incident is likely to have the most enduring effect on Ronald? Shaquilla's drug use, which left her so high that she was unable to remove herself from a toilet someone in the household needed to use? The fight with her boyfriend, John, one of many over the years with this man, who was extremely abusive to Shaquilla? His mother being dragged out onto the street in her underwear for the whole neighborhood to see? His mother being handcuffed and taken away by the police? We would expect any one of these scenes to upset and distress a child, but some of them occur rarely and others are part of daily life. Taken together, they represent a potent brew of toxic circumstances that could have both short- and long-term consequences for a child.

As Shaquilla's narrative suggests, her household was not an ideal environment for children, reflecting the hazards hypothesized in the introduction to be present in the lives of children living with female offenders. Shaquilla had

23

begun using drugs when Ronald was three years old and had progressed several years before this incident to snorting heroin and smoking crack cocaine. Her abusive relationship with John lasted years before she ended it, so Ronald was a frequent witness to their violent clashes. Shaquilla never held a legitimate job, instead earning money by having sex with people she met while dancing at clubs and parties. As is common for poor people, she moved frequently, causing Ronald to change schools several times. When Ronald was nine, the rest of his family finally concluded that his living situation was unacceptable and decided to act. As a result, he had been living in a stable and nurturing environment for two years with his father, his father's girlfriend, and his paternal grandmother. His life with his mother was more chaotic than those of many other children in this study, but it underscores the importance of placing parental incarceration in the context of a child's life and reflects the reality that many such children confront multiple risk factors for harm, including parental substance abuse, criminal justice system involvement, poverty, and violence.

Like the lives of the other children I met, Ronald's was inextricably woven with his parents'. Their decisions, their way of living, the people with whom they chose to share their life—all created the niche into which Ronald was born and from which he would eventually emerge to create his own identity and place in the world. A child's family is the source of early socialization and the place where children develop profound attachments and the ability to become attached to others. Children look to their family as a source of safety and security, and threats or ruptures in that system can reverberate through childhood and beyond. Although children can be resilient even after dealing with adversity—"strong in the broken places," as Ernest Hemingway said—they are also vulnerable. It is precisely because such traumatic events have the potential to affect children in profoundly negative ways that concern about parental incarceration has grown.

In this chapter, I offer a close look at the family life of the children whose mothers were not yet incarcerated to help clarify why some children are affected more directly by parental incarceration than others. Despite their mother's criminality or drug addiction, some of the children in this study live in stable and secure homes, while others have experienced disruptions in their family and physical separations from their mothers. Nearly all, however, have been exposed to a number of experiences, events, and lifestyles that can stress and strain the most resilient of children and lead to maladaptive behavior and emotional reactions among them.

Family Composition: An Overview

Nearly all fifty children I interviewed while their mothers were awaiting trial were living with their mothers; in some households, another adult relative, such as an aunt or grandmother, was present and helped with childrearing responsibilities. In some cases, the children lived full time with other relatives, seeing their mothers only occasionally. These different living arrangements of course would have shaped the children's lives regardless of whether their mothers were involved in the criminal justice system, but they also had potential consequences for the children if their mothers eventually were incarcerated. But first we turn to the children's fathers.

Where Have All the Fathers Gone?

A striking feature of almost all the children's families was the absence of the father: only six (12 percent) of the fifty children were living with their fathers at the time of the interview. Furthermore, their siblings' fathers were also missing. Nearly all the mothers had more than one child (M = 3.2 children), most of whom were fathered by different partners. For instance, in every family where the mother had two children, each had a different father. Of all the families with more than one child, only two (4 percent) comprised children who all had the same father. Furthermore, no adult male was living in most households (62 percent), which meant that none of the children in those families were living with their father.

The children's fathers were absent for a variety of reasons, some of which made it impossible for the children to maintain a relationship with them. In many cases, the fathers lived in the community but no longer had any connection with the mother and made virtually no effort to have contact with the child. In some instances, however, even though the child's parents were no longer involved with each other, the father stayed connected with the child through the paternal grandparents, who frequently helped out and wanted to have a relationship with their grandchild. Visits to their grandparents afforded these children an opportunity to see their father as well. For them, the notion that they could build a relationship with their father remained at least a possibility.

Other children had limited or no opportunity to establish a connection with their fathers. For some, any relationship was precluded because their fathers were unknown or dead. Given the youthfulness of the sample, it may seem surprising that the fathers of 17 percent of the children were deceased. Sadly, this rate of early death reflects the fatal risks associated with being a young man who lives in one of today's poor urban neighborhoods; in many cases, the father died as a result of violence. Other children had a hard time maintaining a relationship with their father because he was in prison; nearly three in ten children (27.6 percent) had fathers in prison at the time of our interview, and two-thirds of the children (66.7 percent) had fathers who had been in prison at some time. Few of the children whose fathers were currently in prison had strong prior relationships with them, and building bonds was difficult because the children had to rely on other adults either to take them to the prison for visits or pay for long-distance phone calls. Most mothers were unwilling to do either, so the children had little contact with their incarcerated fathers even if they wished to see them.

Thirteen-year-old Antoine's situation illustrated the difficulties a child encountered when his father was incarcerated. When Antoine was ten, his father began serving a life sentence for murder in a prison some three hundred miles away. Although he received occasional letters from his father, Antoine did not speak with him by phone and had never been able to visit him, despite his desire to do so. Antoine's mother had no interest in visiting her former boyfriend, so Antoine was dependent on other relatives who might be able to take him, just as they occasionally took him to visit one of his four uncles who were also incarcerated. That uncle—also serving life for a murder conviction—was in a prison much closer to the city, making visits far more feasible. With no adult willing to make the long journey to his father's prison, Antoine was left wishing for someone to help make his dream a reality.

The absence of fathers in these families had significant ramifications for children and mothers alike. Their absence nearly always meant that the mothers were handling parenting responsibilities alone, creating additional emotional and financial stress for them and setting up a fragile situation: the children were vulnerable if the mother was unavailable for any reason. Were she to be sentenced to prison, for instance, she could not depend on the child's father to take over, unlike the imprisoned fathers of the children in this study, who when they were sent to prison had been able to rely on their children's mothers for care.

In addition to the stresses placed on the mother and thus on her family, the missing fathers left an emotional void in the lives of their children, resulting for some in feelings of anger and difficulty understanding why their fathers would choose not to be in their lives. Sean, an eleven-year-old who lived with his mother and four brothers and sisters, felt bitterly disappointed with his biological father, who had recently been released from prison after serving seven years. Sean's disappointment over his father's absence is not attributable simply to his having no male role model in his life, because his mother had lived with another man for several years, although he died several months before her arrest. He had been a father figure to the children, and Sean expressed a desire to be like his "dad" when he grew up. Asked to clarify which father he was talking about, Sean replied: "My real dad I couldn't stand, and the reason I don't want to be like him is because I want to be a good dad and take care of my kids. Don't just have 'em and leave them and then when they're sitting there struggling just leave and then come back seven years later." For Sean, as for other children, being a good dad meant at a minimum being present and taking steps to take care of one's children.

The presence of a biological father did not always ease the strains on the family but at times created additional problems, especially when fathers perpetrated violence against the mothers or children. Sean's father, for instance, contacted the family upon his release from prison and wanted to visit with his children, ostensibly to establish relationships with them. His efforts, however, frequently amounted to little more than unkept promises, leading to feelings of bitter disappointment for Sean. His father also hit Sean and the other children in the family during his visits with them. During one incident he struck Sean's sister so severely that he was arrested and subsequently spent five months in jail as a result of his actions. Other children who lived with their fathers or surrogate fathers (stepfathers, boyfriends) were also exposed to violence perpetrated by these men and, in some cases, by their mothers in response to the abuse inflicted by the men, as illustrated by the scenario described at the beginning of this chapter (see chapter 3).

Although the presence of a father or father figure was not always a panacea for the problems that the children's families faced, some fathers did bring stability and security to the children's lives. Nick, for instance, is an eight-year-old who has lived with his father and grandmother since he was a toddler. His mother, Ivy, has been addicted to crack and heroin for many years and has spent extensive periods of time in prison and in residential drug treatment programs. When she lived with Nick during his infancy, she admits, she was unable to fulfill her parental responsibilities, frequently leaving him alone at night while she went out to seek drugs or money to support her habit, usually through prostitution. She acknowledged that she "couldn't handle being a mother" and thus had not lived with Nick or her other two children for any significant amount of time. In her absence, Nick's father, Jack, had provided a stable, well-supervised home environment with the help of Nick's grandmother. While Jack worked full time, helping enable him to send Nick to a parochial school, Nick's grandmother was home, providing an adult presence when Nick returned from school. Nick was secure in his attachment to his father and grandmother and seemed to have left behind the turbulent life he experienced during his early years alone with his mother. Unfortunately, Jack was an exception even among the fathers who were present in the children's lives. All too often, the women's partners were involved with the criminal justice system themselves, engaged in illegal activities, or were simply unwilling or uninterested in assuming the responsibilities of a parent.

As in Nick's case, grandmothers as well as other female relatives helped provide for several children. Mothers and children benefited from their presence, although at times these arrangements led to overcrowded homes, with many children having to share limited bed space with siblings or cousins. Nevertheless, the presence of other female adults helped insure that some adult would be available to look after the children if the mother had to attend to other business or go to work. Their presence also helped relieve some economic pressure because resources could be pooled, alleviating the need for the mothers alone to take care of the household. For the children, the other adult women in the household represented an additional emotional attachment, someone they could feel close to and in whom they could confide. In cases where a mother was ultimately sent to prison, the children's lives could be minimally disrupted, at least from a material point of view, because the other relatives were already present and could be counted on to take care of the children.

Missing Mom

In view of the large number of absent fathers, the role played by the children's mothers assumes central importance in the children's lives. As the sole parent present, they alone must shoulder the responsibility of providing for the children's needs, whether emotional or material, and ensuring their safety and security. Most of the mothers succeeded at this demanding task, typically made more difficult by their limited economic resources, but variations among the women in their level of engagement in parental responsibilities were apparent. A subgroup of children whose mothers were not fully engaged in parenting, typically because of drug addiction, experienced regular disruptions in their family life. I discovered three levels of maternal engagement: engaged, sporadically engaged, or disengaged mothers. These categories are not static, however. For example, a mother might go from being sporadically engaged to disengaged. Such transitions were nearly always the result of variations in a woman's level of drug use.

ENGAGED MOTHERS. Women I labeled engaged mothers lived with their children, were involved with the children's daily lives, and were available to the children emotionally and physically. They provided good supervision for their children and ensured stability in the children's lives even under less than optimal material circumstances. Most of the engaged mothers had little history of trouble with the criminal justice system and were not jailed before their trial. I categorized a majority (55.4 percent) of the mothers as engaged. They lived regularly with their children and were involved in monitoring their children's schooling, looking after their medical needs, being attentive to who their children spent time with, and engaging in activities with them. They were familiar with their children's teachers, aware of how the children were doing in school, and sometimes volunteered to participate in school activities.

Typical was fifty-one-year-old Dorothy, who lived with her husband and her two youngest children in a well-kept home that they owned. Her youngest child, twelve-year-old Tanya, was a good student in middle school and a talented singer and dancer. Her mother made every effort to ensure that Tanya could develop her talents, enrolling her in dance, voice, and modeling classes, getting her involved in a church choir that performed at home and abroad, and hoping to get Tanya into the public performing arts high school. Dorothy's full-time job prevented her from being as involved in Tanya's school as other mothers could have been, but she monitored Tanya's activities, knew her friends, and had clear expectations of her children's behavior, as she explained when talking about her two older children, both adults:

> Well, I go out and have a nice time and act crazy, but I always try to raise my children to be polite to the elderly, to the sick, to the homeless, whatever. And when my children are here, and we're partying, they are like just two perfect gentlemen, you know, and all kids have peer pressure. You don't know what group to hang in. This kid's goin' down to the corner dealing crack, stealing cars, robbing people. Knock on wood, my boys didn't go that route. And my son, he may smoke a little reefer, but he hasn't gotten to the point where he's on crack or anything. He's never been on crack. 'Cause his father was on crack; my husband was on crack. But he learned to stay away from those Joes, 'cause they knew I would kick ass if I even thought they was trying to do something to harm themselves and harm their family.

As Dorothy's allusion to acting crazy suggests, she was not without her own issues. In fact, it was her drinking problem that led to her arrest on a DUI charge following a serious traffic accident. Indeed, engaged mothers like Dorothy did not necessarily abstain from drug use, but they did find ways to remain committed to their children even if their use became frequent and intense. Danyelle, a thirty-six-year-old mother of four, had a history of drug abuse but had not used for two years. Detained in jail for several weeks before her trial on assault charges, she eventually had been released before her trial. In the following excerpt, she talks about her determination to stay with her children despite her drug problems, particularly because she carried responsibility for her children alone:

> I was so messed up, but I never gave these kids up for nothing. Every one that came out of me, I been there. I was so messed up from sniffing coke, I put myself away to try to save myself. I was tired of hurting them. My kids been through a lot with me without their father, but God seen that I was no harm to them like physically or nothing and we always had somewhere to live. We always had some food, and in rough times God always made a way for me to get. See, he knows my heart and I just had problems on trying to stay strong and fight this rough life I'm living. It's not too rough, because I'm here today, you know. Even when I was locked up, it felt like it was the end of the world but I survived it. But I got to try to stay out here to continue to take care of these kids because I don't

have anybody who is going to take care of them. His dad is in jail. He been in there since he was four months and he is eight years old [now]. My older daughter dad, he just gave up on her. He got a woman and he just step out of her life. Her dad is out here but he ain't doing nothing for her. So it just me and God and these kids.

Although life for children of the engaged mothers was stable, incarceration posed a greater threat of upheaval for them than for other children, unless there was another parent or relative present in the household who could maintain the home in its customary configuration. Otherwise, their mother's incarceration would mean not only separation from their primary caregiver but also disruption to their family, possible separation from their siblings, and in all likelihood a move from their house, which in turn could necessitate a change of school and the loss of their friends and usual activities. In a perverse irony, children whose mothers were engaged were at greatest risk of both material and emotional disruption if their mother ended up in prison.

SPORADICALLY ENGAGED. Many of the children lived with mothers whom I characterize as sporadically engaged in their children's lives. These mothers were in and out of their children's lives, living with them at times but absent at others, creating periodic disruptions in the children's lives. Typically, the sporadically engaged mothers were absent for reasons related to substance abuse. Sometimes they were in jail or prison; at other times they were away from home because of their addiction or their desire to be running the streets. One married woman whose husband could theoretically care for the children in her absence maintained a separate apartment in a distant part of the city where she could spend her days using drugs. This meant that other relatives would care for the children at least part of the time, and that they had to cope with the unpredictable nature of their mother's involvement with them. Demands might also be placed on the older children in these families as a result of their mother's intermittent presence in the household: in effect, they were expected to shoulder the responsibilities their mother did not. Their mother's absences also resulted in children—even very young children—being left without adequate supervision.

Nicole was a sixteen-year-old who lived with her mother, three younger siblings, and her maternal aunt in a house owned by her maternal grandparents. Nicole's mother, Sharon, had been using crack for more than ten years, had been arrested several times, and was not supervising the children adequately. As a result, two years earlier, she had given her sister, Nicole's aunt, what she referred to as temporary guardianship of the children. Before the family moved in with the aunt, however, Sharon's frequent absences from the household when she went out to get high left Nicole in charge and without much supervision. Nicole has clear memories of those days and contrasts them with the way the household is now organized, with her grandmother frequently stepping in to fulfill household duties and impose some supervision:

JS: So your mom was not around a lot of the time?

NICOLE: She was around, but she used to be—like, she'd be around, but she'd be . . . doin' drugs.

JS: Doing drugs?

NICOLE: She'd come home, and stuff like that.

JS: But would there be days that would go by and you wouldn't see her?

NICOLE: My mom livin' here. She not gonna come home and do it [take drugs], you know what I mean? She figure she go out and do it.

JS: But she just wouldn't worry about things like making dinner for you and that kind of stuff?

NICOLE: Yeah. She knew I was gonna do it when she wasn't gonna do it, or my grandmother was gonna do it, I was gonna do it. Somebody was gonna do it. I mean, she was always, "Nicole, when are you gonna get done?" This is how I lived while I be takin' care of her. That's why I don't do nothing now. Because when I was younger, that's all I remember, taking care of my mother. All I remember is always takin' care of them, so I don't be feelin' like doin' nothin'.

JS: Who were they?

NICOLE: My brother—my thirteen-year-old brother—my sister.

JS: So you were given the responsibility and had to take care of them for a long time.

NICOLE: Yeah. That's why I be acting so old now. 'Cause I've always had so much responsibility. And then it's like, I used to do whatever I want. Now, they settin' all these rules on me, all at one time. Like, I went so many years without rules, it's just hard to adjust. Now they try to keep pushing all these silly rules on me.

JS: Who's trying to push rules on you?

NICOLE: My grandmom.

JS: What kind of rules does she have?

NICOLE: Some of them be logical, but some of them are dumb rules.

JS: So, does she have special rules just for you? Like curfews or . . . ?

NICOLE: Yeah, I gotta be in by like 10:30 during the week, and 12:30 on the weekends. She actually take the [unintelligible], she puts them in effect like in the house. You understand? She's too old-fashioned. She need to get with the times.

JS: So before she got involved, you used to be able to stay out till whenever you wanted?

NICOLE: Well, I used to be able to [unintelligible], but . . .

Nicole refers to the time when she "be takin' care of her," meaning her mother, and although their living arrangement had changed and other adults were now fulfilling the responsibilities that Sharon had long neglected, Nicole continued to feel a sense of responsibility for her mother's well-being. The crack house where Sharon spent a lot of time was around the corner from their house and Nicole would go there to check on her mother:

JS: Had you ever been in crack houses with your mom before?

NICOLE: I was just there 'cause I just wanted to make sure my mom was cool. I would go there and bring her food, and go there to bring her some clothes. I would go there to get some money.

Children raised under these circumstances are clearly at risk of negative consequences, even if their parent is never incarcerated, as Sharon briefly was while awaiting the disposition of one of her cases. Before then, Nicole had already gotten into trouble, having been expelled from school two years earlier in the ninth grade. Unhappy with the new school she attended following the expulsion, Nicole eventually stopped attending, missing one hundred consecutive days. Sharon claimed to have no knowledge of her daughter's truancy and apparently took no action to intervene. Nicole had been placed under the supervision of the local child protection agency because she had been designated a child in need of supervision, but that did not prevent her from being involved with a romantic partner who was seven years her senior, an adult with whom she first became involved when she was twelve years old. By both legal and commonly accepted definitions, such a liaison constitutes child sexual abuse, but Sharon was aware of the relationship and did not object to it.[2] Nicole had also been arrested twice and, in a particularly cruel twist, was caught in a police raid of the crack house her mother frequented, leading to Nicole's third arrest.

The sporadic engagement of mothers and the shared child-care responsibility in these families differ from the shared family responsibilities described by Carol Stack in her seminal work *All Our Kin* (1974). In that study, which described adaptations made by urban African American families to straitened economic circumstances, family members assisted each other as a means of survival. The mothers' sporadic engagement observed here led other family members to take on child-care responsibilities not out of economic necessity but in response to crises in the mother's life that prevented her from assuming her parental responsibilities. In addition, in this study these arrangements were not confined to the African American families. Substance abuse problems were a great equalizer, necessitating intervention among families of all racial and ethnic groups when mothers were not adequately caring for their children.

Children of sporadically engaged mothers were liable to be more inured than were children of engaged mothers to the disruption resulting from their mother's incarceration. They had already experienced instability and periodic separations and typically had other relatives who had assumed a caregiving role and would continue caring for them in their mother's absence. Nevertheless, these children had deep emotional attachments to their mothers and viewed them as their primary mother figure; the children felt their mother's absence keenly, whatever the reason she was not with them. If a mother who had been less than fully engaged in her parental responsibilities was sentenced to prison, her departure would still represent an emotional trauma for the child.

DISENGAGED. I categorized a few of the mothers I met as disengaged from their parental role. Disengaged mothers were rarely present in their children's lives, living apart from them while others cared for their children. Often, the separation began early in the child's life because other family members recognized that the mother was not going to provide adequate care for the child. In other cases, the children and mothers lived together for a number of years, usually sporadically, until the mother could no longer take care of her children. In the alternative living arrangements that resulted from their mother's absence, children of disengaged mothers forged strong emotional attachments to other adults who cared for them; this was the case for Nick, who lived with his father and grandmother, as we have seen.

At times, disengaged mothers were absent for extended periods; even if they reappeared for a brief time, they remained relatively uninvolved in their children's lives. These reappearances could be particularly painful for the children, especially if the mother tried to displace the emotional ties the child had built with another adult. Deshanda, for example, is an eleven-year-old whose life had been disrupted by her mother's attempt to establish herself in the maternal role after having relinquished that responsibility when Deshanda was a baby. Her mother, Sheila, had a long history of drug abuse, beginning with heroin use at the age of fifteen. For several years, Sheila supported her drug habit through prostitution until health issues caused her to turn to theft and drug dealing. Sheila had five children, ranging in age from eleven to twenty-eight. Until the birth of her youngest child, she had relied on her parents to help her care for the children because she was frequently absent due to her drug use and periodic stints in jail and prison. I asked if her three older children had lived with her:

SHEILA: Back and forth. After I got out of jail, they'd come back home with me. All my kids have always been around me, I just wasn't around them when I should have been, but I've always been there, you know.

JS: So they would come and stay with you for a time?

SHEILA: When I was around, you know. Like I had them for a long time until they were like nine or ten, then I went to jail, then I was trying to get my life back together, then when I did, they would come in. They would live with my mother, come back over here, get mad at me 'cause I used [took drugs], go back to my mother's. Back and forth like that.

The family experience of Sheila's youngest child, Deshanda, differed from that of her older siblings. She describes her life as "full of drama," and indeed it has been characterized by a considerable number of disruptions. When Deshanda was born, Sheila's mother decided that Sheila was unable to care for a child because of her drug use, which at that point included both heroin and crack cocaine, and took the child to live with her. Deshanda's grandmother died soon afterward, and Deshanda's great uncle and his girlfriend, Maya, took Deshanda into their household. The couple split up when Deshanda was six years old, and Deshanda went to live with Maya and Maya's children. Maya and Deshanda had a mother-daughter relationship, and Deshanda viewed Maya's children as her siblings. When Maya became gravely ill, she made her daughter Monique promise to care for Deshanda in the event of her death. Maya died when Deshanda was eight, and Monique kept her promise, taking Deshanda to live with her and her own four children.

In a life marked for Deshanda by loss, Maya, Monique, and their family have been an emotional anchor, always there to care for her and provide her with a sense of home and belonging. And what of Sheila? During Deshanda's earliest years, her birth mother was rarely present, but when Deshanda went to live with Maya, Sheila attempted to regain custody of her daughter. Instead, the court granted Sheila visitation rights on weekends and in the summer. Monique reported that Sheila's visits have been rare: "Supposed to be every weekend, but she don't ever come, or hardly ever. She drop by when she get herself together, then she don't drop by when she says she's coming to get her."

When I first interviewed Sheila and Deshanda, Sheila had not used drugs for two or three months and had decided that she would try to reclaim her position as mother to Deshanda by having her daughter stay with her for the summer. Deshanda was deeply unhappy with this arrangement.

DESHANDA: I never wanted to live with my real mom. I never want to either.

JS: Why is that?

DESHANDA: Because I don't. I like my other family better, and I will always like my other family better. And I love them both the same way, but my other family treats me better than this family. My real mom, she don't, like, pay much attention to me.

Deshanda's despair was profound. Here she speaks about living with her mother at her sister's house during the summer: "I just wish none of this happened to me, like this. Like [when I'm] at my house [the house she lived in with Monique], I wish I could come here, but then no. Because that's why I came here this summer, to see how it feels. I live here, but it don't feel right to me. I can't have it like I have it at my house. I can't have, like, clothes and stuff, like that. I know I can't. I can't eat what I want. I can't go to the store. I just wished this never happened to me. I hate my life."

When asked what she would wish for if she could be granted one wish, Deshanda replied: "To stay with my other family forever." One week later, she learned that her mother was smoking crack in the house, so she called Monique's grandfather and asked him to come get her. She packed her things, left the house, and returned to her "real family." Two weeks passed before Sheila called her.

Like Deshanda, children of disengaged mothers typically built strong relationships with other caregivers that helped buffer them from some of the difficulties children of sporadically engaged mothers encountered through their exposure to their mothers' behavior. Consequently, the disengaged mothers' absence during incarceration was likely to be less materially disruptive to them than such an absence was to the children of engaged or sporadically engaged mothers, because they already had an established home elsewhere. Nevertheless, as it was for the children whose mothers were sporadically engaged, their mother's incarceration could be a difficult event for them. Even children who have never had any relationship with their mother retain strong feelings about her. A woman who had raised her niece from birth recounted how devastated her niece was when she went to visit her mother in prison, even though mother and daughter had no relationship during the girl's lifetime.

Mothers who absented themselves from the family at times created a different family configuration from the one the child would have had otherwise or would have wished to have had. For instance, Lucinda was a thirty-eight-year-old mother of six children by four different men; her oldest son was an adult, but the rest of the children ranged in age from six months to ten years. She had been a heavy crack user for twelve years but had lived off and on with her children and mother until the oldest of her minor children was seven. After Lucinda was reported to the authorities because she had taken her children with her when she went to buy drugs, the children went into foster care. Since then, her mother had obtained custody of two of her minor sons, her sister had taken her two daughters to another state and refused to let her see them, and her six-month-old son had been given up for adoption. Her parental rights to her daughters were eventually terminated, and the family was considering putting the girls up for adoption as well. Lucinda's sons saw her from time to time when she came to stay with them and her mother for a few days, but there was little other contact between them. Lucinda's disengagement, coupled with the children's fathers' abandonment of their offspring, resulted in a reconfiguration of the family as the younger children had known it. The youngest children were so young as to have had few memories of their early family life, but the two sons who lived with their grandmother remembered it well. Ian, the ten-year-old, really missed his sisters and identified them as the people in his family to whom he felt closest and with whom he most liked to play, even though he rarely talked with or saw them.

Sporadically engaged and disengaged mothers had much in common, and some who appeared disengaged might try to reengage with their children at times of sobriety, typically with poor results, as shown by Sheila and Deshanda. Other women attempted to care for their children for a time but were able to do so only intermittently before becoming disconnected from their parental responsibilities, either because family members decided to intervene or the mother turned her children over to family members for care. The more serious the mother's involvement in the criminal justice system, the more likely she was to be only sporadically engaged in or disengaged from her maternal role. Time spent out on the street looking for and using drugs, punctuated by repeated stints in prison or jail and occasional stays in treatment, were impediments to carrying out regular parental responsibilities. Although not all the mothers who were jailed after their arrest were sporadically engaged or disengaged, they were more likely to fall into those categories than those who were at home awaiting the disposition of their case. The jailed mothers typically were more heavily dependent on drugs, had more criminal justice involvement, and were more likely to report that they had suffered from some mental illness. Thus, the women in jail—those most likely to end up being sentenced to prison—were also those whose children were most likely to be exposed to multiple risk factors if they were living together. In other words, those who ultimately would become prisoners' children were already vulnerable to the depredations associated with parental imprisonment because of their tumultuous home environments.

Teen Parents

During the course of my research, I met some children who had a child of their own. Generally, the children I interviewed in the city were young, with an average age of 11.7 years. Thus, most were not of childbearing age. Only nine children were above the age of fourteen, but four of them (44 percent) were already parents, a percentage far above the expected rate for adolescents between the ages of fifteen and nineteen based on national data. Three of the teenage parents were female, and all of them were caring for their children; the fourth was a male whose daughter lived with her teenaged mother and grandparents. He was initially very attached to his child but his relationship with her became much more distant after he became romantically involved with another teenager and broke up with his child's mother.

The teenaged parents came from families with certain similarities. Three of the four had mothers who could be characterized as chronic offenders: they had been arrested numerous times and were in jail awaiting the disposition of their case following their arrest. Throughout the children's lives, two of these mothers spent so much time in and out of jail and on the streets that they were rarely available to take on parenting responsibilities, thus falling into the category of sporadically engaged mothers. Indeed, because of her drug habit and frequent encounters with the criminal justice system, one mother had given up custody of her child to the child's grandmother when the child was three years old. When she was able to do so, however, she did live with her children for brief periods. The third chronic offender mother had managed to avoid spending time in prison despite her numerous arrests, but her life with her son John was nevertheless also characterized by disruptions to their household, with frequent moves, periods of homelessness, and a changing family composition as different romantic partners moved in and out. Life in all three families thus was characterized by a lack of stability and emotional turmoil caused by the shifting circumstances in which the children were growing up. Even Mandy, the one teenage parent whose mother was not a chronic offender, had experienced disruptions in her life. Although she was living with her parents, her father and mother had separated twice; each became involved with other romantic partners during the separations. During one separation, Mandy's mother was arrested and imprisoned for four months as a result of her boyfriend's illegal activities. Mandy's parents had since reunited, but family life was further disrupted when her mother gave up a child fathered by her boyfriend for adoption, and another sister was sent to live in a group home for troubled children.

The teenage parents' mothers were not the only family members involved in the criminal justice system. Three teen parents had fathers with criminal records; only Mandy did not. John's father had been incarcerated for murder when John was a baby; he died in prison when John was three years old. The fathers of Aleesha and Ronice, the other two teenage mothers, were both serving life sentences for murder and thus could not help the girls out with their parental responsibilities. Furthermore, as if in a tragic recreation of their own mothers' situations, Aleesha and Ronice both bore children with men who were serving time, one in an adult prison and the other in a juvenile facility. And, in an apparent cycle of intergenerational criminality, Aleesha and John had also spent time in juvenile facilities after being adjudicated delinquent.

Life for the teenage parents is not easy and their future prospects are bleak. All four of them had dropped out of school, and although some of them spoke of planning to resume their education, the logistics of caring for young children while attending school made it difficult to envision how they would do so, particularly without either financial resources or parental support. Even those whose mothers were only sporadically engaged had hoped to rely on them for help with their babies and were disappointed when their mothers were unable or unwilling to help. Seventeen-year-old Ronice, for instance, had lived only occasionally with her mother, Jacinta, who had been in and out of prison numerous times. Ronice was fifteen when her baby was born and since then she had moved around, staying at times with an aunt and at others with Jacinta. At the time of Jacinta's arrest, Ronice had been living with her for six months; she continued living alone with her toddler in her mother's apartment when Jacinta was detained in jail pending trial, until the apartment manager realized she was there without adult supervision and forced her to leave. Without her mother, Ronice felt overwhelmed and depressed. Not only did she have to navigate the welfare system to try to get assistance to support her child, but she also had to try to pay the bills for her mother's apartment to ensure that her mother's utilities and lease would continue during her temporary absence. Feeling trapped in her aunt's house by her need to care for her child, unable to attend school or to socialize with her friends, and bearing many adult responsibilities, Ronice kept her unhappiness to herself. The only person she thought could help her was Jacinta, but there was little her mother could do for her from jail.

Whether the situation of the teen parents portends the future for the younger children in this study is difficult to say, but the turmoil and traumas these adolescents endured while growing up were not dissimilar to the experiences of the younger children whose mothers were sporadically engaged. Consider the case of nine-year-old Jeremiah, for instance. By any measure, Jeremiah seemed far from a likely candidate for teenaged parenthood or a stint in juvenile detention. He was a good student who did not get into trouble in the neighborhood or school. The one sign that all was not well was his desire for counseling, precipitated by sadness at his separation from his mother, Tiffany, in jail pending her sentencing on an aggravated assault charge. Her incarceration had also elevated Jeremiah's concern for her health: Tiffany had AIDS as well as bipolar disorder and depression, and everyone in her family worried about the care she would receive in jail. However, besides his mother's incarceration, much more in Jeremiah's life might have upset him. Tiffany was an alcoholic who also used crack; Jeremiah and his brother were frequently left to fend for themselves when their mother was drunk.[3] Her alcoholism and drug use contributed to her frequent arrests and occasional periods of incarceration, the longest of which began when Jeremiah was six months old. Neither Jeremiah nor his brother could look to a father for help; his brother's father was dead, and Jeremiah's father had never really been part of his child's life and had begun serving a life sentence for murder when Jeremiah was seven. Tiffany had never been employed, and their meager finances had led the two boys and their mother, together with Tiffany's longtime girlfriend, into a nomadic existence, staying at various relatives' houses until they wore out their welcome.[4] As a result, Jeremiah attended five schools between kindergarten and third grade. How long, I wondered, could he continue to excel at school when his family's moves disrupted his education so frequently?

Will Jeremiah's apparent resiliency allow him to overcome the odds that seem so stacked against him? He was such a winning child that I sincerely hoped so. Even children who seem relatively resistant to the effect of adverse life events at a young age can become vulnerable as such events accumulate over time. As the younger children like Jeremiah approach the age of the teenage parents who were the oldest participants in the study, the balance between vulnerability and resiliency may slip and they may find themselves in similar situations. Further disruptions, such as parental incarceration, could tip the scale and place once resilient children in danger of undesirable outcomes.

Family Characteristics

The quality of family life for children like Tanya, whose situation was relatively stable despite her mother's drinking, was quite different from Nicole's or Jeremiah's, with their frequent disruptions caused by their mothers' drug use and poverty and a concomitant lack of parental supervision. Such differences carried with them varying levels of exposure to potential risk factors associated with the quality of family life. In other respects, however, the families I interviewed shared similarities that could jeopardize healthy outcomes for the children.

Moms and Drugs

Drugs are a major reason why women become involved in the criminal justice system, either because of a drug offense or a drug-related crime, as noted earlier. In addition, nearly a quarter of women in prison fit the criteria for alcohol dependence (Mumola 1999). My interviews with mothers and children in the city confirmed that children whose mothers were involved in the justice system were exposed to parental drug use in unusually high numbers and, to a lesser extent, to alcohol abuse. Although only about a quarter of the women I met were currently charged with a drug offense, drug use and dependence were far more prevalent among the mothers than that figure would suggest. Approximately eight out of ten women (81 percent) said they were current or former drug users, nearly all of them describing themselves as dependent on the drugs they used. The problem was especially acute among the women who were being held in jail following their arrest: only one of them did not have a past or current self-described drug abuse problem.

The descriptions of the mothers in this chapter indicate that drugs were a significant factor in determining their children's family structure and the quality of their relationship with their mother. These factors in turn were likely to be important in shaping how a child might react to a mother's incarceration. However, even for children whose mother's drug use did not cause them to be separated, their exposure to drug abuse constituted a risk to them because of the potentially harmful consequences known to be associated with parental substance abuse.

Mothers with serious drug dependency problems frequently acknowledged that their drug addiction had cost them their maternal role. Jacinta, Ronice's mother, said:

> I felt like a failure as a parent. I mean, just comin' back and forth to jail. Like my daughter havin' a baby at a young age and me not bein' there, and she feelin' she wants something that's gonna always be there and love her. You know, and like, you know, even when I came to the point, it goes against our religion and I had to, like, say: "Ronice, you can't have this baby." She said, "Yes, I am," because she knew that baby's always gonna be there. That baby gonna love her, you know what I mean, in spite how babies, you know—I mean, I'm not always gonna be there. This baby is. You know what I mean? So she made the decision that she's gonna have this baby 'cause she knows this baby's always gonna be there, she wanted to be loved. You know, and that was her purpose. So I felt like I failed as a parent because I'm never there. Like I'm in and out her life, and like she's the type o' person that been through a lot. I never knew how to raise a child. You know what I mean? And I was just learnin' as I went along. Like I didn't have anything. I didn't have a blueprint. I didn't have everything mapped out like the average person would.

Jacinta's disappointment in and regret for her perceived failings as a mother were not uncommon among the women. During a cycle of abstinence from drugs, many would vow to become better mothers and make amends for what they felt was the harm they had caused their children. Pam, for instance, was a thirty-four-year-old mother of four children ranging in age from one to twelve years. She had a history of having used cocaine, marijuana, and pills, but her life changed dramatically when she started snorting heroin at the age of thirty-three. At the time I spoke with Pam, she had stopped using after having completed a drug rehabilitation program a few months earlier. Pam realized that she had not been attentive to her children during her addiction. Describing her state of mind when she was using heroin, she said: "I was just living today . . . living today. The kids were just basically there. And every thought of mine was where are we going to get another bag from? What are we going to do now? What kind of schemes are we going to come up with to get money? What can we sell?

You know, stuff like that." Although relatives ensured that the children had food, Pam and her boyfriend spent virtually all their disposable income on drugs.

> We wasn't paying any bills. A lot of stuff we did back then, we still dealing with it now. When we first came home [from drug rehabilitation], the water was shut off. And the gas was shut off. And they started to turn the electric off. So we tried to get all that paid up, and it's hard now 'cause we're behind on the bills and stuff. But the kids weren't getting sneakers. They weren't getting new clothes. They weren't getting haircuts 'cause he [her boyfriend] cut hair. So we always tried to find ways around of doing stuff. And, they would have plenty of food.... That was not a problem. Food wasn't a problem. They didn't get much of anything else. Like if they wanted change or a dollar to go outside to the store or ice-cream truck, never that. Never that.

Reflecting on how she had behaved as a mother, Pam clearly recognized that her behavior during this time was detrimental to the children, and she vowed to make things up to them: "I hated for them to know. I hated myself. But all I kept thinking about was, I'm going to get better and I'm going to make it better for them. And I'll make it up to them. That's all I kept thinking about."

Unfortunately, within a few months of our first conversation, Pam relapsed, as did her boyfriend, and her children's lives were disrupted once again when she left to enter rehabilitation. Drug addiction frequently entails periods of sobriety followed by relapses and renewed drug use, but each such relapse can result in the mother absenting herself from the family and her children as she becomes enmeshed in a world where little else besides getting drugs matters to her.

Children were bothered by their mother's drug use and blamed it for their mother's trouble with the law and their sometime inability to act in ways the children believed they should. As one mother said of her children: "They hated the life I was in—they hated it. They'd get mad at me. Like, 'Mommy, why you keep doing that?'" Children seemed to find it hard to understand why their mothers would not just stop using, seeing their drug dependence as a choice. Here Aleesha, one of the teen parents, talks about her mother, a user of several types of drugs:

ALEESHA: I'm so mad at her.

JS: What do you think she should have or could have done differently?

ALEESHA: Changed her life around.

JS: Yeah. How?

ALEESHA: By doing stuff differently.

JS: What do you think she could have done differently?

ALEESHA: What she did to get her where she is. She should have thought twice.

Aleesha's remarks reflect the frustration many children felt about their mother's drug use and their inability to stop engaging in behavior that was clearly damaging the family and the children. They also reveal a belief that these mothers had a choice to continue or reject their drug use, showing how difficult it can be for children to understand the challenges associated with terminating drug dependence, which frequently occurs only after several cycles of sobriety and relapse, as well as their mothers' pathways to drug use. Most of the mothers began using drugs when they were young, before they had children. Some were introduced to drugs at very young ages by other family members, well before they were able to make an informed decision about the consequences of their action. In addition, many of them had adverse experiences when they were growing up, including child abuse, that could have led them to start using drugs. Giving up a nearly lifelong drug habit is difficult, even after a woman undergoes treatment and even when she seems motivated to quit. But for children, abandoning the desire to have a mother who will be a steady and dependable presence in their life is just as difficult, so the disappointment and frustration many expressed about their mother's persistent drug use is certainly understandable.

Crime: A Family Affair

"Like mother, like daughter." "Like father, like son." These phrases are part of our vocabulary because they neatly summarize the fact that children so often resemble their parents, not just physically but also behaviorally. Small wonder then that one of the major concerns about children of incarcerated parents is that they themselves may become criminals, and may even be locked up in the same prison as their parent. Although we don't yet have conclusive evidence that parental incarceration increases the risk of children's criminality, we do know that parental criminality—regardless of whether the parent is imprisoned— heightens the likelihood of delinquency (Farrington et al. 2001; Lipsey and Derzon 1998; Loeber and Dishion 1983; Osborn and West 1979). While there is some evidence of a hereditary component to this intergenerational phenomenon (Walters 1992), a child's environment seems to play a far more significant role in this cycle. Children whose relatives engage in criminal activity have within their family both role models for behavior and mentors to teach them the attitudes, rationales, and beliefs that enable people to break the law.

In addition to having mothers who had been arrested, the children in this study had relatives who were in trouble with the law. One of the most disturbing interviews I conducted was with Lucinda, the disengaged mother of six, only three of whom were still in her life. Although I first met Lucinda in the city jail, she was later transferred to a jail in another county, where she was wanted for violating her probation. This facility provides no private rooms for confidential conversations that prisoners might have with lawyers or researchers. Instead, prisoners were brought to a large cafeteria-like space, where they sat at separate tables for such meetings. It was in this room that Lucinda and I sat one late fall afternoon at a table across the room from the door used by prisoners coming in for private meetings. She and I had been talking quietly for about an hour when this door opened to reveal a male prisoner standing in the doorway. I did not pay particular attention to his entrance, but Lucinda certainly did: she suddenly burst into tears, sobbing loudly and inconsolably, slumped on the table, her head resting on her arms. What on earth, I wondered, could have triggered such an intense reaction? Was it the sight of the prisoner in the door? Indeed it was, for the young man in prison garb was Jack, her twenty-two-year-old son. Lucinda had not known that he was incarcerated in the same facility as she; seeing him there brought home her disconnection from her children and her sorrow for what she perceived were her failings as a mother.[5]

Mother and son were not the only members of the family in this jail: Lucinda's brother and sister were locked up in the same facility. From Lucinda's ten-year-old son Ian's perspective, his mother, brother, aunt, and uncle were all incarcerated at the same time in the same place for different offenses.

Ian's family was unusual but not unique in having so many family members in jail or prison at the same time. Far more common were families in which various members had been to prison in the past, with perhaps one member currently incarcerated. In the city sample, 39.5 percent of the children had family members who had been incarcerated, including grandfathers, uncles, aunts, and brothers, and another 14 percent had siblings whose fathers had been in prison. Others had relatives who had been in trouble with the law but not incarcerated. Imprisonment, therefore, was far more normalized for these children than for others. When I asked Antoine what he thought about his father and four uncles all being in prison for different crimes, he simply shrugged and replied: "I don't think about it." Despite the prevalence of incarceration in the family, however, these children found the prospect of their mother going to prison frightening and disturbing, especially if they were living with her and especially if she had never been to prison before.

Having a relative in prison was not the only way in which children were made aware of crime in their family. Many, of course, knew about their mother's illegal drug use, but some were exposed firsthand to other criminal behavior their mothers engaged in, such as fights or assaults. A few had accompanied their mothers when they went out to crack houses: a solution, from the mother's perspective, to the problem of having no one to look after the child if she left the house. One mother was arrested and jailed for shoplifting when she was serving as a chaperone on her eight-year-old son's school trip; her unexplained disappearance left her son and his classmates and teachers bewildered. This mother ran a drug-dealing business from her home at night, with a walk-up window for customers. She sent her son, whose father was in prison, around the corner to sleep at her sister's, but he knew that his mother was doing something illegal. Many of the children in this study likewise had opportunities to observe behavior that could serve as a model for them. Of course, that does not mean that the children wanted to model their behavior on their mother's. All the children thought it was wrong to steal, for example, and several viewed their mother's behavior as wrong. Others were angry with their mother because they felt her drug use had created so many problems for the family that they had been deprived of having a normal life. Nevertheless, the extensive exposure to family members in trouble with the law raises serious concerns about the children themselves becoming involved with crime, especially because the odds of having a criminal record are far higher for those who have a family member with a history of arrest (Farrington et al. 2001)

Living in Poverty

Ten-year-old Dayesh remained standing during our first interview. We were in his bedroom, and when he gallantly offered me a folding chair, he was left with no place to sit. After leaving the house Dayesh shared with his mother, Siena, his three siblings, and a nephew, I described the setting in my field notes:

> I got lost driving to Siena's house, so I called to tell her I wasn't sure where her street was. She insisted on walking out to where I had stopped in order to guide me back to her street, which was probably a good thing: the street runs one way and the route we took to get there was one I never would have found. It led over streets that looked bombed out and were crisscrossed by old railroad tracks. Abandoned factory buildings lined the streets. Her street is a narrow one lined with rowhouses, many of which are vacant or abandoned; some have been posted by the city as off limits.
>
> The house is in poor condition and in need of repairs and renovation: walls stripped of wallpaper but then not refinished, worn flooring, a large hole in the bottom step of the stairs, no bathroom door (a piece of fabric hangs in its place), etc. Dayesh's bedroom is probably about eight feet by eight feet. The walls at one time had wallpaper on them but they have been mostly stripped. The ceiling, which has an empty light socket, has suffered tremendous water damage. There is very old deteriorated furniture in the room, including something that used to be a bunk bed. The bottom bunk is still intact, with two mattresses on the bottom of it. However, the top bunk had collapsed onto the two mattresses and is leaning to one side quite badly and that's apparently where he sleeps. There's a television set in the room, a wardrobe that's in bad condition (the wood is delaminating), and a kind of storage container with a big garbage bag on top of it and some dirty clothes on top of that. The room's

one window is covered over with a big poster board that someone has a drawing on and an old raggedy shade. There's one light fixture in the room with a bare light bulb in it. When we first came upstairs, there was a red light bulb in it so it was very dim in the room. You really essentially couldn't see anything, and he had to go downstairs and get a regular light bulb for it.

While other children I met in the city lived in better physical surroundings than Dayesh's, his neighborhood and house were typical of many of the children's homes. Virtually all the children I interviewed following their mother's arrest were living in low-income households, not surprising given that low incomes are far more prevalent among female-headed or even single male-headed households than in two-parent families. However, even the few children living in two-parent families were in the low-income bracket. Being from low-income families meant that the children lived in deteriorated neighborhoods characterized by neglect, abandoned houses and, frequently, high levels of violence (see chapter 3). Often, the furniture in the children's houses was similar to Dayesh's, with few furnishings beyond basic necessities such as beds and perhaps a couch in poor condition. The beds sometimes consisted of mattresses on the floor that were shared with other children in the household, which was consistent with the overcrowded living conditions in some homes. Several children lived in apartments or houses with a room clearly intended to be a dining room with no furniture at all in it. Thus, there was no place where the family could sit together to share a meal, had they been so inclined, a significant shortcoming because shared family meals are associated with many positive outcomes for children (Pearson, Muller, and Frisco 2006; Sen 2010; Tubbs, Roy, and Burton 2005).

Children from more affluent families in the United States usually have dozens of toys, purchased in part for the perceived developmental advantages they can impart. The children in this study, however, tended to have few—if any—toys, save for a video game, which several seemed to own. Almost none of the households had any children's books. The constant companion in almost every household was a television, usually tuned to programming inappropriate for young children.

The children clearly felt the financial constraints of their family circumstances. Asked what they would wish for if they could have one wish, a large majority of the children expressed a desire for improved material circumstances. A big house where a girl wouldn't be ashamed to invite her friends, all the toys in the world, a million dollars, riches for the entire family—these were the sort of wishes the children expressed. One nine-year-old girl made clear that she associated her family's difficulties with their financial situation: "I wish I had a lot of money. Then I could buy a big house and get away from a lot of our problems." Indeed, as already noted, research has shown that poor children have an increased likelihood of numerous problems in various domains.

What is known about the effects of low income on children is not encouraging for prisoners' offspring. Evidence suggests that parents in prison—especially women—are very poor, as most of the children in this sample appeared to be. Just over half (51.9 percent) of mothers in state prison said that before they were incarcerated, they had provided the primary financial support for their children. Nearly one in three of them had an income of less than six hundred dollars the month before they were imprisoned (Glaze and Maruschak 2008). Children in such low-income families would be considered to be living in extreme poverty, which would make them more vulnerable to poverty's ill effects. In addition, a significant minority (18.3 percent) of prisoners' children are under age five (Mumola 2000), which places them among those for whom poverty exerts the most direct influence on cognitive ability and achievement. Older children may be affected through the community factors just noted. And the poor home environment that can ensue as a consequence of poverty can adversely affect children of any age. The financial situation of the children I met constrained them to households and communities that shaped their social worlds in potentially harmful ways, as we will see.

Mom's Mental Illness

Approximately one-quarter of the mothers in the city sample spoke openly about suffering from mental illness, reporting either that they had been diagnosed with a disorder or that they had been in treatment for one.[6] Most often, these women reported suffering from depression, but some also reported anxiety disorders, schizophrenia, and bipolar disorder. Some were taking medication, and a few reported having been hospitalized because of their illness. Some had attempted suicide.

Life with a mother suffering from mental illness can present special challenges to children, including having to cope with time spent apart from her. Melissa, for example, was a ten-year-old living with her mother, Catherine, after a separation of seven years, during which Melissa lived continuously with one foster mother. Melissa and four of her five siblings had been removed from the house by the city's child protective services agency when she was three, because Catherine was neglecting the children. Some of the children were sent to stay with relatives, but Melissa and her older sister, both of whom appeared to be intellectually delayed, were placed in foster care. After the children were taken from her, Catherine was hospitalized because she suffered a nervous breakdown. She had been on antidepressants ever since.

As might be expected, Melissa had become extremely attached to her foster mother. Her diary contained page after page of lines that read, "I love you Mom Carrie," referring to her foster mother. She had been living with Catherine for only three months when I first met her, but she was trying hard to feel that she loved her biological mother as much as her foster mother. Catherine, however, was difficult to deal with, and Melissa was struggling to reconcile her desire to be with her mother while still feeling profoundly attached to her foster mother. Catherine's behavior and attitude toward her children showed why the children had been removed in the first place. She was tyrannical and capricious toward them, imposing strict rules in an atmosphere of threats. When I met her, she had been arrested on a charge of beating one of her sons, who lived with his father, and if she did not physically punish the children, she did not hesitate to threaten them with such consequences. Here is an excerpt of notes following a visit to the house several months after Catherine and Melissa's reunification. Catherine had prepared dinner for the children, which consisted of tuna fish served in part on crackers and in part on a paper plate. The children were not given utensils, so Melissa's older sister, June, who was impaired intellectually, was eating with her fingers.

> Catherine started yelling at June, telling her to get that smartass look off her face and to "stop doin' that." I asked her what June was doing and she didn't answer me. All I could see was that the girl was apparently eating the tuna fish with her fingers, presumably because she had no cracker to eat it on. I asked her again and she said something about how June is always rolling her eyes around and getting an attitude. Not long afterward, June went upstairs and her mother yelled at her not to clomp her feet that way. Then Catherine told her to stay upstairs and she said she was coming back down. Catherine then hollered "You're gonna get punched in the face if you come down here." She repeated it again and added "I'll punch you right in the mouth."

In addition to Melissa and June, three very young children were in the house, sitting quietly on a couch.

> Catherine hollered at the four-year-old to shut up, even though the child was simply sitting on the couch talking quietly to the others. There was no shrieking, no giggling, no running around out of control. Instead, the kids sat on the couch watching TV the whole time I was there. Catherine is very large both in height and breadth and after she told the child to shut up, I watched her bear down on the child while I was still talking to Melissa. Everyone held their breath because her walk across the living room from the kitchen was so menacing. She towered over the child and told her to "get up there," meaning presumably to pull her legs up on the couch and not to move. The children were not doing anything wrong, but she has absolutely no patience with them at all. It was truly frightening to witness. . . . She shows no signs of affection or love toward them, and I didn't hear her say a single kind thing to them.[7]

When I first met Melissa, she said that her one wish was to learn to listen and be good, which no doubt reflected Catherine's repeatedly telling her to do just that. Months later, however, Melissa's wish was simply to return to live with her foster mother. Melissa had told her caseworker of her desire, but the plan when we last spoke, some months afterward, was to put both June and Melissa up for adoption.

Conclusion

Melissa's story was among the saddest I encountered, but the family life of many children I met revealed numerous factors that could jeopardize their well-being before their mothers ever went to prison. Most notable were four conditions that together produce a powerful combination with potential negative outcomes for children: parental substance abuse, poverty, family criminality, and fragile family structures—single mothers and absent fathers. Many children were residing in households where multiple risks were present, intertwined in ways that sabotage efforts to get out from under their influence. The net effect is that the children are enmeshed in environments and family situations that can put them on trajectories toward undesirable consequences.

The prevalence of substance abuse among the mothers in this study was consistent with a solid body of evidence indicating that women offenders have far higher rates of drug use than occurs in the general population (Bloom, Owen, and Covington 2003). In fact, substance abuse is a key factor in what feminist criminologists refer to as a gendered pathway to crime among women: a trajectory that often begins with their victimization as children and adults and consequent drug use and drug-related crime (Belknap 2001; Chesney-Lind 1997). Despite their involvement with drugs, however, most of the mothers I met remained engaged with their children. The drug habit for a minority, however, became their paramount need, subordinating even their parental responsibilities. Their dependence on cocaine, heroin, alcohol, or other drugs led to their sporadic engagement with their children and families or to disengagement from them. Apart from a mother's earlier incarcerations, her substance abuse generally was the greatest cause of disruption in the children's lives; their mothers connected with them for a time, only to leave again when seized with the need to use. Mothers at greatest risk of incarceration—those in jail awaiting trial—were those most likely to be sporadically engaged or disengaged, meaning that the children most likely to experience maternal incarceration were those subject beforehand to the greatest disruption due to maternal drug abuse.

Family disruption was not the only consequence of a mother's drug habit: these drug-addicted mothers turned to crime and earned little money, impacting the family economy for the worse. Money that might be spent on necessities for the children instead went to feed a habit, as Pam made clear when she voiced regret over her behavior while she was addicted to heroin. Supporting their dependency typically meant that mothers resorted to illegal sources of income, such as theft or prostitution, and conventional employment was usually of short duration at low pay. Even without the complication of drugs, however, most mothers' employment options were limited by their lack of education, occupational skills, and work experience. As a result, families were mired in economic difficulty. Growing up in households with such meager economic resources may compromise children's development in multiple domains, including physical and mental health and cognition (Brooks-Gunn and Duncan 1997; Seccombe 2000; Smith, Brooks-Gunn, and Klebanov 1997).

Most of the families' financial difficulties were further exacerbated by the absence of fathers. Unlike the case in many U.S. families, these fathers are absent not due to divorce, but rather to incarceration, death, or lack of involvement. For this group of children, fathers were more likely to be in prison than to be living with them. In families where fathers were alive and not incarcerated, twice as many children had fathers who were not involved with them as had fathers living with them. As Danyelle said of one of her children's fathers, "He just step out of her life"—as if he were watching a movie he did not particularly enjoy so got up and left the theater, the movie's story unfolding behind his indifferent back. This detachment was compounded for nearly all the children by seeing other men become fathers to their siblings, only to disappear from their lives as well. The combination of missing fathers and instability in the mothers' intimate relationships—evident from the numerous families with multiple fathers—represents yet another threat to the children's well-being, placing them at risk of undesirable behavioral and psychological consequences (Ackerman et al. 2002; Najman et al. 1997; Osborne and McLanahan 2007). Single parenthood also produces strain on mothers, leading to more stressful family environments and increasing the risk of maternal mental health problems and pressures that have been theorized to lead to the mothers' further criminal behavior (Agnew 1992, 2001; McLanahan 2009).

Fathers who were missing because they were in prison were not the only family members in trouble with the law. Many of the children had uncles, aunts, grandparents, and siblings who had been arrested, in addition to their mothers. The idea that crime runs in families is not new (Dugdale 1910), and researchers have found that offending is indeed concentrated in families (Farrington et al. 2001). In addition, women who engage in antisocial behavior are more likely to become romantically involved with men of the same bent (Krueger et al. 1998), which was certainly the case for the women I interviewed. Various theories have been advanced to explain why particular families have high rates of arrest, but one likely explanation is the continuity of exposure to environmental risk factors, such as family disruption, poverty, living in disadvantaged neighborhoods, and inadequate parental supervision. Whatever the explanation, such extensive family criminality does not bode well for the children's futures, because family members' arrests—particularly a father's arrests—have been found to be robust predictors of boys' arrests (Farrington et al. 2001).

The portrait of the children's family life that has emerged here demonstrates the importance of viewing parental incarceration via a life-course perspective to help explain the complexity of the forces at work. Many of the children had already experienced disruptions and resultant separations from their mothers, and some had developed strong attachments to other family figures who cared for them. Although these relationships might mitigate the trauma that could accompany a parent's imprisonment, they did not necessarily inure children from the effect of disruptions to their family life and to other risk factors that might be present. Seen from this perspective, incarceration becomes a point on a continuum of multiple traumas, any of which could produce negative emotional and behavioral reactions. Indeed, research has shown that a variety of stressors, such as being abused as a child, witnessing violence, parental divorce, or poverty can produce outcomes similar to those observed in prisoners' offspring. In other words, some problems observed in childhood and adolescence do not result from specific traumas but instead are outcomes that can be associated with a diverse range of negative life events (McMahon et al. 2003) like those the children I interviewed were experiencing.

The troubling family circumstances of many of these children had consequences for their social worlds, as we see in the next chapter. Both family structure and poverty influence a child's social mobility and accumulation of social capital, and thus a child's life trajectory (Biblarz and Raftery 1993), limiting access to prosocial forces that could counterbalance the potentially harmful effects of the family setting.

2

Outside the Curtained Windows

It happened time and again: walking into a child's house, I would be struck by its dimness. Only after the first few interviews did I begin to realize that the houses had something in common that created these darkened interiors: makeshift curtains shrouded their front windows—blankets, bedsheets, lengths of material, and even on occasion some old curtains. Unlike drapes or curtains that can be closed or opened to provide a view of the outside and allow light in, this expedient blocked the windows from view. In truth, the scene outside many of the houses was decidedly unlovely. Occupied homes badly in need of renovation stood side by side with abandoned and boarded-up houses. Littered and potholed streets. Trash-strewn vacant lots. No trees to relieve the bleak urban landscape and offer shade in the hot summer months. If these curtains were not intended to block the view of the streetscape, why were they hung? The likely reason was to protect the family's privacy and prevent passersby from seeing inside. The houses were typically in neighborhoods where residents and visitors sat on stoops or front porches to pass the time, and an exposed window made a showcase of a house's interior. Nevertheless, the drapes often felt like barriers, isolating the people who lived in the house from the outside world and trapping the children in a setting that at times seemed oppressively insular—disturbing, given the environment in which the children were enmeshed.

Although many of the children were living in situations that could presage negative consequences for them, as we have seen, a less than ideal family life does not doom a child to an unhappy, trouble-ridden childhood followed by more of the same as an adult. Many children deemed at risk do not follow the script society has written for them and instead achieve a satisfying and fulfilling life and a sense of well-being. Even those whose behavior or circumstances seem to portend long-term difficulties, such as delinquency or teenage parenthood, often are deflected from such paths and achieve a good quality of life in adulthood (Mahoney and Magnusson 2001; Moffitt 1993; Werner and Smith 1992).

What factors can help at-risk children overcome the odds? Researchers who have followed children over time from birth or early childhood have identified several. Some, such as a child's disposition, are not amenable to change. For instance, children with sociable, easygoing temperaments apparent from the first years of life are more likely to be invulnerable to the risks posed by a home characterized by poverty, distressed family relations, parental alcoholism, or mental illness (Werner and Smith 1982). More mutable factors involve how the child interacts with and performs in the environment outside the household. Performing at grade level in school, graduating from high school, having support from teachers during adolescence and a positive attitude toward school, and having access to adults outside the home for support, guidance, or advice have all been found to contribute to resiliency (Werner and Smith 1992). Positive influences encountered in the world outside the home therefore represent one way to help offset the potential harmful effect of adverse family circumstances. Unfortunately, the draped windows I saw in so many homes heightened the impression that their residents were cut off from such outside forces.

"I Don't Trust People"

When we think back to the people who were important to us as we were growing up, many of us include in that group someone outside our family. A beloved teacher, a demanding sports coach, an understanding member of the clergy, a close family friend, a caring neighbor—any one of these or others may have helped us navigate childhood and adolescence. The significance of these individuals in our lives demonstrates a central premise of human development: although a child's immediate family is vital to his or her growth, once the child is exposed to the world beyond the household, other sources of socialization and influence take on importance as well. Most influential are people with whom the child interacts regularly, including other family members, friends, neighbors, schoolmates, and nonrelated adults, such as parents' friends or teachers. All these individuals become part of a child's social network, an aggregation of people with whom the child engages in activities and develops relationships of support, friendship, guidance, and reciprocal exchange. Social networks have an important place in children's lives, connecting them with others who can provide emotional support, intellectual stimulation, play, and counsel. Networks also contribute to the development of social capital, which in turn can enable children to achieve goals that position them for improved life circumstances.

How exactly do adults other than parents contribute to a child's healthy development? In 1979, Moncrieff Cochran and Jane Anthony Brassard, child development experts, provided a framework for understanding this phenomenon.

Ties to adult social networks, they theorized, could benefit the child through direct support as well as indirectly, through their parents. Indirect influence occurs because networks of adults provide parents with both emotional and material support, role models for parenting, and opportunities for their own personal growth through exposure to new experiences and aspects of the outside world. Adults in parents' social networks can affect children directly by providing cognitive stimulation, engagement in a range of activities different from those parents alone offer, and additional social support. Network members can also provide additional role models for children.

Consistent with Cochran and Brassard's theoretical framework, research has demonstrated that the extent to which parents introduce their children to other adults in their own network is important to enhancing their development. Children's connections with adult networks have been shown to promote healthy development in domains such as social competence, emotional well-being, and academic achievement (DuBois and Silverthorn 2005; Greenberger, Chen, and Beam 1998; Rishel, Sales, and Koeske 2005; Woolley and Bowen 2007).[1] As we have seen, many children had, in their parents, role models whose behavior even the parents themselves did not want them to emulate. Certainly the mothers did not wish their children to have a future that included drug addiction or prison, like so many of their children's fathers. Mothers—especially mothers of adolescents—worried that their children were in peril of becoming involved in drugs or antisocial behavior. One mother with a long history of drug addiction, arrests, and time in prison said: "I just don't want my son to be like myself or his dad."

Despite their concerns, the mothers had limited ability to give their children access to more positive role models in their daily lives. That so many of the children's fathers had prison records or were murdered, usually because of their involvement in crime, is a good indicator that the mothers' social worlds often involved association with men at a considerable remove from conventional society. Furthermore, many of the women seemed socially isolated. Time and again, when asked how many close friends they had, mothers replied, "None," and I classified a majority (59 percent) as having few or no friends. Some women had intentionally cut off relationships with people who were part of their social circle when they were using drugs. Now clean and sober, these women wanted to avoid associations that could trigger their relapse. Groups like Narcotics Anonymous warn recovering addicts to avoid the "people, places, and things" that were part of their drug-using life, and these women took that advice to heart. For instance, Lynn, a forty-two-year-old mother living with her daughter and fiancé, explained why she had no friends now, although she had as a teenager:

LYNN: Like, most of them [her former associates] are into stuff, and they run
    the street and all that, and I don't do that anymore. I stay home, so I don't

want to be bothered with people who're still out there. Like, I changed, and they changed. They should change, 'cause they got more kids than me. And besides, I really don't like people anymore.

JS: Why's that?

LYNN: 'Cause they try to get you into a lot of stuff, and people ain't really your friend, and I just really like being alone.

Lynn's concluding remark hints at the probability that the social isolation of many of the women was related to their profound mistrust of other people, their expectation that others would betray or hurt them. As another mother put it: "I don't trust people. I don't trust people to be my close friends. You know what I mean? I really don't. I know I could be a good friend to you. I don't trust people to be good friends to me. I helped them get a job, did everything. They turned their backs on me every time."

Some women who distrusted others had been involved in relationships with fellow drug users whom they perceived as using others to get drugs. At least one woman acknowledged that she had acted this way, viewing other users as "disposable people" whom she would "use for what I want, then let them go." Other socially isolated women not only seemed to distrust others but also had a generally antisocial orientation that appeared to date from their own childhoods. They described themselves as having been belligerent and aggressive for most of their lives, as did Donna, a thirty-one-year-old mother of two:

DONNA: I don't really want no friends. I had more male friends than I did female friends. You feel like you can talk to a male better than you can talk to a female without the confusion and the "he say, she say" stuff. And I'm getting too old to be out there fighting people.

JS: Did you used to fight people?

DONNA: All the time. I used to fight every day.

JS: Physically fight?

DONNA: Uh huh.

JS: Who would you fight with?

DONNA: Anybody. Anybody who got in my face, I was fighting on them.

JS: Yeah? Why was that?

DONNA: I don't know. I'm just that type of person. I don't like nobody in my face. Don't talk to me in any old kind of way, I'm grown just like you grown, or when we was kids, don't talk to me like that. Don't get in my face.

JS: Were these people you knew or strangers?

DONNA: They was people I knew. They talk about me, I beat them up. Way back then they had a tendency to do things like that.

Whatever the reason women chose to avoid friendships, the result was that their social network was considerably narrowed and their households felt insular to me, an impression intensified by the makeshift curtains that shut out the world. Lynn said she wished she could "live on an island by myself," together with her fiancé and daughter. In some cases, this preference for isolation was compounded by concern about the perils of the neighborhood, which led mothers to conclude that it was unsafe for the children to play outside. Such insularity has consequences for both parent and child. For the mothers, the absence of a social network can add to the stresses that any parent experiences, because they have no one to turn to for advice or support when unexpected, worrisome, or frustrating events occur. The children do not receive the benefits of contact with adults in a parent's social network, including the development of social capital. Their parent's isolation also deprives children of a model of how to become integrated into the community.

Not all the mothers were as isolated as those just described. Some provided a model of positive engagement for their children, who seemed more engaged as well. Margaret was a fifty-year-old grandmother who had raised three of her grandchildren from early childhood. Her son, the children's father, was a drug addict who had spent long stretches in prison and had never taken responsibility for the children's care. On the day he was released from one of his prison terms, he went to see the children at the apartment where they lived with their mother and discovered that she had left them alone for three days—the children were three months, one year, and two years old. The authorities removed the children from the house, and Margaret and her husband took them into their home and raised them. Their mother never made an effort to see them again, and their maternal grandparents turned their backs on them as well. Margaret was the only mother they had ever really known.

Margaret had worked for many years until she became disabled by a stroke. Her recent arrest on a fraud charge was the only time she had been in trouble with the law. She had good relations with her family and a strong circle of close friends with whom she socialized regularly. She volunteered at her church, the community center, and the children's school. The grandchildren went to another city nearly every year to spend the summer with their great-aunts, who engaged them in a variety of recreational and cultural activities. The children therefore were part of a larger social network in which adults other than their grandparents provided stimulation and encouraged their participation in a broader range of activities than their grandparents alone could have managed.

Kanishia, the oldest grandchild, was thirteen years old when we met. She was an excellent student who enjoyed participating in sports and spending time both in the library and with her large circle of friends. After school, Kanishia worked at the local playground for two or three hours a day, helping younger children with schoolwork and recreational activities, for which she was paid a nominal amount. The recreation program director had become a mentor for Kanishia, taking her places once or twice a week and buying her small things, thereby giving Margaret a break from some of her responsibilities, which had weighed more heavily on her since her husband's death a couple of years earlier. All the neighbors liked and admired Kanishia, who was always helping them out by babysitting or taking children to the library, where she taught them how to use computers. Following her grandmother's example, Kanishia was very engaged in the community and was clearly building social capital for her future. In contrast, Lynn's daughter, nine-year-old Kelly, was growing up in the kind of insular environment described earlier. When asked what she would wish for if she could be granted one wish, Kelly replied that she wanted to be "big," because big people "get to see a lot of people." Although she loved and admired her mother, Kelly felt the absence in her world of others beyond their immediate family.

The children's relationships with relatives outside the immediate family mitigated the effects of the absence of a parent's friends or work colleagues. By necessity, children whose mothers were sporadically engaged or disengaged had developed strong ties to other relatives who could care for them, but many other children also had relatives outside their nuclear family to whom they felt close. These relatives—grandparents, aunts, uncles—engaged the children in activities, were available for them to confide in, and often served as the role models lacking in the children's immediate family. Donna's fourteen-year-old daughter, Crystal, for instance, had formed a strong bond with her grandparents, with whom she had lived for the past few years after her mother had gone to jail for a period of months. Her mother had been home from jail for some time, but Crystal preferred to stay with her grandparents, although she saw her mother daily. Crystal was disappointed in her mother, saying that women should not use drugs because they "mess their lives up, their careers," as her mother had done. However, she found a positive role model in her aunt, whom she spoke of with admiration and whose life was far different from Donna's: "I would probably want to grow up and be like my aunt. She has a job. She has one child, but she had her after she was married. She didn't get married too early. She was, I think, twenty-five years old when she got married. Her marriage is still lasting. And she's in the church, which I like to do."

At times, the contrast between the models that children had at home and in their extended family was pronounced. Like Crystal, twelve-year-old Chantay lived most of the time with her grandparents in their clean, well-furnished, and inviting house in a working-class neighborhood. Her grandparents were retired after having worked all their adult lives and raised two daughters. One daughter had become a nurse; the other, Chantay's mother, Darlene, had become a crack user. Married, with three other children and another on the way, Darlene lived in a rundown, sparsely furnished house in a very poor neighborhood to which Chantay would return on weekends. Darlene's marriage was tumultuous, marked by infidelity and violence. Darlene was arrested twice in six months for assault. Chantay had opted to stay with her grandparents, where, as she said, things were quieter and she had her own bedroom. In addition, she was able to attend a better school than was available in her mother's neighborhood. Her grandmother was quite engaged in Chantay's education and activities, making sure she did her homework and encouraging her involvement in other activities. In contrast to what was on offer in her home with her mother, Chantay's grandparents provided stability and security.

In addition to serving as potential role models, confidantes, and sources of support for the children, these relatives also provided a support system for the mothers, assisting them with the constant responsibilities so many of them had as single parents. Furthermore, as we will see, these extended family members could be counted on to care for the children if the need arose, as it would if a mother went to jail or prison. Without the support of others in the family, finding someone to take the children in would be very problematic.

Some of the children had few relatives outside their immediate family who were part of their network because their mothers were estranged from their families or had bad relations with them. Like their children, several of the mothers had virtually no relationship with their own fathers, even in childhood. Their mothers and maternal relatives were the only part of the family with whom the mothers in the city sample maintained a tie. If those relationships were compromised, the mothers and children had limited opportunities to expand their networks through family members. In addition, as we saw earlier, incarceration was common in many families, meaning that members of the immediate and extended family might provide models of antisocial behavior instead of positive role models the children could emulate. As a result, troubled or undesirable family relations could shrink the children's potential positive social networks and add to the insularity of some families.

School: Safe Haven or Cauldron of Trouble?

Peter was six days shy of seventeen when we first met, but he wasn't sure what grade he was in. When asked, he replied that he was taking tenth- and eleventh-grade classes, trying to make up for having failed one year and for time lost a couple of years earlier when he all but stopped going to school after his father died. Small wonder that he was vague about his grade: at best, school had been only a tenuous part of his life. Just when he should have been starting school, he and his mother were living on the streets, sleeping indoors when a friend would let them stay but essentially homeless for years. Finally recognizing that she was unable to care for her son because of her drug abuse, his mother left Peter at his grandmother's house when he was nine years old, hoping she would take care of him. The one wrinkle in this plan, however, was that his grandmother did not want Peter living with her, so she called the city's child welfare agency—OFS (Office of Family Services). OFS took Peter into foster care and, when he was ten years old, was able to send him to live with relatives outside the city who enrolled him in the fifth grade. This is Peter's earliest memory of attending school.

It is doubtful that Peter had never attended school at all before he went to live with his relatives, but the chaotic life he had lived with his mother during his first years of life had obscured any recollection of his early education. The chance at redemption that life with his relatives had presented was fleeting. After he had spent a year with them, his mother reentered his life, now clean and sober but still not completely stable. Peter went to live with her, this time in secure housing, but the family moved frequently, forcing him to change schools several times. Once he started high school, he had a difficult time because of the deficiencies in his early education and his upbringing. He brought a defiant attitude to school, which created problems for him, as did his lack of money.

PETER: I think I got suspended one time when I wasn't in school 'cause they said there was a dress code. Of course I was like, like, "Come on, I can't afford that shit right now, man." Like they let me in school, but they gave me a detention. I can't afford the shit that everyone be wearing. I come with what I got. Whatever I wear is what I got. I cursed the lady out.

JS: You told the lady what?

PETER: I told her that she was a bitch. I don't want to hear that shit.

JS: What's the dress code?

PETER: You gotta wear khakis and a button-down shirt. I don't wear that shit, first of all. Second of all, I'm not buying this shit and I can't afford it.

JS: So what did you wear to school yesterday?

PETER: I wore a jersey and a hat, and they let me in that day. They didn't say nothing to me.

JS: Well, what have you been wearing since the beginning of school?

PETER: Same thing I wear every day, usually like a T-shirt, a pair of jeans, and a hat. Some boots.

JS: So they let you in those other days, but today they said they had—

PETER: Yeah, they just want to bust my balls.

JS: And so did they tell you you were suspended?

PETER: Yeah, so I walked out. I just left.

This incident was characteristic of Peter's shaky career in school. Nevertheless, Peter still wanted to graduate with a high school diploma, recognizing that life without one was not easy. Ultimately, Peter realized that the route to his goal lay outside a traditional high school; the last time we talked, he was hoping to get into an alternative school, where other teenagers he knew had succeeded after failing elsewhere.

Schools are a principal venue for children's development outside the home, a place where they acquire not only academic skills but also social competence. For some, school offers safety and security from the type of chaotic family environment Peter experienced or from a tough neighborhood. Academic achievement and the development of athletic, creative, or intellectual talents are important elements of a child's lifetime trajectory. Indeed, schools play a vital role in children's lives and are increasingly looked to as institutions that can compensate for some of the deficiencies many low-income children experience in other domains. But can they overcome the kinds of disadvantages a child like Peter was living with at home?

Parental incarceration is part of the spectrum of disadvantage children may bring to the classroom with them. Like so many of the children I met, Peter had a father who was in prison during much of his childhood. His death occurred mere months after his release from his latest stint there. If someone had asked Peter's father about his child's academic performance while he was in prison, he might well have said that his son was not doing well. Indeed, in several studies, parents and caregivers have noted that prisoners' children's academic performance has been adversely affected by parental incarceration or that a child in that situation has been getting into trouble at school. There is evidence as well that children with a parent in prison have lower grades than their peers (Trice and Brewster 2004). Considering Peter's life apart from his father's incarceration, however, how much of Peter's academic difficulties can we ascribe to that circumstance?

Although one researcher has noted that academic performance among jail inmates' children was poor before the parent's incarceration (Stanton, 1980), information about children's school performance and conduct before their parent's imprisonment is largely nonexistent. My conversations with the children in the city about their schools and their school performance and conduct shed light in this area and reveal that a parent's imprisonment is not the only explanation for his or her children's academic difficulties.

All but four of the children I interviewed who were still in school attended public schools in the city. Of the rest, one attended a parochial school, one attended public school in a suburb right outside the city, and two attended public school in a nearby city, the state's poorest and home to a troubled education system. Like those of other large U.S. cities, the public school system is characterized by inadequate resources, aging facilities, and a disproportionately high number of students performing at subpar achievement levels in nearly every grade. Many children who cannot afford private schools but have some resources seem to have enrolled in charter or magnet schools, abandoning the traditional public schools, with the result that at a majority of the these schools, fully 100 percent of the students are considered low-income; at some grade levels, virtually every child is considered economically disadvantaged.[2]

Although many question the utility of standardized test scores in assessing academic achievement and knowledge, statewide achievement tests do provide some measure of how students fare relative to their peers in other school districts. Scores for city students have been improving in recent years, but the schools still lag far behind the rest of the public schools in the state. Two-thirds of the city's fifth-grade classes fall into the lowest quintile, or the bottom 20 percent, of all schools in the state on standardized tests. By the eleventh grade, the test scores of 78 percent of the classes in the city are in the bottom quintile. The picture improves somewhat when schools are compared to others with a similar socioeconomic composition, but it is clear that students in these schools are falling far behind their peers in other locales.[3]

The school environment the children described makes it understandable why learning and achievement would be a challenge. Some children went to schools that lacked adequate resources, while others were in classes rife with disciplinary problems, causing significant disruptions in the classroom. Tanya was in seventh grade in an urban middle school that reflected what happens when schools are deprived of sufficient resources, both human and technological. She had identified Ms. Williams as her favorite teacher that year because "she respects us and we respect her" and was explaining what Ms. Williams taught during a computer science class:

TANYA: She was the teacher, 'cause there wasn't no teacher for us, so she would give us math, English, and basic subjects, 'cause we didn't have no computer science teacher, so she would just give us some subjects to keep us occupied.

JS: So I don't understand this. You were supposed to have computer science. And, so, during the period when you went to computer science, there was no computer science teacher? [Tanya nods] And so there was Miss Williams and she would teach you math and English and different things?

TANYA: She wouldn't teach, she would just look at our work to see if we already know the work.

JS: So she would be almost like a tutor or something, for the work you were already covering in other subjects?

TANYA: Uh huh.

JS: Were there computers in this classroom?

TANYA: No. We didn't have enough circuits for that in the school.

JS: What did you think of that?

TANYA: I thought it was wrong. A lot of teachers and things we didn't have. Like we didn't have any English-language teacher; we had different English-language teachers all year. We had about three different English-language teachers.

JS: Why?

TANYA: Because we didn't have no proper English-language teacher.

JS: What did you think of that?

TANYA: I thought that, I mean, that we wouldn't be able to get no work done if we was switched around to all these other teachers and it ended up that they never really taught us anything. The only period of the year that we really got taught English language with our proper English-language teacher was fourth marking period.

With a changing cast of teachers and inadequate or nonexistent equipment, it was small wonder that Tanya felt that "if we didn't have enough teachers, then we wouldn't learn much." The rotating cast of teachers in Tanya's school, as well as in others, was one factor that made classroom environments inimical to learning. As another student noted: "The teachers don't teach and the kids don't learn too much and the teachers don't do nothing about it and the kids play around." Students instinctively knew which teachers they could take advantage of and which teachers would enforce discipline. In the case of the former, students would show little restraint in the classroom, leaving their seats when they wished, talking freely among themselves, and challenging the teacher. Many children described similar classrooms, and in some cases the children in the city sample were among those who were disruptive. For instance, seventeen-year-old Aleesha, one of the teen mothers, had stopped attending school in the ninth grade after being suspended several times.

JS: When did you stop attending school regularly?

ALEESHA: When they kept suspending me.

JS: When did that start happening?

ALEESHA: A month after school started.

JS: In what grade?

ALEESHA: Ninth.

JS: What were they suspending you for?

ALEESHA: Being in the hallways!

JS: What were you doing in the hallways?

ALEESHA: Just standing there talking to people.

JS: When you were supposed to be in class? [*Aleesha nods*] So they would come up to you and say, "Aleesha, go to class," and you would say . . .

ALEESHA: No. And then I'll go to school and my ID will go off, they would give me detention, I wouldn't go [to detention], I go back and they suspend me.

JS: And how many times were you suspended, do you know?

ALEESHA: Ten.

JS: And this was all in the ninth grade?

ALEESHA: Yes.

JS: And before that, had you ever been suspended?

ALEESHA: Yeah. In middle school.

JS: What were you suspended for there?

ALEESHA: Fighting and being bad.

JS: What does "being bad" mean?

ALEESHA: Disruptin' the class.

JS: How would you disrupt the class?

ALEESHA: Make noise.

JS: And were you disrespectful towards the teachers?

ALEESHA: Yes.

Aleesha was not unique. Among the thirty-seven children in the city sample who discussed the issue of suspensions, twenty-one (56.8 percent) had been suspended from school for disruptive behavior or fighting at school, 67 percent of them multiple times. Clearly, disciplinary problems predated maternal incarceration for many of these children. The seeds for their misbehavior were probably sown in their troublesome home environments, but their growth was no doubt nurtured by the lack of prosocial networks in their worlds and by schools where disorder and disrespect occurred in the classrooms and hallways. Even with a mother at home, the children had insufficient constraints and supervision to prevent them from having significant problems in their schools.

Behavioral problems were not the only issues the children had in school: many were struggling academically—28 percent had been left back at least one grade. For some, achieving academic success was challenging due not only to the school environment but also to their home situation. Finding a quiet place to study and do homework in an overcrowded home is difficult, and many children lived in households where their education did not seem to be highly valued. Even those with good grades and aspirations to continue their education after high school had scant support for their dreams, despite their mothers' desire to see their children advance. Dequan, a tenth grader and eager learner, was interested in subjects as diverse as science and poetry. He reported being the recipient of a scholarship that would pay part of his college expenses and said he planned to use it to attend college. However, neither he nor his mother had any knowledge of what was required for college preparation. For instance, neither knew about the standardized tests required for college admissions, and no guidance counselor or teacher had ever informed Dequan of the need to prepare for or take these exams. In fact, none of the five youths in high school who said they would like to attend college knew about the SAT exams and, as a result, none were engaged in preparing for them. Their college prep experience was far different from that of more privileged students, who have support from their schools and families in the form of SAT preparation courses, involved guidance counselors, and even private tutors.

In his college aspirations and engagement in learning, Dequan was more the exception than the rule among the teenagers I interviewed. The younger children's academic struggles in elementary school were mirrored in the adolescents. Becoming a parent meant an end to school, at least temporarily, for the teens in this sample, as we have seen. Although all four teen parents had stopped attending school, caring for their babies was not always their primary reason. Cumulative past circumstances sometimes resulted in their being in classes below the grade level appropriate for their age. Aleesha, for instance, was seventeen years old but still in ninth grade, the result of having been arrested at age fourteen and placed in juvenile correctional facilities for two years, after which she had a baby. When she returned to school, she was placed in the ninth grade but attended only one day. As she remarked, "I was supposed to be in twelfth, and I didn't want to look like a big dummy in ninth grade and being seventeen years old." Several teens who were not parents also had difficulties in school. Of the remaining seven who were high school age (fourteen and older), three were below their expected grade level because they had been left back. Some of them, like Nicole, who was profiled in the preceding chapter, had all but given up on school. At age sixteen, she was only in the ninth grade. When asked why she had been left back, she replied that she had just stopped going to school:

NICOLE: I went to [School A] for a little bit, then I had got kicked out of there and I had to go to [School B], but I was just mad. I don't know why. It was boring. I don't know, we didn't do nothing. We just used to sit there.

JS: At [School B]?

NICOLE: Yeah. I just, I said, "Oh well, I won't go today." Then I said, "I won't go tomorrow," and then when I did try to go I be so far behind, I was just like, "Dang, I ain't gonna pass." Then I didn't go. Then it became a habit, it got so hard for me to actually go. I got in trouble with truancy and everything. I don't know, it was just like I didn't want to go.

It is apparent that several of the children in this sample were encountering academic difficulties, whether the cause was schools with inadequate resources and classrooms with conditions that interfere with learning, home environments that make studying difficult, individual circumstances and behavioral problems, or a combination of these. Although it was encouraging to see that some of the adolescents were doing well in school and aspired to continue their education after high school, more were struggling in school or had left before graduating. The younger children who had already been suspended, had been left back, or were frequently disruptive in class seemed at peril of similar difficulties in secondary school. If parental incarceration does create school problems for children, it would exacerbate already troubled academic careers, based on the histories of the children in the city.

The Underscheduled Child

The media depict today's middle-class youth as occupied with a multitude of activities, juggling participation in sports, lessons, clubs, youth organizations, and, for the very young, scheduled play dates. We hear of children equipped with electronic calendars to keep track of their many activities. Many middle-class parents appear to be competing to ensure that their children are exposed to the maximum number of developmental enrichment activities. Whether motivated by parents' perceived need to give their children a competitive edge or their belief that so much engagement is beneficial for their children, the result in many cases is what has been dubbed the "overscheduled child."

Although some controversy exists over the validity of this issue—whether middle-class and affluent youth are overscheduled or the media has distorted the reality of children's lives—research shows that an overwhelming majority of children do participate in such activities. In a 1999 survey of U.S. families, more than 80 percent of children and teenagers reported participating in at least one sport, lesson, or club during the previous year, although participation by low-income children was less than that of more affluent children (Moore et al. 2000). Such widespread participation is encouraging because there is evidence that children benefit from taking part in extracurricular activities. Involvement in school- or community-based activities is associated with higher academic achievement, stronger attachment to school, a greater sense of well-being, and improved social and interpersonal functioning. Children and adolescents who take part in such activities are less involved in such risky pastimes as underage drinking, drug use, minor and serious delinquent behavior, and sex at an early age (Eccles et al. 2003; Mahoney 2000; Rose-Krasnor et al. 2006). There is also evidence that parents' consistent involvement in community activities is associated with a decreased likelihood that their children will engage in persistent offending from adolescence into adulthood (Mahoney and Magnusson 2001). Thus, participation in such activities has the potential to offset some of the negative risk factors that we have seen in the lives of the children in this study.

The portrait painted by the children and their mothers, however, reveals a phenomenon opposite that of the overscheduled child: the underscheduled child. Like other poor children in the United States, these children's participation in extracurricular activities was far less frequent than that of their more affluent peers. Only seven (14 percent) of the children participated in after-school activities, such as student council, the school band, or a club. Four other children reported that they belonged to a school sports team, even though many of the boys—and the occasional girl—liked to play basketball in their neighborhood pickup games. Six other children reported that they participated in activities with their church, a neighborhood sports league, or a community center. Only one child was taking any type of private lessons, in this instance dance lessons. A partial explanation for this relatively low rate of participation is that, as the children often reported, their schools offered no after-school activities and had no clubs in which they could participate, a further reflection of the underresourced schools that they attended. Low family income was no doubt the reason why almost none of the children were enrolled in private lessons.

The children who were involved in extracurricular activities were thus not representative of this group of youths. A typical day for most involved attending school, returning home, doing homework, playing either indoors or outdoors, and watching television. Like other children, they enjoyed playing, which most did with their friends and neighbors, although some liked solitary pastimes. In addition to the pickup basketball games that many boys took part in, several also liked to play football or ride their bikes around in the neighborhood, and virtually all of them enjoyed playing video games. Interestingly, many homes seemed to have video games, which was striking because the absence of nearly any other toys was notable in a majority of homes. Young girls liked to play with dolls or engage in activities like jumping rope or skating with their friends. Watching television was a common way to have fun for all the children. Computers were a rarity in their homes, but several children enjoyed visiting Web sites when they had access to computers in school or at the library. In sum, the younger children enjoyed the same sort of activities that most children enjoy, but their economic situation deprived them of many of the enrichment programs enjoyed by more affluent children, and thus of another potential means of building social networks and social capital that could assist them.

For most of the nine older adolescents in the city sample (those above the age of fourteen), participation in extracurricular or organized activities would have been difficult even if they had desired it. In some cases, because of their mother's involvement in the criminal justice system, they had to take on adult responsibilities that prevented them from taking part in their peers' activities, as we will see. The three teenage mothers had parental duties that kept them anchored to the house and out of school. Others in this group were alienated from school and engaging in antisocial behaviors that were the opposite of the activities thought to contribute to healthy development.

"Living a Life of Crime and Loving It"

Of all the outcomes thought to be associated with parental incarceration, delinquency is the one that evokes the most concern. Both common wisdom ("like mother, like daughter," and "like father, like son") and more formal propositions (e.g., social learning theory) posit that children are liable to follow the example laid down by their parents. The mothers themselves certainly feared this would be the case. Often, mothers said they worried that their children would follow in their footsteps or those of the children's fathers if they were involved in drugs or in trouble with the law. Some of their concern was based on signs of early antisocial behavior in their children; other children had already become involved with the juvenile justice system (see chapter 3).

It is difficult to look at an adorable, laughing, playful eight-year-old and imagine that he might someday become a thuggish adolescent in trouble with the law. Nevertheless, the prevalence of delinquency among the older children in this study was so great, it was as if a neon sign were flashing "Warning! Warning!" in an ominous foreshadowing of what could await the younger children engaging in misbehavior that might escalate over time. At least six (67 percent) of the nine adolescents over the age of fourteen had been arrested, some of them more than once. Only one of them explicitly adopted the persona of a street-smart thug, but the other teenagers who had been in trouble with the law were socializing with peers who engaged in antisocial behavior and did not seem to have been rehabilitated by their experiences in the juvenile justice system. The social worlds of these teens were characterized by friendship with antisocial peers and engagement in antisocial behavior. My conversations with two of them reflect the influence of these peer relationships for both younger and older children.

Richard was a ten-year-old who had not been in trouble with the police but who frequently got into fights and had been disciplined at school for stealing. He seemed to be headed for the same fate as the delinquent older children, given his behavior and that of his friends. In this excerpt from our first interview, Richard had just talked about getting into trouble at school for stealing someone's pencil because he didn't have one himself.

JS: Have you ever stolen anything else?

RICHARD: Lots of things from the store.

JS: How come you steal things from the store?

RICHARD: 'Cause I don't have money to be buying stuff.

JS: Do you think it's okay [to be stealing]?

RICHARD: Yeah

JS: How come?

RICHARD: I don't think it's okay, but I can't help it.

JS: Why?

RICHARD: Because I done it too many times. I'm used to it now.

JS: Do your friends steal?

RICHARD: Yeah.

JS: When did you start stealing?

RICHARD: When I was growing up, like when I was eight.

JS: What made you steal the first time?

RICHARD: All my friends had money and I didn't have enough, so I just took it. They told me to take it.

JS: And you listened to them?

RICHARD: Yeah.

For Richard, this pattern of behavior had become established. As he said, he had done it "too many times," presumably meaning that he no longer saw a way to retreat from the misbehavior his friends now expected of him, and so he continued stealing. What he stole—candy bars, for instance—was of little value, but the troubling aspect of this pattern was the risk that his behavior would continue and escalate in severity. Richard had told his mother that he was stealing, and she told him not to steal "around her," so he knew that she did not approve (albeit with the apparent qualification that he not do so in her presence), but that was not sufficient to deter him. Nor was the threat of getting caught and arrested: Richard thought that if he were caught, he'd have to "go to jail or something," which he viewed as a bad thing. However, like other children who think themselves invincible, he doubted he would be caught. After all, he was a fast runner.

The types of delinquency in which some of the younger children reported engaging, typified by Richard's small acts of shoplifting, are minor when compared to those committed by some of the older teenagers. What they were doing was serious enough to warrant arrest, adjudication, and placement in juvenile facilities. Sixteen-year-old Peter, whose school experiences were described earlier, illustrated how serious this involvement could become and reflected the negative influence of his associations with antisocial peers. As we talked, we discussed his numerous tattoos, and Peter mapped out his plans for future "tats." Pointing to a large blank space on one arm, he explained that it was reserved for a scroll he planned to have tattooed there emblazoned with the

phrase "Living a life of crime and loving it." He presumably thought the statement would be a badge of honor in his world, which he portrayed as dominated
by drug dealers, street-fighting men, and thieves.

Peter did indeed seem to love street life and the thrill he derived from
committing crimes, although his embroilment was unsurprising, given his
upbringing. His mother, Patty, was immersed in the drug culture at the time
they entered the study and was in jail awaiting trial when we first met. His father
had been imprisoned for most of the ten years before he died. Although Patty
expressed concern for her son and regret for her past behavior, her mothering
style placed her among the sporadically engaged. In addition to the periods of
homelessness that Peter had endured when living with his mother and the long
separations from her, Patty had more than once left him on his own in a locked
apartment for two or more days when he was a preschooler. She had done little
to shield him from her activities and had enlisted his assistance in obtaining
drugs. "My mom used to keep me out on the streets all night with her," he told
me. She also sent him out to purchase drugs for her.

PETER: She always had me drivin' shit, she [unintelligible] had a bench warrant,
she had me drivin' down, um, Northside every day to get bags of dope
and shit.

JS: How old were you then?

PETER: Fifteen, sixteen. I've been drivin' for a long time. A couple years. Soon as
I learned how to drive, I was out on my own. Ma let me get the car. Took [it]
all night. And she used to be so fucked up she would gimme the car keys
and be like, "Come back in an hour." I come back, she's knocked the fuck
out. So I just be out all night. Break o' dawn drivin', I'd be watchin' the sun
come up. Come home and she still be out and then eight, nine o'clock
comes around, I'm just wakin' up. She'd be like, "Go back down North and
get another bag o' dope," and then after that she's done and gonna do
things all over again.[4]

As the words Peter intended to etch on his arm indicated, he was engaged
in far more serious types of behavior than young Richard was. He appeared to
have moved smoothly into illegal practices as a natural part of the world his
mother inhabited, in which people survive by ignoring some legal niceties.
Here, for instance, Peter was talking about having just "beaten" a firearms
possession case in juvenile court, saying that the court wanted to see if he was
attending school and whether he was fighting there:[5]

JS: So have you been going to school?

PETER: Yes. It's stupid not going, there's nothing to do. What are you gonna do,
sit around? Smoke weed all day? There's no point. It just gets boring.

JS: Do you smoke a lot of weed?

PETER: Oh yeah. A little bit. I go out to the bar on Saturdays too.

JS: And they serve you?

PETER: Yeah. I be getting shitfaced down there too. Oh my God . . . like every weekend we go down there. Like I don't use [unintelligible], I just like to have a good time with my friends.

JS: How long have you been going to the bar?

PETER: Not long, I started probably this year. My mom knew. She used to let me go. My mom has a lot of rules but she's real cool though. But if you disrespect her, she'll get on your ass.

JS: And how old are your friends you go with to the bar?

PETER: Eighteen or nineteen, twenty, twenty-three. We used to drive down there, but the cops took my car though. This is like the sixth one.

JS: The sixth car that they took?

PETER: I was getting a new car like every three weeks.

JS: How were you getting a new car every three weeks?

PETER: My grandmom was helping me out. Get around. I was doing stuff, like food shopping. . . . Before, she [his mother] was in a rehab for like six months. I think it was like four or five months. I was here by myself. So I had to get a car to do things, like get out, to go up and see her.

JS: So your grandmother would give you money to buy a car?

PETER: Yeah, no problem.

JS: Well, why are the police taking your car? Don't you have the registration for them?

PETER: Like, that's what I learned. For like the first few cars, I just threw a bullshit plate on them and [unintelligible].

JS: Where did you get the bullshit plates?

PETER: I don't know, I had them laying around from like my mom's old cars. So I would just take them.

JS: So wait a minute, when you bought the cars, did you get them from dealers or from individuals?

PETER: No. Off the street. One of my cars broke down on me. Either the last car I had or the one before that.

JS: So wait, where do you buy them on the street?

PETER: Oh, from anybody, you see a car for sale, three hundred dollars, you go tell them you want to see it, drive it, then tell them you want it.

JS: And you just buy it? And they don't give you paperwork?

PETER: Yeah, you gotta go over to the place and switch the title. Sign my name on it.

JS: Okay, so you switch the titles, and then so why would there be a problem? Wouldn't you get a temporary tag?

PETER: No, you gotta have insurance. If you don't have insurance they don't give you your license plate. And insurance is high, because it's a first driver, and I don't have no license so they can't give me insurance.

JS: You don't have a license?

PETER: Nope, that's why they took my car. I've been driving since I was like 13.

JS: Who taught you to drive?

PETER: My mom.

JS: So why don't you get a license?

PETER: I don't know, I got too many tickets. I should though. My last car I just had, man, I loved that thing, I wish the cops didn't take that one. That one was legal. It had plates and insurance and brand-new inspection stickers.

JS: How did you get plates and insurance?

PETER: A good friend of mine let me use his name.

Some of the behavior Peter describes in this exchange, such as underage drinking and smoking marijuana, is not that different from what many high school students do (L. D. Johnston et al. 2007). However, his mother's tacit acceptance of his drinking behavior and of his illegal driving is certainly not the norm for most teenagers, nor would most teens likely have such easy familiarity with the strategies employed by those without the means to do things by the book. In his mother's world, however, and thus in Peter's as well, one did such things to get by. Peter also took part in more serious forms of antisocial behavior. One of his specialties was stealing car radios, and he told me quite explicitly how to break into various makes and models of cars (including mine) to accomplish this. Although he drew the line at stealing cars, both because the punishment was more severe and because he felt that the market for stolen vehicles was not that lucrative, he did engage in other offenses that carried serious penalties, many of them motivated by a desire for money, as was the case with Richard. Peter's closest friends were older than he and apparently spent a lot of time hanging out on street corners, selling drugs, and participating in other kinds of illegal behavior, including the buying and selling of guns, robberies, and assaults, all of which Peter had been doing along with them. Like his mother, his friends were deeply involved in the drug culture, and Peter realized they were facing a future that was "going nowhere." Peter had enough self-awareness to realize that he was on the same path, but he said it would be difficult for him to move in a different direction: "It's just that the money's so fast and bein' on the bricks [out on the block] all night, it feels good." However, after being adjudicated delinquent—convicted of an offense in juvenile court—and placed on probation for the gun possession charge he thought he had beaten, he claimed not to be engaging in the illegal activities he and his friends enjoyed, even though he continued hanging out on the corner with them.

Despite Peter's participation in criminal activity, glimmers of a young man who aspired to a straight life in which he would become a skilled tradesman shone through his tough-guy persona. Although he spoke disparagingly of school, he wanted to graduate because he believed "you need that high school diploma." However, he was rarely attending school and, when he did attend, was frequently being put in detention or suspended "for not listenin' and talkin' to the teachers like shit." His future prospects seemed bleak, especially since no adults were providing real supervision for him. A few days after my first visit with Peter, he was evicted from the house where he had been living with his mother before her arrest. He then went to live with his grandmother, who had little control over him. When Patty got out of jail, she had not returned to live with Peter but instead was staying with friends, using drugs once again. The one indication that Peter might eventually complete school was that being on probation seemed to have persuaded him to refrain from the antisocial behavior that was the norm for his friends, despite his continued association with them.

Peter was trying to cross the border between street life and the straight world, recognizing that there was a legitimate route to a world where a person could "make eighteen, nineteen dollars an hour and come home to a house with a 63" TV and money and a beautiful house, white piano, white car." Yet he had been born into a world that erected many roadblocks to his ability to make that crossing, and he had few positive role models or peers who might ease his way, especially since he had invested so much in his self-image as a gangsta.

The other adolescents who had been in trouble with the law also had relationships with delinquent peers, but no other teens seemed as totally—and perhaps irretrievably—caught up in a deviant lifestyle. For instance, John, one of the teenage parents, had been in trouble with the law and was involved with crime, by his own account. Nevertheless, he was not invested, as Peter was, in demonstrating his love of crime. He was fifteen years old when we first met. By any gauge, he was another youth who had been dealt many difficulties in his short life. His mother was a chronic offender, as noted earlier, and his father had served several years in prison before his death. As was true for Peter's mother, the only social world to which John's mother could expose him was filled with drugs and crime, and so it is not surprising that John associated with youths involved in antisocial activities, as he describes here. However, as this excerpt also demonstrates, his world was broader than the exclusively criminal one in which Peter was involved.

JS: What do you do with your friends?

JOHN: Well, basically, we sit there and smoke pot and talk, with certain friends. And then you got the trouble-making friends and you got the drug-dealer friends and people who are rob-people friends. I got categories of friends. If one day if I want to go play on a computer, I go to my friend Michelle's. One day, I want to go play football, I visit my friend Matt. One day I want to steal cars, I go visit my friend Andy. All different things.

JS: So, are you still doing stuff like stealing cars? And robbing people?

JOHN: Robbing people? No.

JS: But stealing cars?

JOHN: I stole a car, what, three weeks ago.

JS: And what do you do when you steal a car?

JOHN: Just drive. Well, I'm too young to drive and I like driving, and if I want to learn to drive, I just go over and teach myself. It's not like I have a father figure to teach me how to drive a car. So I just teach myself. And it's the only way to keep myself learning how to drive a car.

Unlike Peter, who spent his days hanging out with his "bulls" on a street corner, John had friends with whom he could enjoy more conventional activities like playing computer games or football, but his future will be shaped in part by which group of friends prevails. And, of course, by what happens to his mother after her trial.

Conclusion

As children mature, the relationships they build outside their families take on increasing significance. The social networks young people create become the foundation through which they connect with others who can ultimately facilitate their access to the educational or employment opportunities that many parents hope will improve their children's quality of life. The children do not build networks alone: parents, family members, and other adults—family friends, teachers, coaches, or clergy—help them along the way by providing both role models and opportunities for them to develop skills in intellectual, social, spiritual, creative, or physical domains.

The ease with which prosocial networks are constructed and the type of connections that are made in a child's network vary as a function of socioeconomic status (Lareau 2003). Families of higher socioeconomic status benefit from access to networks that pave the way to greater opportunities. For instance, children from such families live in communities with schools that afford children safe and secure learning environments and enriched curricula that prepare children for higher education or the acquisition of skilled trades. Their schools also provide intellectual, creative, and athletic extracurricular activities that can enrich a child's development. Parents with sufficient economic means can also ensure that their children have opportunities to participate in the activities offered by organizations like scout troops, community centers, or sports leagues, or to receive private instruction, such as music lessons, dance classes, tutoring, or sports training. All of these afford children the opportunity to forge relationships with other adults and with children who are also engaged in such prosocial pursuits. These activities not only provide children with educational opportunities, cultural enrichment, and skills development, but also represent preparation for entrée into a world beyond their community, a world where higher education is within reach and successful careers await the children.

Children embedded in the lower socioeconomic strata, including the children in this study, do not enjoy similar access to the individuals and activities that facilitate linkages to the networks to which more affluent children are connected. Poor children simply do not have the means that bestow advantages on peers whose families are better off financially. They are disadvantaged educationally because of the schools they attend and the activities in which they can participate. Not surprisingly, then, poor children are less likely to graduate from high school (Kaufman, Alt, and Chapman 2004) and are more likely to become poor adults than are children of higher socioeconomic status (Bowles, Gintis, and Groves 2005; Corcoran 1995).

The perimeters of the social worlds inhabited by the children I met indeed were largely demarcated by their socioeconomic position, which placed them in environments with meager resources and few of the advantages enjoyed by more affluent youth. The children were acutely aware of their families' economic hardships. When asked what they would wish for if they had one wish, the nearly universal response was related to the acquisition of wealth. Simply put, they wanted to have a lot of money, whether to buy their family a nicer house, have all the toys in the world, or help other people. The probability of attaining this goal seemed remote in light of their circumstances. Conventional pathways to wealth, or even to middle-class status, include a good education and the social connections to people and institutions that can facilitate upward mobility. For the children I met, gaining access to such pathways would require helping hands that were not immediately present for most. The communities in which they lived suffered from inadequate resources, and their families too often lacked the types of connections that more prosperous families rely on to invest in their children's future.

Although the problem of underresourced communities applied to all the children regardless of race, the issue is of particular concern for African

American children because of the disadvantages associated with living in poor African American neighborhoods, which are less racially integrated than are poor white communities. A significant body of research has found racial residential segregation to be one of the major reasons for "systematic variation in life-chance opportunities along racial lines at the low end of the American class structure" (Wilson 2007, 219). Areas of concentrated poverty such as those where poor African Americans live produce neighborhood effects that are detrimental to residents' well-being and opportunities (Farley 1996). These include diminished sources of employment; inferior institutions, such as schools, that might provide a pathway out of poverty; limited access to the networks that connect individuals with information about work opportunities; and psychological consequences, such as "dampened career aspirations; the formation of counterproductive values such as fatalism and resignation, and finally, the development of the seeds of an 'oppositional culture'" (Wilson 2007, 220). In other words, even though the white children lived in similarly poor neighborhoods, they did not face the structural impediments to moving out of their position that the black children did.

For all the children, the limitations of the communities outside the families' homes were compounded by the mothers' social isolation and backgrounds, which restricted the children's access to positive role models who might widen their perspectives and help connect them with others who might serve as bridges to the opportunities that would help them achieve their dream of prosperity. The encouraging news, however, was that most children did have close relationships with other adult family members, many of whom could fulfill that role for them, even if they too lacked significant connections with individuals and institutions that could boost the children's opportunities for success. Nevertheless, their mothers' constricted networks reduced the social support that can be so beneficial to parents and help build social capital that might assist their offspring.

Social support and social capital are both important for creating social environments that nurture individual development and help children flourish. They can help children build social skills such as empathy, trust, and notions of reciprocity. Social capital can facilitate children's access to various institutions and milieus that improve their chances of success in future endeavors. For families, social support "serves as a form of insurance against poverty and economic hardship and is expected to improve the quality of the child's home environment by reducing parental stress" (McLanahan 2009, 126). Such support also can mitigate the harmful impact of the multiple negative life events many of the children experienced, which are associated with less favorable developmental outcomes, by serving as a buffer between those circumstances and the psychological and behavioral problems that might otherwise ensue (Carothers, Borkowski, and Whitman 2006). In fact, social support has repeatedly been identified as one of the key factors in promoting resiliency in those exposed to adverse childhood conditions (Garmezy 1983). Furthermore, children who report having mentoring relationships are more likely to have positive outcomes, such as better educational achievement, less problematic behavior, and greater psychological well-being, although having a mentor is not sufficient by itself to offset the issues at-risk youths like those I interviewed face (DuBois and Silverthorn 2005). The support that many of these children found in their relatives was therefore encouraging. For those whose mothers were socially isolated or enmeshed with others who took part in antisocial behavior, however, the implications are troubling. They not only miss out on the benefits that social support can confer but also may be at risk of misconduct and depression if the nonparental adults who are important figures in their life engage in illegal behavior themselves, as associates of many mothers did (Greenberger, Chen, and Beam 1998).

Not all children can build the sort of prosocial networks that lead to the development of social capital and to outcomes generally valued by society at large. Some become involved in networks that lead to connections with deviant peers and antisocial behavior. In fact, the influence of antisocial peers is one of the most important predictors of serious delinquency and aggression among adolescents (Lipsey and Derzon 1998; Moffitt 1993). John's and Peter's stories reflect the consequences of having friends who are involved in illegal behavior, and the high arrest rate of the high school–age youths in this study was one of its most troubling findings.

How many of the children will end up in trouble with the law obviously is an unknown at this time. However, the behavioral model presented by the teenagers is not encouraging if the younger children follow in their footsteps, and the exposure to violence in their worlds raises additional concern about their futures (see chapter 3). The narrow social world in which the children were living—often peopled by many undesirable role models and few positive ones, coupled with a lack of opportunities for enrichment and exposure to a broader array of activities—made it obvious that the children would not have an easy time escaping the poverty that engulfed them, particularly in light of the barriers to upward mobility imposed by the social structure.

3

The Ubiquity of Violence

Jasmine is thirteen, and playing basketball is her passion. She plays as often as she can and lifts weights to build up her muscles, so Jasmine is a strong young woman. That's good for her not just because it improves her playing but also because Jasmine fights. She'll fight anyone, but mostly she fights boys because the girls are scared of her. No sissy girl fighting for Jasmine: she knows how to throw a punch because her older male cousin taught her how. When she fights a girl, she's liable to hurt her, as she did in this fight she described that took place not long before we first met: "She said some words to me when I sat on her desk and she pushed me. I told her if she pushed me again, I'd black her eye. She pushed me again, so I hit her in the eye. And she fell. I let her get back up and we started fighting, so I hit her in the eye again, and she had a black eye."

Jasmine started fighting in second grade and has fought frequently since then, mostly in the neighborhood but sometimes at school. What really provokes her is when someone says something about her father, who was murdered before Jasmine was born. Jasmine's mother's explanation of his death was matter-of-fact: "He was selling drugs. You know how it goes—one thing leads to another and, you know, he got shot."

Children fighting. Moms being victimized. Dads getting shot. Fights at school. Fights in the neighborhood. Relatives teaching children how to fight. Such was the reality of life for many children I interviewed while their mothers were awaiting trial. The amount of violence in the children's lives before parental incarceration was one of the most striking and disturbing aspects of the children's narratives, and it insinuated itself into the children's worlds at home and beyond. These young people were both victims and witnesses of violence, as well as, in many cases, perpetrators. Although they expressed dislike for the violence in their communities and several refrained from fighting, the violence was so common that many people I interviewed seemed resigned to its inevitability. As Jasmine's mother said, "You know how it goes." Viewed in conjunction with the other troubling aspects of the children's private and public worlds, the violence presented itself as a serious risk factor for worrisome consequences.

The violence in the children's lives manifests itself in a variety of ways. Children can be exposed to violence both directly through their own victimization and indirectly as witnesses to violence perpetrated against others. The violence can occur at home, in the community, and at school. Wherever it occurs, children who experience violence respond to it variously, sometimes by adapting their own behavior to cope with it. There is a notable similarity between the outcomes reported to be associated with parental incarceration and those linked with children's exposure to violence, which suggests that the children's frequent contact with violence may provide additional context for understanding the conduct of children whose parents are incarcerated. I did not embark on this research specifically to assess either the extent or the impact of violence in the children's lives, but its ubiquity was so pronounced that it cannot be ignored, particularly if it helps explain why prisoners' children are considered so vulnerable a population.

No Safe Haven

Ian is the ten-year-old boy introduced earlier whose older brother, aunt, and uncle were all locked up in the same county jail as his mother, Lucinda. Ian lived with his mother and father until they separated when he was four or five. He never saw his father again. Ian was taciturn, but he was willing to talk about the reason for his parents' separation:

IAN: My mom got a divorce because he was abusing her.

JS: How was he abusing her?

IAN: Pouring bleach into her eyes. Threatening to stab her.

JS: Did you see any of that happen?

IAN: Yeah.

JS: Did you see him throw the bleach in her eyes?

IAN: Yes.

JS: How did that make you feel?

IAN: Angry at him.

JS: Did you say anything to him about it?

IAN: No. Me and Steve [Ian's brother] were too scared. We were hiding in the corner.

What young child wouldn't be terrified by the sights and sounds that took place during this incident? Ian's fear and anger were similar to the feelings of other children who described having witnessed the victimization of their mother. Some also talked of wanting to intervene to protect their mother. Ian at least had found some refuge in his divorced maternal grandmother's house, where he had been living for nearly seven years because Lucinda had been unable to care for him and his siblings due to her drug abuse. His grandmother's life was more ordered and violence-free than the world in which his mother lived, working as a prostitute and sleeping in crack houses. Even so, his home life was not ideal. In addition to Ian and his grandmother, Ian's younger and older brothers lived in the house, along with his uncle and his uncle's girlfriend. Like Lucinda, Ian's older brother and uncle were drug addicts and were in and out of the house because they were either out on the street or in jail, as they both were when I first met Ian. His uncle's girlfriend likewise used drugs, but her life was stable enough that she was able to help the grandmother with the children.[1]

A child's home is the one place we would like to believe that the child can feel safe and secure, even if the world outside is violent. Yet homes across the country, like Ian's when he lived with both his parents, all too often are not safe havens. Family violence affects millions of households in the United States (Rennison 2003; Tjaden and Thoennes 2000) and as many as ten million children may be exposed to such violence annually (Onyskiw 2003). However, some groups of children are more likely than others to be exposed because their mothers are at higher risk of violent victimization at the hands of their partner than are other women. Compared to other women, a greater likelihood of being victimized by an intimate partner exists for low-income African-American women living in urban environments with someone to whom they are not married (Rennison 2000; Tjaden and Thoennes 2000; Yllo and Straus 1981), and for women with a history of violence in their family of origin (Hotaling and Sugarman 1986).

A majority of the children's mothers I met fell into these at-risk groups, which was not unexpected because female prisoners are disproportionately low-income, African American, and single, with high rates of victimization as children and as adults (Belknap 2001; Browne, Miller, and Maguin 1999; DeHart 2004; Morash and Schram 2002). The mothers awaiting trial were no more immune to violent victimization than were women in prison. Several, including Lucinda, talked about their childhood histories of either physical or sexual abuse. Many continued experiencing victimization as adults, this time at the hands of their romantic partners. Many women saw a connection between those experiences and their use of drugs or alcohol, which in turn led to their involvement in criminal behavior, some of it violent. As one mother who started using heroin when she was fifteen said: "I was abused as a child. As an adult, I realized that was a part of my problem all the time. And people say you leave that behind you, you're too old for that. But I got to bring that pain up. That caused me to feel good in that addiction. That is the cause, but you can't put that down. Your childhood, you got to go there to recover for real."

Ian saw his mother being victimized, but other children were present during events in which their mother either initiated violence or fought back against someone who was victimizing her. In such cases, children may face the difficult choice of condemning their own mother's behavior or absorbing the lesson that violence is acceptable under particular circumstances. Chantay, for instance, was the twelve-year-old who lived most of the time with her grandparents in their well-ordered home. Her mother, Darlene, was a crack user, and her father was murdered when she was six years old. When she lived with her mother, the household was frequently visited by violence, including some that Darlene perpetrated. A thirty-two-year-old mother of four, Darlene had been married for ten years to a man who was the father of her two youngest children and of the child she was pregnant with when she and Chantay first talked with me. Darlene had been repeatedly abused by her husband over the years. Recently, during her pregnancy, he had punched her in the ear, pushed her down the steps, knocked out some of her teeth, and injured her badly enough to require stitches and trips to the emergency department. His abusive behavior was not directed solely at Darlene; he also targeted his stepson, Chantay's brother. The children had often witnessed these events, and Chantay, as the oldest child, took responsibility for shepherding the younger children upstairs when fighting erupted. The family never discussed the fights, and no help was sought for the children.

Over the years, Darlene had called the police on several occasions when her husband had assaulted her, but they always failed to arrest him. Eventually, in retaliation for his abuse, Darlene cut him in the abdomen with a razor, and the police arrested her. Her case lingered in the system for several months until the prosecutor dropped the charges against her because her husband refused to testify against her. Three weeks after the case was dropped, Darlene stabbed her husband in the abdomen.

Chantay had turned thirteen by the time her mother stabbed her stepfather. Before the birth of her mother's baby, Chantay had been living with her maternal grandparents during the week, returning to live with her mother on most weekends. However, a few weeks before the stabbing, she had moved back in with her mother to help take care of the baby, born while Darlene was awaiting trial for the first incident. When her stepfather was stabbed, Chantay was in the house, although she says she was asleep. When she came downstairs, she saw her stepfather lying on the floor bleeding and wrapped in a blanket. Her mother told her to go over to her grandmother's house, threatening to beat her if she told her grandmother or anyone what had happened. The threat of the beating was real enough that Chantay indeed did not reveal to her grandparents what had taken place in her house. They learned of the injury only when Darlene called to ask them to come to the hospital where her husband had finally been taken, reportedly hours after the stabbing. He was in serious condition for several days. Darlene was arrested again, charged with aggravated assault, and sent to jail to await trial.

Children faced with violence such as occurred in Chantay's household cope with a complex array of feelings that may include fear, anger, love, guilt, and animosity. Chantay developed a deep antipathy toward her stepfather. When she went to the hospital with her grandparents the night of the stabbing and realized the severity of what had happened, she believed that he probably was going to die. Asked how she felt about that, Chantay replied: "I wanted to yell at my mom for doing it, but I just didn't really care," that is, whether her stepfather died. She was angry with her mother not because of the stabbing itself but because of the consequences: she knew that her mother would be arrested again and probably sent to jail. Chantay thought that her mother's use of violence was wrong, but she did not believe that punishment and imprisonment were the appropriate consequences, particularly because she blamed her stepfather for provoking her mother through his use of violence and other behavior that Chantay believed reflected marital infidelity. Instead, she thought that her mother needed treatment and help, and that she should be put somewhere other than a jail for a short time to think about what she had done.

When I spoke with her, Chantay betrayed little emotion about any of the events that had transpired in her life and made it clear that she did not discuss her feelings with her mother or any of her friends. However, she was more fortunate than many children in similar situations because she had a place of refuge to which she could turn. Her grandparents' home and community represented a calm, stable, and safe environment where she could escape the turmoil of her own home and attend a better school than those available closer to her mother's house. Even though no professional counseling was offered to Chantay to help her cope with what she had witnessed or with the separation from her mother following her second arrest, her grandmother and grandfather gave her the type of support that research has shown can moderate the effect of violence on children (Groves and Zuckerman 1997; Osofsky 1999). Despite all that had transpired in her family, Chantay was doing well in her own sphere. Her grades were consistently well above average, she was never in any serious trouble at school or in the community, and she was actively engaged in extracurricular activities.

The violence the children observed at home was not restricted to that between their mother and a romantic partner. Some of the children saw their mother engage in fights on the street with neighbors or other people, and a few had become involved in their mother's fights to assist her. In some families, a ready resort to violence seemed all too familiar to the children. On one occasion, for example, I was interviewing eleven-year-old Dayesh on the second floor of his house when shouting began downstairs. I had barely noticed it, but Dayesh, showing consternation, went to ask his family to quiet down. A few minutes later, after he had come back upstairs, the shouting resumed and the sounds of physical fighting broke out downstairs: grunts, shouts, furniture being banged around. Dayesh flew down the stairs and I followed him. When I reached the first floor, his mother was on her front porch, exchanging obscenities at full volume with her teenaged neighbor. Within a short time, she grabbed a tricycle and brandished it above her head, threatening to hit him with it. The young man she was confronting had been inside the house and had stood on her sofa. That disrespectful action had triggered the argument, which turned physical and then led to the confrontation I was witnessing. Dayesh's adult sister was also in the house and, after trying to summon help by phone from a friend, ran to get a hammer to wield against the neighbor as well. The confrontation ended when the neighbor retreated with a threat to return that night and harm everyone in the house. Dayesh was in no mood to talk following the incident, so I left with a promise to return soon.

Fortunately, the neighbor did not make good on his threat. When I called the family that night to see how Dayesh was, his mother, Siena, told me he had left the house shortly after I had and had still not returned several hours later. She seemed unworried and told me that similar encounters with the young man were frequent. Everything was fine, she said, minimizing the incident and dismissing it as "a black thing" that a white woman like me would not understand. Siena may well have been referring to the unwritten rules of the inner city that may dictate that someone treated disrespectfully, as Siena felt she had been, respond aggressively, as sociologist Elijah Anderson (1999) has documented in his studies of African American urban neighborhoods. Residents of such neighborhoods understand these rules, whether they subscribe to them or not. Siena was correct in thinking that such rules were not part of the behavioral guidelines I was taught. Although Dayesh may have been absorbing these lessons, he seemed unhappy about adopting them. The incident had clearly left him frightened, angry, embarrassed, and upset. When we next met, he explained that he had feared that his sister might get hit and die and that his mother might inadvertently have caused his sister's death if she had thrown the tricycle.

Although Siena alluded to what had happened as "a black thing," few racial differences emerged in this study with respect to the children's exposure to violence. Indeed, a white family in the city sample illustrates another troubling aspect of the children's home environments: the lessons they are taught about the use of violence. Family members' use of violence under given circumstances implicitly conveys to children that this is the appropriate response to particular forms of provocation. More explicitly, family members routinely told children that they needed to defend themselves if necessary, and some parents schooled their children in the ways of fighting.

John, for instance, had absorbed attitudes toward fighting from his family. By any measure, his life has been particularly difficult. His father, a drug addict, died of AIDS in prison when John was three years old. His mother, Linda, also a drug addict, was arrested numerous times and spent short stints in the county jail. Now fifteen, John had stopped going to school and had fathered a child. He had witnessed a good deal of violence in his community and at home and reported fighting extensively when he was younger. From his mother, he adopted beliefs about the appropriate ways to respond to provocation. In this excerpt, John discussed an episode in which one of his mother's boyfriends, whom he referred to as his father, was stabbed. In retaliation, Linda took the car, used a ruse to lure the people who stabbed her boyfriend out of their house, and then ran them down. The victims did not die and the extent of their injuries was unclear, but John saw his mother's actions as justifiable:

JS: So what do you think about this idea that your father gets stabbed and then she goes over there and gets in the car and runs them down?

JOHN: That's just how it is. You stab my father, you get run over, you know. When you stab somebody, that's personal. I could see if you threw something at them or something, but you stab somebody, that's close and personal, that's sheisty [shady, sneaky], ya know, that's jail shit. That's something people do in jail. That's some sheisty shit. So you do something like that, ya know, it's personal, it's real personal. Ya know, especially Italians. Like, I'm Italian, I'm old-school because I was raised old-school.

In this incident, Linda followed the unwritten rules that prevailed in her environment and responded to a wrong with personal aggression, just as Siena did. Of course, standing on someone's sofa, as Siena's neighbor did, is not as serious as stabbing someone, but both women believed that these transgressions needed to be avenged and that violence was the appropriate response. In both instances, the mothers delivered a powerful message to their sons about righting wrongs and the use of violence.

John's "old-school" education apparently included lessons from his mother about defending his honor, fighting fair, and not backing down.

JOHN: Whenever I fought, my mom went with me. I always got my mom in this; I knew it would be a fair fight. If my mom's there, I figured my mom's gonna protect my security.

JS: If you were having trouble with a kid in the neighborhood or something, you would go home and you would tell your mother?

JOHN: Yeah.

JS: And how would she get to the fight? I mean, how would that work, in terms of you bringing her to the fight? What would you say to her?

JOHN: I would say: "Hey, Mom, I'm havin' a problem, I'm gonna beat this kid up. And she would be like, "Wait, I'm comin' with you." That's the way it would be. My mom always stuck by me like that. My mom would always make sure I wouldn't get hurt.

JS: So she would watch the fight.

JOHN: Yeah.

JS: And if you were getting too hurt, she would . . .

JOHN: I never got hurt, if my mom's there. My mom says, "If you lose the fight, I'll whip your ass." So, I'd rather kill the kid than get beat by my mom. I'm gonna win this fight no matter what. There was just one time, there was these three kids and they started fightin', they were like three years older and they were gettin' high. And I say, "All right, I'll be right back." I ran home, I grabbed the dog chain—it was one of those spiky ones, it had little spikes on it. I grabbed that, and I wrapped it around my hands, and I was just gonna go fight 'em all. My mom said, "No, no chains, no weapons. Just go over there and fight 'em one on one."

That fight concluded with John inflicting what he described as a serious beating on one of the boys after the boy said something derogatory about Linda. Asked how he felt about it afterward, John replied: "I felt good. When you win a fight, you feel good afterwards. If you lose a fight, you feel like shit."

Linda's insistence that John settle his disputes through the use of physical force or face the possibility of a beating at her hands was unique among the children I interviewed. Other mothers, by word and by deed, conveyed similar messages about the necessity of fighting, but none were as extreme or overt as Linda. The type of lesson Lily received from her mother was more common. Lily was a ten-year-old girl whose mother was awaiting trial on an assault charge, having been accused of hitting her common-law husband's teenage children, who lived elsewhere, with a bat. Lily's mother had laid out for her the rules for fighting, although as this exchange shows, Lily had some rules yet to learn. Here, Lily was discussing an incident involving her aunt. Her mother was present during part of our conversation because on that stifling summer day, we had sought refuge in her bedroom, the only room in their house with air conditioning. Lily's mother lay sprawled on her bed watching soft pornography on TV while Lily and I talked.

LILY: Then my aunt comes out; she smacks me in the face, so I smack her back.

JS: Why did she smack you in the face?

LILY: I don't know.

MOM: 'Cause she's a smart-ass too, my sister.

LILY: So I smack her back.

JS: You smacked her back?

MOM: Yes, I told her, anybody hits you, you hit them back. They can't respect you, you don't respect them.

LILY: Even my aunt. Same thing with my grandmom. She hit me, I hit her back.

MOM: You didn't!

LILY: No, I'm saying, *if* Grandmom hits me!

MOM: And you won't hit her back.

LILY: Why not?

MOM: Because she's older. That I don't go for. My sister, I don't care. But my mother!

Clearly, Lily's mother had a set of rules in mind that she wanted to teach her daughter. The explicit lessons parents conveyed to some of the children also included fighting technique, which Dayesh learned from his father. Dayesh's father had moved out of the house five years earlier but the two still saw each other. Dayesh feared his father, however, because he frequently saw him beat his mother. Witnessing that abuse made Dayesh want to hit his father, but, as Dayesh said, "He was too big and he would hit me back."

DAYESH: He hit me a lot of times . . . with his hand. He taught me how to fight and stuff so I won't get hit. Me and my brother used to stay gettin' into trouble. 'Cause we just be arguin', me and my sister be arguin' sometimes and he just starts hittin' us with a belt or something.

JS: So he would hit both of you?

DAYESH: He just hit me. Because I'm the boy and I should know better.

JS: How did he teach you [to fight]?

DAYESH: He used to just hold his hands up and he told us to punch it. And if you go like this, you mean uppercut and all that [*demonstrates some of what his father had shown him*].

JS: And he told you how to duck punches also?

DAYESH: Uh-huh. Because if you go like this with his hand and he would swing at us and you have to duck real quick.

Both John's and Dayesh's accounts of their parent's role in teaching them lessons about fighting contain references to the use of physical force, or the threat of physical force, against them. They were not alone among the children in this study. The use of corporal punishment by parents is widespread in the United States, and nearly every child in America has been spanked

(M. A. Straus and Gelles 1990), so I was not surprised to learn that the children were being hit. However, the types of punishment inflicted on many of the children in the city sample are considered the most severe forms of physical punishment, more likely to cause injury than a spanking. Several children talked of being beaten or whipped with belts, spiked athletic shoes, sticks, or other objects. Typically, the mothers and children spoke of the physical punishments used in the household in a matter-of-fact manner and downplayed their severity, the children rationalizing it as deserved because of their behavior. In this exchange, Peter, the sixteen-year-old self-proclaimed "gangsta," discussed his drug use and what his mother would do if she knew that he used PCP. She was aware that he smoked marijuana and had warned him not to get "high high," but apparently she would have been quite upset if she knew that he was also using PCP.

PETER: If my mom knew about that she'd beat my ass.

JS: She'd beat your ass?

PETER: Aw, man. She beat my ass with a hockey stick.

JS: Were you okay?

PETER: Oh yeah. I understand. She was just trying to teach me a lesson. 'Cause she be punching me with her hands and it don't hurt me, so I just stand there. She punched me with a fist in my face, and I was like, "What's that? That don't hurt."

Peter's thuggish self-image as a tough guy would require him to seem impervious to his mother's actions, although, given his age and size relative to his mother, her fists probably could not really hurt him. Regardless of whether Peter's reaction was false bravado or not, his remarks illustrate an important point about children and corporal punishment. The use of objects such as hockey sticks—or belts, sticks, or shoes with spikes—may physically injure children, which is typically what distinguishes corporal punishment from child abuse in legal decisions. In all likelihood, the children themselves—and certainly their mothers—would not characterize these forms of physical punishment as abusive despite their potential to inflict injury. As Peter said: "She was just trying to teach me a lesson." Yet the lesson delivered to the children was that the use of violence is an appropriate means of handling problems and responding to provocation. It was a lesson Peter and many others had absorbed all too well and applied in their community.

Violence in the Community

We have seen that the children's homes are far from safe havens. But what about their neighborhoods? How safe are they? Children who live in the type of low-income urban communities that the children in the city called home are exposed to violence at rates far higher than their suburban or rural counterparts are—or even children living in more affluent sections of the same city (Buka et al. 2001; Reiss and Roth 1993; Stein et al. 2003). From an early age, children living in such high-risk neighborhoods say that they have seen not only fights and beatings but also killings or dead bodies in the street. Just as troubling, many child witnesses of violence report having been victimized in the community themselves, although not as often as they have seen others victimized (Campbell and Schwarz 1996; Fitzpatrick 1997; Fitzpatrick and Boldizar 1993; Richters and Martinez 1993).

In view of what is known about these urban communities, the words the children I interviewed used to describe their neighborhoods were ones I expected to hear. "Bad," "not safe," "messed up," the children routinely and emphatically declared when I asked them to describe the area around their homes. They pointed out that people were selling drugs on the street and that they frequently saw fighting and heard gunshots. Some also spoke of hearing that people had been shot and killed in the neighborhood and of seeing blood-soaked pavement following a shooting; others had seen people murdered. Sixteen-year-old Nicole spoke of the turmoil that lay behind the façade of her decent-looking neighborhood:

NICOLE: It looks better than it is.

JS: So what's wrong with it?

NICOLE: There's a lot going on around here.

JS: Really? Like what?

NICOLE: It's terrible! There's shooting and everything! And everybody's fighting. You just gotta be there. If you're in your house all the time, then you'd probably think everything was different, too. But, if you were out there and seeing it . . .

JS: Do you ever hear people shooting?

NICOLE: Yeah! Sometimes I'm at the wrong place at the wrong time. That's why I don't even go outside like that. That's why I'm glad that when I got locked up [following one of her arrests]—the two days after I got locked up—I had that curfew and I had to go in at eight o'clock. And sure enough, when I went in, that night there was shooting. And they were shooting at my friends that I be with. And I was like, I'm glad I got that curfew, 'cause I would have been right in the mix. Right there. And I don't know what I would have done, you know what I'm saying. I might have done something and gotten right in front of the bullets. I'm really glad I got that curfew. It keeps you out of certain trouble. You know what I mean? 'Cause a lot of things happen at night. Most of the things that happen, happen at night.[2]

The mothers were well aware of the dangers of the neighborhood, and several kept their children indoors to protect them. Certainly, part of the motivation behind the lessons parents taught their children about using force stemmed from their wanting their children to be able to protect themselves outside the house. As one mother put it: "You hear shooting wherever you go, no matter what neighborhood you go in. It's not a good neighborhood for him. I grew up in this neighborhood, but it's not really good. I mean, you got drugs on this corner right here. Everywhere, there's drugs, shootings, and stuff. So I don't let him go out." This legitimate concern for their children's safety that led mothers to keep their children indoors contributed to the sometimes claustrophobic sense I had, described earlier, of the children's being shut off from the outside world. Like children elsewhere who live in communities where violence is a frequent occurrence, the children in this study reported having been victimized in their neighborhoods. Most often this took the form of fights with other children in the community and at school, although one youth had been shot during a robbery. Describing the neighborhood where he had lived, John put it like this: "Yeah, it's just everywhere, every neighborhood, there's disputes, there's kids, 'Oh, I don't like you,' and this and that, and they get in fights. You know, everybody fights. If you ask anybody in the neighborhood, they at least got in fights."

Numerous studies have found that children who are exposed to violence, whether at home or in the community, are themselves more likely than other children to become aggressive.[3] Given the frequent contact with violence that the children experienced at home and in their neighborhoods, coupled with the implicit and explicit lessons they learn at home, it would not be surprising to find that many of them engage in aggressive behavior. Indeed, among both boys and girls whose mothers were awaiting trial, fighting was a common occurrence. Nearly eight of ten children who discussed the topic said that they engaged in physical fights in their neighborhoods or schools. Many had been suspended from school for fighting, including those in elementary school. Much of the fighting described by the children, especially the younger ones, was relatively minor, like that reported by Lily, which involved no weapons or serious injury.

The first time we met, on a January day, Lily arrived home from school and barreled into the kitchen where her mother and I sat talking. No hugs or kisses greeted her. When asked how her day was, Lily's reply was solely about her fight at school that day. An accidental push by another girl in the schoolyard had led to a fight between Lily and Joseph, one of her classmates, each hitting the other. Later, during music class, Joseph threw an eraser at Lily that struck her on the head, leaving a bruise right next to her eye. Although Lily sought attention and sympathy from her mother, pointing out the mark on her face and removing the Band-Aid on her knee to show the abrasion she had received during the schoolyard incident, she got little in return. Instead, her mother told her to go put her things away, dismissing her from the kitchen so that she could resume talking about her own situation with the justice system.

Her mother's reaction is perhaps explained by the fact that Lily, despite her young age, had a long history of fighting. As a result, her parents appear to have become accustomed to hearing that she has been in a fight, not all of them as relatively minor as the one just described. Lily's aggressive acts were so frequent and so disruptive at school that she had been assigned wraparound services, which meant that an adult monitor was provided to stay at school with Lily all day to control her behavior. Even so, her father maintained, Lily's teacher thought that she was not overly disruptive and that other students in the class behaved even worse. If so, the teacher's comments are indicative of the level of misbehavior that goes on in the schools many of the children attended and the relative lack of severe sanctions that seemed to be the schools' response. For instance, when Lily and I met on a subsequent occasion, she said that she had "almost" been suspended from school for a month and went on to describe the fight that had gotten her in trouble:

LILY: Because, one of the kids started with me, right? I wasn't shocked when the teacher broke me and her up, because she punched me in my nose. I was about to have my nose broke. I don't allow that. So I swung right back at 'em. I accidentally hit the teacher. I apologized, then kept on fighting. So I knocked her in her nose. Her nose bled to death. Her nose was running right on her desk. So me and her were fistfighting. I got her down on that floor. I grabbed her by her hair—well, her weave, her black weave. Swung her around twice. She's not too heavy for me; she weighed less than me. I pulled her weave out of her head, threw it in the teacher's face, started punching her in the face, 'cause I had my [professional football team] jacket on, I couldn't see nothin', 'cause she had just grabbed it by the back and just pulled it right in front of me, so I couldn't see nothin'. So she couldn't get in my face. All she did was scratch me right there. So I grabbed her by her hair, squealed [sic] her on her desk, started punching her in her face. She grabbed my arm, my jacket, and swung it off of me, grabbed my hair, swung me around. Her head was right here. On my hand. And my hand was on her desk. Goin' like this, right into her face [demonstrates punching the girl].

JS: So you were just punching her in the face repeatedly?

LILY: She hit me in my nose, and I was about to have a nose broke, and I never had that before.

JS: But it was her nose that was bleeding, right?

LILY: Right.

JS: So what happened? So you were punching her in the face, and then what?

LILY: She got me on the floor. Started punching me in my tummy, tummy hurted that day 'cause I was sick. She got her cousin into this. So I got one of my big—my friends, the one in black right there. I got her. Actually, I didn't get her, I told her, make sure that that girl don't touch me. She touch me, I hit her back.

The fight ended when the school security officer was called to the room and Lily was taken to the nurse's office and then to the assistant principal. She was suspended for a one-day trial, with the threat of being suspended for a month, a threat that failed to materialize. Instead, Lily was permitted to return to school, where she continued getting into fights.

Some might contend that Lily's behavior is likely to change as she gets older and that the extensive fighting reported by the children is a function of their relative youthfulness. However, the teenagers in this study reported fighting as well. In thirteen of fifteen interviews with teenagers whose mothers were awaiting trial, the subject of fighting either arose naturally or I asked directly whether he or she ever fought. Of those thirteen, one girl reported never having fought and one boy had fought only when he was younger. The remaining eleven talked about recent fighting in which they had been involved. In fact, one-third of them had been arrested because of their fighting, some of it far more serious than what the younger children were involved with. For instance, Peter, who wanted the tattoo proclaiming that he was "living a life of crime and loving it," reported frequent fighting as well as more serious offending. Shortly after we first met, he had been placed on probation by the juvenile court for carrying a gun. He also reported being heavily involved in a variety of criminal activities, including drug dealing and robbery. When he was about twelve years old, he had become involved with a group of older men who apparently allowed him to take part in their drug-dealing activities. Peter recounted taking part in a significant amount of fighting on his own, but he also engaged in fights with this group:

PETER: Like when I was growin' up, they like my old heads. They're all twenty-three, twenty-two. When I was growin' up, I was like eleven, twelve, when I met them dudes. And they saw something in me. And all my boys is black and I'm white. I'm a fighter too, so they saw something in me. I was the kind of young boy where they have a problem, they be like, "Okay, go right handle it." I just be bold fucked up. They be like, "Yo, yo, Peter, handle that for me, dog." I just start [*makes growling noises*] gassin' 'em and beatin' 'em up.

JS: So you showed them that you were . . .

PETER: Yeah, like I know I'm not no bitch from the door. I ain't, I ain't no chump. Like if I gotta fight, I gotta fight. I like to fight. I, I really think it's fun. I like fightin' by myself, it's fun. But it, it makes you more of a man. Puttin' your hands up instead of pullin' out a gun and shootin' at 'em. You throw your hands up, you fight, you straight. But it's fun though.

Peter also recounted some brutal assaults he and his group of "bulls" perpetrated that resulted in serious injuries. Peter's self-image as a tough street criminal was unusual among the teenagers in the study, but many of the other teens had also taken part in serious fights. There seemed little doubt that Peter's mother's involvement with drugs and her use of him in her illegal activities had introduced him to a criminal world where he had found a home.

The amount of fighting the children spoke of during their interviews far exceeds that reported in national surveys of schoolchildren and adolescents (Bureau of Justice Statistics, 2005, table 3.60), although it was similar to levels found among children living in inner-city neighborhoods (DuRant et al. 1994) and even closer to those among children considered at risk of delinquency (Snyder et al. 2003). The extremely high levels of fighting reported by the children in this study therefore may in part reflect behaviors common among children in their communities whose lives put them in the category of at-risk youth. Many of the study's children fell into that category even before their mother's incarceration, not just because they faced the prospect of separation from their mother but also because of violent home lives that taught them to use violence.

Conclusion

Violence is truly ubiquitous in these children's lives. It permeates their homes, their communities, and their schools. Both they and their mothers are victims, witnesses, and perpetrators in these various milieus. The children's own participation in fighting and other forms of violent offending is of particular concern, not least because it may lead to juvenile justice system involvement, as it had already for several of the adolescents interviewed, and the possibility of intergenerational incarceration.

The potential consequences associated with such extensive exposure to violence are deeply troubling. A large body of research has consistently found that those who experience violence, direct or indirect, are more likely than other children to exhibit a variety of behavioral, emotional, social, and cognitive problems (Margolin and Gordis 2000). Table 3.1 lists some of the psychological and behavioral effects found among children exposed to violence. The second and third columns show that child witnesses and child victims suffer similar problems with adapting to what they have experienced. Reported psychological symptoms include depression, anxiety, withdrawal, and somatic problems. Children are at risk as well of involvement in acting-out behavior,

TABLE 3.1

Comparison of outcomes observed among children of incarcerated parents and children who witness or are victims of violence

	Child witnesses of violence	Child abuse victims	Children of prisoners
Internalizing problems			
Anxiety	✓	✓	✓
Depression	✓	✓	✓
Withdrawal	✓	✓	✓
Low self-esteem	✓	✓	✓
Sleep disorders	✓	✓	✓
Behavioral problems			
Poor academic performance	✓	✓	✓
Acting out	✓	✓	✓
Delinquency	✓	✓	✓
Aggression	✓	✓	✓

Note: The check mark (✓) signifies that empirical studies have documented an association between an outcome and the category of child.

which includes disciplinary problems at school, delinquency, and especially aggression. Analyses across studies have concluded that approximately 65 percent of children who experience these forms of violence develop these or similar symptoms or fare worse than children not exposed to violence.

Others have pointed out that there is considerable overlap in the reactions attributed to different forms of violence children experience, which table 3.1 clearly shows (Saunders 2003). The fourth column of the table also reveals that the symptoms observed in children exposed to violence match those reported among children of prisoners. This comparison is not meant to suggest that the effects of parental incarceration are inconsequential or attributable instead to violence exposure. Rather, it is intended to highlight the commonality of children's reactions to a variety of traumas. Furthermore, many children experience multiple traumas; the effects thought to be attributable to one type of trauma may in fact be a consequence of a different trauma or of a combination of experiences. As I noted in the Introduction, isolating the impact of one trauma and identifying it as the sole source of problems observed in children not only is difficult to accomplish but also overlooks the complex network of forces in children's environments that influence how they will react to their life circumstances.

Consistent with this perspective, it is important to recognize that violence exposure alone may not explain the children's antisocial behavior or the other outcomes that prisoners' children have in common with children exposed to violence whose parents are not incarcerated. A number of characteristics of individuals, families, and communities have been identified as correlates of these outcomes, and several are present in the lives of the children in this study. For instance, parental criminality, poor academic performance, school behavioral problems, and parental substance abuse have all been found to increase the likelihood of youth violence and serious delinquency (J. D. Hawkins et al. 1998; Lipsey and Derzon 1998). Several studies that have compared abused children to low-income children have found few differences between them (Margolin and Gordis 2000), which highlights the corrosive effects on children merely of living in poverty. Likewise, children separated from their parents for reasons other than parental incarceration exhibit many of the behaviors found among prisoners' children (Sack, Seidler, and Thomas 1976). Some or all of these correlates are present in the lives of the study's children, and we must keep them in view as we try to fully comprehend the nature and level of the risks they face.

The list of risk factors in the children's lives is daunting, and adverse consequences may seem inevitable. However, with respect to the risks posed by violence exposure, it is important to point out that there were variations in both the amount of violence in the children's environments and the attitudes toward violence within their homes. Elijah Anderson's (1999) ethnographic study of violence in inner-city Philadelphia provides a useful framework for understanding the children's situations. As noted earlier, Anderson observed that a set of unwritten rules govern behavior on the street and the appropriate response to infractions of expected behavior. He dubbed these rules a code of the street. Showing "respect"—as defined by those on the street—is of primary importance, and the code stipulates that acts of disrespect be answered with violence under particular circumstances, which was the response of Dayesh's and John's mothers. All families in these communities, Anderson maintains, are aware of the code and must find a way to negotiate life on the street under this set of rules.

Anderson identified two types of families with differing orientations to the code: "decent" and "street" families. Decent families are more accepting of mainstream values of hard work, personal responsibility, and engagement with social institutions; they believe in the possibility of a better life in the future. Street families, by contrast, feel relatively hopeless about the future and are more fully invested in the code of the street. Anderson also notes that many people "exhibit both decent and street orientations, depending on the circumstances," and that people in a given family may differ in their level of acceptance of the street life (1999, 34). I met families who maintained a "decent" orientation and children who seemed to have resisted being drawn into the culture of the street. Often, the children's use of violence seemed situational; few had adopted a street persona as entirely as Peter had. His view of the world mirrors the hopelessness Anderson documented among those with a street orientation:

PETER: I started hanging out on the corner probably about 3 years ago. I be a young buck and then my old heads, you know, you got old heads, they schoolin' you, teachin' you about life on the streets and this is how you learn about the weight scales [for drug sales] and how to get guns and how to, how to get over and shit. Like, and basically how to get over on people and how, how to get, get people for shit. And rob and steal. And the streets ain't nothin' but a circle. It keeps on going around and around and around.

JS: What do you mean by that?

PETER: It ain't gonna end up nowhere.

In contrast to Peter's bleak outlook, Chantay maintained an optimistic, forward-looking view of life despite the turmoil and violence in her family. Her grandparents' home provided her with a safe refuge from her mother's and stepfather's violent relationship in a community where violence was far less common than in her own neighborhood. Furthermore, her grandparents conveyed to Chantay their strong disapproval of the violent behavior she had witnessed. From the grandparents' perspective, Chantay's mother was the aberration in their otherwise decent family, the one child they had who had succumbed to the street. As the evidence in this chapter makes clear, violence in the lives of female offenders' children cannot be ignored. Violence deserves a prominent place on any policy maker's agenda, especially those who are concerned about the children of incarcerated parents and other youth living in this type of high-risk environment. Reducing harm for the children in this case also requires confronting the victimization their mothers face. Witnessing such victimization is potentially harmful to the children as well as the mothers. Furthermore, most of the violence the mothers perpetrate and that sometimes results in their involvement in the criminal justice system is a response to abuse directed at them by their partners. These violent encounters serve as templates on which the children may model their own behavior so that when they step out into their communities and schools, they are primed to respond to provocation with violence, as far too many of these children have.

PART TWO

4

When the Criminal Justice System Comes Calling

Imagine this.

You are ten years old, getting ready for school in the early morning of a cold December day shortly before Christmas. You are still drowsy at this early hour. Your mother is helping you and your sisters and brothers get washed up and dressed when someone bangs on the front door. Your older sister goes to the door and suddenly the house is swarming with police officers and other men and women with badges clipped to their clothes. Your mother tells you and your brothers and sisters to help her hide and runs into a closet, where you all pile clothes on top of her, desperately trying to conceal her. The police have announced that they're looking for your mother, and they and the nonuniformed adults begin searching the house for her. They go through all the rooms, banging open doors, checking under the beds and in the closets, peering into every recess, the private spaces of your family's life. The atmosphere is thick with tension: you and your siblings are wide-eyed, breathlessly waiting to see if they will discover your mom. Your seventeen-year-old sister has taken on the role of adult in charge and is berating the police, telling them that your mom is not here. She is screaming at them, and the police threaten to arrest her if she doesn't stop. They look into the closet where your mother is hiding but turn away from it and continue searching. You breathe a sigh of relief, but just as it seems that your mother has successfully eluded the search, a woman in plain-clothes says she wants to recheck the closet and begins poking at the pile of clothes covering your mother. Eventually, inevitably, she finds your mother. She grabs the collar of your mother's nightgown and drags her screaming across the floor. While your mother is still on the ground, the woman pulls her hands behind her back and handcuffs her. Your mother screams and shouts, arguing with the officers, who spray mace in her face. As they lead your mother to the door, she pleads with the officers to let her change out of her nightgown and put something on her bare feet before they take her out into the cold. They refuse, hustle your mother outside into a waiting police car, and drive away.

You don't know it yet, but you have just begun your first day as a child of a prisoner.

Imagine that.

Such was the fate of Rhodaisia and her five sisters and brothers when their mother was arrested yet again. This time was different, however, because this time the police had come to the house to get her instead of picking her up on the street, as had been the case when she was arrested before. This arrest carried the added trauma of the children witnessing their mother literally being dragged away. So begins the odyssey of children left behind when the criminal justice system comes calling.

Only after the parent has been through several steps in a process of which incarceration is nearly the end point does one become the child of a parent in prison. The process begins with an arrest, followed by various court proceedings, such as bail hearings, arraignments, preliminary hearings, and a trial. If the sentence includes incarceration, the defendant begins serving time in prison. Along the way, a person may serve time in a local jail, usually run by the county, that serves two purposes: holding people who are awaiting trial, sentencing, or some other criminal justice system procedure such as a transfer to another jurisdiction, and incarcerating people with short sentences, usually of less than a year. The entire process from arrest to sentencing can take months, and children must endure it along with their parent. This chapter offers a rare opportunity to see how children fare after their mother's arrest and to hear their thoughts and concerns about their own changed circumstances following this event.

Arrest

Relatively little attention has been paid to what children experience when a parent is arrested.[1] My interviews with mothers and children revealed that, depending on the circumstances of the arrest, the situation that arises can be complicated and frightening for children. Three broad categories of experience emerged: the child was absent, the child was an observer, or the child was a participant.

Getting Arrested

A person can be arrested either at the time a crime is committed or after investigation leads the police to identify that individual as the criminal. Arrests can also occur when a person has violated court-imposed requirements, such as failing to appear in court for a hearing. Routine police procedure calls for handcuffing persons being arrested before leaving the location of the arrest.

The police typically take the arrestee to a precinct for booking (taking finger-prints, photographs, etc.). Once arrested, a person is in police custody and not free to leave the premises. Therefore, the person is placed in a cell, either at the police station or at some other lock-up facility. The city has a central lockup at the police administration headquarters, where arrestees are held for several hours or in some cases for a few days until they appear before a judicial officer who decides whether the person can be released before trial and, if so, whether and how much bail is required to secure the release. Those who can post bail or are released without having to make a monetary deposit are then free to return home to await further judicial processing. Those unable to pay their bail are transferred to the county jail, where they may be held until their bail is paid or their case is over.

Some people who are arrested are already under criminal justice super-vision at the time of their arrest, typically because they were on probation or parole. Getting arrested for a new offense is a violation of their supervision con-ditions and can lead to the revocation of their supervision and a decision to incarcerate them instead. In such cases, people are typically taken to jail until the supervisory office decides what should be done. If the person is on proba-tion, the probation officers usually defer a decision until the new case is concluded so that they can determine the appropriate course of action in light of the outcome of the new case, but at a minimum they require that the person be detained in jail until the conclusion of the case. Arrestees not under super-vision may have outstanding arrest warrants for other incidents, either in the jurisdiction in which the arrest occurred or elsewhere. They too are detained in jail until their new case is concluded. If they have a pending case in another jurisdiction, they are usually transferred to the other jurisdiction's jail once the authorities in the new case decide that the person can be released, which happened to some of the women in this study.

As this overview indicates, getting arrested means that the person will not be able to return home for at least several hours and in some cases for days, weeks, or months. Even a brief absence, however, means that temporary care must be provided for the children, which can be a challenge for the parent to arrange. Advance warning of an arrest is usually not part of the police game plan, so parents have virtually no time to arrange such care. This concern is less when a parent is living with another adult who shares responsibility for the children, such as another parent, but as we have seen, nearly all these children lived in single-parent families. How then does this process play out for mothers and children?

Arrests When the Child Was Absent

The most common experience was that the child was not present for their mother's arrest. More than six in ten children were in this category. Some fell into this category because they were not living with their mother at the time of her arrest and therefore were unlikely to be present. More often, however, the child was absent because the mother was arrested away from home or the child was at school or elsewhere. If the child was home and the mother was arrested elsewhere, eventually the child began to wonder where she was and why she had not yet returned. If the child was at school when Mom was taken into custody, he or she would either return to an empty house or be left waiting at school to be picked up by a mom who never arrived, which is what happened to eleven-year-old Sean. His mother, Diane, was on her way to pick him up from school when she was arrested and taken in for booking. She eventually managed to reach her mother to ask her to pick Sean up at school, but her mother did not go to get Sean because she thought Diane was joking, as she had never been arrested before. Unbeknownst to Diane, Sean had one bus token with him and thus was able to get himself home.

Shereece was a thirteen-year-old eighth grader whose mother, Roneika, was arrested for shoplifting and held in jail pending the outcome of her case. Shereece's remarks reflect the sequence of events surrounding the arrest and their impact on the children. At the time of the arrest, Shereece and Roneika had been staying at Shereece's grandmother's house while their house was undergoing renovations.

SHEREECE: Our house is getting done over so we had to leave, so we had to pack our stuff and move to the next [unintelligible]. So we had to stay at my grandmom's. And we needed clothes and he [her mother's boyfriend, father of Shereece's half-brother] wouldn't bring us clothes so she went out and she never came back that day. So we was already with my grandmom.

JS: So how did you find out where she was?

SHEREECE: 'Cause she was with my aunt. And my aunt came home and told us, and she [Roneika] called me that night.

JS: So when your aunt came home, what did she say happened to your mom?

SHEREECE: I don't know, she just was just, like, "She got arrested." She wouldn't tell us. She got arrested by an undercover or whatever, she said. I wasn't listening because my mom, regardless, she wasn't coming home.

JS: How did you feel?

SHEREECE: I cried. I cried every day up until when I came to my dad's. I used to wake up crying and go to bed crying and stuff like that.

"I wasn't listening because my mom, regardless, she wasn't coming home" reflects the core reality that confronts the children: Mom had gone out and was taken away, unable to return home. Shereece's mother, in this case, would be away from home for quite some time, spending several weeks in jail awaiting the resolution of her case. Other children were luckier: their mothers were held for only a day or two, as was Sean's mother, who returned home at 2:00 AM two days after she was picked up, bearing reassuring sub sandwiches and chips for her children. Whatever the duration of their mother's absence, children whose mothers were engaged with them shared Shereece's reaction of sadness along with anxiety, not only about their mother but also about what would happen to them until she returned.

Children as Observers

Some children were present when their mother was arrested, often witnessing not only the arrest but also the events that precipitated it. These children at least did not suffer the uncertainty and concomitant fear experienced by children who did not know where their mothers were because they were not present at the arrest. Nevertheless, the events they observed, such as their mother being handcuffed and taken away by the police, were frightening for those who were present when their mother was arrested, even those who did not witness the drama Rhodaisia did. Many of these children reacted with fear and sadness. The most common response when asked how they felt while the arrest was taking place was "scared"; most children also said they had cried. Some expressed anger, typically directed at the person whom the child perceived to be responsible for the mother's arrest.

Perry was a twelve-year-old boy whose mother was arrested three times within a fairly short time based on complaints from her former boyfriend, Theo, who she claimed was fabricating allegations against her to make trouble for her. Theo was not Perry's father, but he was the father of Brian, Perry's infant half-brother. According to Perry's mother, Theo had been harassing the family, so they had moved in with her parents temporarily. Here is how Perry described what happened on one occasion when he witnessed his mother's arrest:

JS: Can you tell me what happened when she was arrested?

PERRY: Um, I was living at my grandparents' house because of Theo. I was sleeping downstairs and I heard these loud knocks on the door, so I wasn't going to open the door. I thought it might be Theo. I didn't know what to do, so I came upstairs, found my grandmom awake. We heard loud knocks on the window, so I didn't open it. It turned out to be the police. My mom had woken up and come upstairs too, and she got dressed and they said she had been charged for abusing her child, abusing Brian or something, so they just put her in handcuffs and put her in the police car.

JS: So you saw them put the handcuffs on her?

PERRY: Uh-huh.

JS: And they put her in the car? How did you feel when this was going on?

PERRY: Angry. I mean my whole family knows that she wouldn't abuse Brian. I'm not sure why the cops couldn't have at least looked into it more so my mom wouldn't have to go to jail.

JS: So you were angry at the cops?

PERRY: No. I was angry at Theo for lying.

JS: At Theo. Okay. And how did you feel while this was happening, besides angry?

PERRY: Just angry at Theo.

JS: And where did you think she was going when they took her away?

PERRY: I wasn't exactly sure. I thought they were just going to take her to jail.

JS: What did it mean to you when they said they were going to take her to jail? What did you think would happen when she went to jail?

PERRY: She just wouldn't get treated right. She'd have nasty food. She wouldn't get to take a shower. She'd have to be in a small cell, and I just think about that when I was in class. I was just praying that she was all right and that nothing happened to her and that she'd be back home.

The concern Perry expressed for his mother's well-being was also a common sentiment voiced by the children, many of whom feared that something bad would happen to their mother if she went to jail, although Perry's concerns were more specific than most. In some cases, the mothers had illnesses, such as diabetes, that heightened the children's fears for their well-being. Being unable to communicate with their mother also exacerbated the children's anxiety.

Not all children had someone else they could blame for their mother's arrest. Some were in the uncomfortable position of recognizing that their mother had done something wrong. This was true especially in cases where a mother was only sporadically engaged in the parent-child relationship. As we already know, this typically resulted from a woman's serious drug use, which in turn also usually meant that the woman had been arrested more than once. As a consequence, some children were more inured than others to the effects of the arrest, having become more accustomed to their mother being arrested and taken to jail. Similarly, they had experienced their mother's eventual return from jail, so the arrest did not carry the same level of uncertainty and ignorance about the outcome it did for others. Children in these situations recognized that their mother had done something likely to get them in trouble with the law and were not particularly surprised when police arrived to take her into custody. Crystal, the fourteen-year-old introduced earlier, spoke of one of her mother's arrests as a rather unremarkable event. Her mother, Donna, had been arrested four or five times, according to Donna's own count. She had twice spent several months in jail when she had been convicted of offenses connected with her drug use. Her substance abuse led her to cede custody of Crystal to her own mother when Crystal was six years old. Because Donna sometimes lived with Crystal and her mother and sometimes not, Crystal had become accustomed to the notion that her mother might leave abruptly and later reappear. Although Crystal was not present at her mother's most recent arrest, she recounted what happened on an earlier occasion: the police arrived at the house where Crystal lived with her grandmother to arrest Donna, who apparently had walked out of a court-mandated treatment program.

JS: Could you tell me what happened?

CRYSTAL: She left the house, the program that she was at, she left and they arrested her.

JS: And what happened?

CRYSTAL: The cops knocked on the door. They woke everybody up.

JS: Did they wake you up?

CRYSTAL: Yeah. [unintelligible] They woke me up.

JS: What did you think was going on?

CRYSTAL: Nothing.

JS: What did you think they were doing there?

CRYSTAL: Taking her.

JS: Yeah? Where did you think they were taking her?

CRYSTAL: Back to jail.

JS: And how did that make you feel?

CRYSTAL: She knew they'd be coming.

JS: Yeah? Before they came, you mean?

CRYSTAL: Uh-huh.

JS: How did she know?

CRYSTAL: Because she left the program and she wasn't finished her time in the program.

JS: And why was she in the program?

CRYSTAL: From being on drugs and stuff.

JS: Did you know she was on drugs?

CRYSTAL: Uh-huh.

JS: And how did that make you feel, that she was on drugs?

CRYSTAL: It made me feel, like, nothing.

JS: Okay. And when the police came, did they talk to you?

CRYSTAL: No.

JS: And how did you feel while that was happening?

CRYSTAL: I was just [unintelligible], and then after they left I went back to sleep.

Secure in her own home with her grandmother, Crystal's witnessing this arrest was far less fraught with emotion than it was for other children. In addition, Crystal was well aware of her mother's behavior, even recognizing that her mother was at risk of arrest because she had walked away from the drug rehabilitation program she was mandated to attend as a result of an earlier conviction. Crystal had in a sense anticipated that her mother would be arrested because she had failed to follow the rules established for her.

Children as Participants

The most troubling arrest incidents were the few in which the children went from observers to participants, because they either were involved in the incident that led to their mother's arrest or were called upon by the police to help them find their mother. Such incidents made them feel responsible—at least in part—for their mother's arrest. Children who were involved in an incident that eventually led to their mother's arrest seemed able to deflect blame onto the other person involved. Ten-year-old Richard, for instance, had an altercation with some children and their mother in his apartment complex, which led to a fight between his mother and the other woman and his mother's subsequent arrest. Richard quite matter-of-factly said that he "didn't feel no kind of way" about his mother's arrest. He was confident that even if she had to spend time in jail, she would be able to defend herself because she often confronted and hit people in the neighborhood who had bothered him.

Children called upon by the police to help them find their mother have to decide whether to cooperate or attempt to protect their mother, as Rhodaisia did when she and her siblings hid their mother in the closet. Being put in this position of course can add to the emotional turmoil the children experience when their mother is arrested. Peter, the "tough guy" profiled earlier, and Tremelle, an eleven-year-old, were two of the children who faced this situation but who had very different reactions to their role in it.

Peter had been through difficult times with his heavily addicted mother, Patty, throughout his life: homelessness, foster care, immersion in her drug culture. Although Patty had remained clean for several years, she had relapsed recently and was heavily involved in drug use again at the time we met. Eventually, she entered a rehabilitation facility for treatment, but she had run away from it after a short time. Now aged sixteen, Peter was angry and exasperated by her behavior, as was his maternal grandmother, who called the police after Patty locked her out of her own house, stole her jewelry and money, and fled. Although the police could not find Patty, Peter and his grandmother saw her at an intersection known throughout the city as a notorious drug-dealing corner. Here he discusses his decision to inform the police of her whereabouts:

PETER: Yeah. She was getting so fucked up where to the point she was trying to rob my grandmother. She tried to rob my grandmother, and at first I told my grandmom, "Don't press charges," but she got away from the rehab and then we drove by and saw my mom on the corner of Crawford and Warren. Sittin' on the ground. I said, "Mom-mom, if she's at Crawford and Warren, you gotta go press charges." Cop came around and picked her up, pressed charges, and now my grandmom's not going to court no more. She just wanted her to do a couple months in prison to stop what she was doing. Me and my grandmom both made that decision. We'd rather have her over there, not doing drugs, than out here, gonna die.

JS: You felt like that was gonna happen, she was gonna die?

PETER: Yeah, because that's my mom, I still love her and all, but [unintelligible], that's why I got her out of it.

JS: And you feel responsible for helping her?

PETER: I don't feel responsible, I just felt like she needed help.

When asked how he felt when he saw the police put her in handcuffs and take her away, Peter replied: "I felt good about myself because finally she's getting the help she needs."

Tremelle, in contrast, tried in vain to protect her mother, who also had a serious addiction problem. Tremelle and her mother, Denisha, had rarely lived together, although Denisha sporadically came around to see Tremelle and her siblings, who lived with their grandmother. Denisha had been arrested on previous occasions and had spent time in jail, so Tremelle was aware that if her mother was arrested, she was liable to be jailed again. Here she recounts what happened when her mother was arrested most recently, when the police came to her house at 2:00 AM:

TREMELLE: And they knocked on the door, and I was sitting on the couch asleep, 'cause me and my grandmom was watching TV and we just fell asleep and they knocked on the door and my grandmom woke up and said, "Who is it?" They said, "The police." So, they came in, they checked around the house with a flashlight, and they woke my cousin up. And then they said, "Can I come in the kitchen," 'cause they had a lot of questions about when was the last time I saw my mom and everything. And where my mom lived. And for that one, I lied, 'cause I don't want my mom to get locked up. 'Cause I know that was coming. I knew that she lived on—I forgot what street. Something near Elm Avenue. She lived six houses from the corner, and I said four, 'cause I didn't want her to get locked up. 'Cause I knew that was going to come.

JS: And how did you feel when this was going on?

TREMELLE: Scared.

JS: What did you think was going to happen?

TREMELLE: I knew that she was going to get locked up. That's one thing I knew for sure. And my last thought was that I was going to have to go to court. 'Cause I was scared. I just had all these kind of thoughts in my head! [laughs] There were a lot of thoughts. I was really scared.

Despite Tremelle's efforts to deceive them, the police found Denisha, who was arrested and jailed while awaiting the disposition of her case. Tremelle's involvement in her mother's arrest left her shaken and traumatized. By her own account, her behavior had changed since the day Denisha was arrested: she had begun fighting and talking back to her grandmother. The incident had taken an emotional toll on her as well: "Sometimes I cry, and my heart start pounding, 'cause I'm scared, and I always worry about that day when she got locked up and everything." According to Tremelle, she had never reacted this way to her mother's previous arrests, which she had not witnessed, so clearly her encounter with the police and what she perceived to be her role in her mother's arrest had a significant impact on her.

In rare cases, children's participation in their mother's arrest occurred because the child was simply with the mother at the time an incident took place and the police mistakenly thought the child was implicated in the criminal wrongdoing. These incidents were especially frightening for the youths involved because they were not only observers but also suspects. In one such incident, fifteen-year-old Dequan, his brother, and his younger sister were present when their mother, Evelyn, became embroiled in an argument with their downstairs neighbor. Evelyn and this woman engaged in a fight, and the woman phoned the police. When they arrived, they arrested Evelyn and took the other woman to the hospital. The police then returned and arrested Dequan's brother, claiming he too had been involved in the fight. Dequan by then had left the house, but he learned that the police were looking for him as well. "Nervous, under pressure, worried," Dequan went to his father's house, but the police never came for him. Both his mother and his brother, however, were ultimately placed on probation. As Dequan said, "It felt like a downfall like for a family in one day."

The second incident in which a child was judged a participant involved Nicole and had more serious consequences. Nicole is the teenager described earlier who felt responsible for looking after her crack-addicted mother, Sharon, which led her to visit the crack house her mother frequented to check up on her or simply to see her. On one occasion, Nicole went to the crack house and asked her mother for money to get something to eat. Her timing was unfortunate. The twenty-dollar bill her mother handed her was a marked bill, one that undercover police officers had used earlier in the day to buy drugs to gather evidence of dealing in the house for a subsequent drug bust. Nicole described what happened when the police raided the house:

JS: Were you scared when they came in?

NICOLE: Yeah, I didn't know what was going on!

JS: Did they handcuff you and everything?

NICOLE: Yeah. 'Cause I wasn't a [crack] smoker, you know, [which was] what they thought. I was in there. I was like, "That's my mom." And they just ran in, just bust in and then they just came rushing upstairs. They handcuffed me. They threw me against the wall, then they ran this scanner thing across my hand and was like, "Yeah, we got them." Me and my mom. Then they locked both of us up.

Later, I asked Nicole how the police had acted toward her.

NICOLE: Ruthless.

JS: Really?

NICOLE: They ran up to the bedroom and put the gun up to my head, [saying] he's going to get the cops to F me up if I don't tell him where the stuff was and all this junk. I'm like, "What is you talking about? I mean, I don't even got nothing." He wasn't trying to hear it though.

JS: And there was your mother, also getting arrested.

NICOLE: Yeah. She had the money mark on her hands too. And so did I 'cause she gave me the money. But she didn't know it was no undercover thing.

JS: So, how did you feel while she was being arrested and you were being arrested?

NICOLE: I was like, this can't be happening. I was like, "Dang!" Just looking at the whole situation, like, "Who is just fell into this shit right here?" Excuse my language. They put her in the cuffs. I was already in the cuffs. Then you knew something was definitely going down.

Nicole and Sharon were taken to the precinct, where Nicole's father came and picked her up. Despite her bystander status, she was charged as a juvenile and was placed under supervision even before her adjudicatory hearing. Months later, we find both Nicole and Sharon locked up. Sharon had finally been sentenced to jail for the incident in which Nicole had been arrested, but Nicole had been arrested on different charges when she was caught selling drugs out of her house. Adjudicated delinquent, she was sent to a juvenile facility some three hundred miles from the city for a minimum of a year's confinement.

Police Behavior During an Arrest

Nicole was the only child who had such a traumatic experience with the police during their mother's arrest (although, as noted earlier, most of the teenagers in the sample had their own experience of being arrested for offenses they had committed). Clearly, however, the police officers' behavior can contribute to the degree of trauma that children may experience during their mother's arrest. Furthermore, the procedures they follow can make the immediate aftermath of a woman's arrest more or less complicated and difficult for the children and their mother.

Most of the women who were arrested when their children were present portrayed the police as indifferent to the children's situation, especially if some of the children seemed old enough to look after any younger ones, as in this scenario of an earlier arrest described by Marcia, a mother of two children who were upstairs in their house when the police came.

JS: So the kids were up there by themselves, crying. And this is three years ago? So Shantay was thirteen, and Nicholas was eight?

MARCIA: Uh-huh.

JS: And what did the cops say about the kids being there alone?

MARCIA: They didn't say nothing. They felt like Shantay was old enough to watch her brother and they called, because in the process when I was putting on my clothes and stuff like that I was, I said, "Can I make a phone call?" and they was like, "Sure." So I made a phone call and I told Shantay to call this one, call that one, and you know . . .

After the police took Marcia away, one of her friends came and picked up the children, who stayed with her for a day and a half before Marcia returned. However, despite the apparent disregard expressed by the police in Marcia's account, no women reported any experience where the police arrested them and left young children alone in a house without an adult. In such cases, the police would have taken the children to the city's child protective services agency (Office of Family Services, or OFS) for emergency foster-care placement, an outcome that women absolutely wanted to avoid for fear that they would lose their children over the long term. For instance, Darlene, whose assault on her husband was described earlier, was defiant and resolute when the police tried to take her away before someone could get there to take charge of the children, suggesting that they would take the children to OFS instead. At the time of the arrest, three of her four children were in the house; they ranged in age from six to eleven.

DARLENE: So they came and arrested me. They kicked my door in. They had no warrant, they read me no rights, they kicked my door in, and me and my children were in here in the bed.

JS: What time of day was it?

DARLENE: 1:30 in the morning. They had no warrant, no nothing.

JS: And so the kids were here when the cops busted down the door?

DARLENE: And they shining lights all in my kids' face and stuff like that.

JS: How did the children react?

DARLENE: Well, they just laid there like, you know, and I called my mother to come here and, um, to get them because he [her husband] wasn't here. They never got up, my mother was here before they [the police] left, they talking 'bout, "Well, we gonna have to . . ." And I said, "You not taking my kids no damn place because, first of all, you had no business kicking my door in, that's for number one. I did not see no warrant and you not taking me anywhere until somebody get here to come take my kids." "We'll take your kids to OFS." I said, "Well then, where you think you're taking me? I have rights just the hell like you do." You know, I don't know who they think I was, I was like, uh, no I'm not scared of no cop, you are human just like I am human. And when you start talking about my kids, then you have a problem. The problem is no longer mine, it's yours, because I'm a make it your problem. Don't mess with my children. And he started to say, "Well, we're only gonna wait . . ." I said, "You're gonna wait as long as it takes." And I sat here, right there [*gestures toward a chair*], for an hour. They said, "Well, we have to go outside," and I said, "Well, get the hell out then." "Well, we have to take . . ." "You don't have to take me anywhere, I don't see no warrant." And they waited for an hour and a half. I said, "You can sit down if you want to. I don't care, but I'm not going nowhere until somebody get here and gets my kids."

The situation was quite different when a woman was arrested without her children present, which in this case meant a majority of the women. Virtually all these women told the same story: the police did not ask them if they had children and, when informed that they had children at school or home, did not seem to care whether the women could make arrangements to get someone to look after them. Again, no women told of an arrest experience in which young children were at home unattended, and it is unlikely that the police would not have taken action had they been informed that very young children were home alone. Nevertheless, there was no effort to ensure that the children would be taken care of, apart from allowing the women to make a phone call once they reached the police station.

Summary

Virtually all the children who witnessed their mother's arrest or became quasi-participants in it reported having felt frightened by the experience and sad because of their mother's removal from the family. Their fear arose from both the immediate circumstances of the arrest—armed police officers coming into their house, sometimes breaking down the front door—and their longer-term anxiety about their mother's well-being and about what would happen to them. Rarely did mothers or children depict the police as having been concerned about the children, although in some instances police extended some courtesy, such as waiting until the children had left the room before handcuffing a woman. In situations where the children were not present when their mother was arrested, their mother had to try, with one phone call, to make arrangements for temporary housing for the children if it appeared that she would not be released soon.

The Aftermath of Arrest

The children's living arrangements were not uniform, as we have seen: some lived alone with their mother, others with their mother and some adult, and still others apart from their mother. What happened to the children as a result of a mother's temporary absence following her arrest was a function in large part of their household situation: children whose household included another adult who could care for them were far better situated than those who lived alone with their mother. Furthermore, what happened to the mothers—and consequently to the children—was in some cases determined by her social networks, which as we have seen were frequently tenuous. The extent of the arrest's impact on the children beyond the immediate experience itself was also significantly affected by whether the mother was held in jail before trial.

What happened to the children once a woman was arrested also varied as a function of how long she was held. Once she was taken to the police station and booked, she was placed at least temporarily in a holding cell there until she appeared before a judicial officer, who decided whether she could be released pending the disposition of her case or she had to be held because there was an order to detain her. A detainer is a legal document authorizing detention pending further action; as noted earlier, detainers were typically issued because the woman had an outstanding arrest warrant either in the city or in another county, or because she was already on probation or parole and her new arrest meant that she could be found to have violated the terms of her supervision. Women in this situation remained in jail, usually for several weeks, pending the outcome of their case. Women who were unable to pay their bail also had to wait in jail until the disposition of their case was decided. Virtually all the women in this latter group did not have the money available to pay the bail, even if it was a relatively small amount of one or two hundred dollars. Their social isolation and family difficulties, as described earlier, influenced the outcome of their situation. People who need money for bail typically ask family members and friends to pitch in and help by putting up the money for their release. After all, if the woman returns to court as required, the amount of the bail, less any administrative fees, will be returned to whomever posted the bail. The women's weak social ties meant that they had few individuals to whom they could turn when needed to obtain their freedom.

In some cases, women whose family would not bail them out knew that their relatives did not have sufficient funds; in other cases, family members simply refused to help. Fed up with a woman's repeated arrests, angry at having to step in to take over the job of caring for her children, hopeful that perhaps a stint in jail would get the woman on the path to sobriety—all these were reasons for the refusals to help. Peter's grandmother, for instance, was both angry and concerned about her daughter: having just been robbed by her, the grandmother thought that a period of time in jail might straighten her out and get her to change her ways. Although the grandmother had filed the complaint that led to Peter's mother's arrest, she did not intend to show up at any hearings, figuring that the case would be dropped. Her plan was to let her daughter spend a few weeks in jail, staying off drugs and perhaps emerging from jail better able to care for herself and her son.

However long the women were ultimately held, the arrest triggered for most a panicked effort to get someone to care for the children and let the children know what was happening. Typically, it was not until they arrived at the police station for booking that the women were permitted to make a call to try to find someone to go get the children from the house or to pick them up from school and take them somewhere else to stay. Here is how Diane described her efforts to reach her mother to tell her to pick Sean up at school:

> I had kept begging them [the police officers]. I had to practically beg them, "Please let me a least make a phone call to my mother. My son is around the corner waiting on me to pick him up from school." They were like, "You'll get a phone call, you'll get a phone call." Different things, and I'm like, you know, so when they were like, "We are ready to take you downtown to [another] district," and I had to ask then like one more time, "Could you please let me call my mother and let her know I need her to check on my kids and let her know where I am or whatever?" So he was like, "Okay." So they finally brought the phone over and dialed my mother and I let her know where I was or whatever. But she said she actually thought I was joking when I told her [what happened]. She's like,

"Yeah, right." I said, "I am serious. I have to go now and I will call you when I can." So she actually thought I was joking until a few hours went by and the kids was like, "We didn't hear from my mom yet." And she said that's when she realized she [Diane] must have been serious. She called my sisters: "Is Diane over there? Is she with you?" They were like, "We have not heard from her."

Like Diane, the mothers often could call only another adult, so the children could not speak to their mother for reassurance that she was all right, nor could the mothers be reassured that their children were safe and being looked after properly. After their one call, the women often were left wondering what had happened to their children. Here Latoya describes her concerns after both she and her husband were arrested at the same time on fraud charges. They had received a letter instructing them to appear at the prosecutor's office on a specific day, without informing them that they would be arrested when they got there. They brought their two youngest children with them, thinking they would be going home after their meeting, but their two older children were in school. Once they learned they were not free to leave, they called Latoya's mother-in-law and asked her to pick up the two children who were at the prosecutor's office with them. Latoya and her husband thought they would be released after a few hours, but they were held for two days.

LATOYA: Two days! I couldn't talk to my kids! The one phone call I got to make was to make sure they got home safe. I couldn't talk to them. They didn't have a change of clothes. I wasn't sure where they were or if they had enough food and stuff. It was no way that I could be like, "Look, go to the bank. Take anything out if there's anything there." There was no way I could give them any keys or nothing. You know, they missed work—my kids' grandma and their aunt—they missed work to take care of them.

The mother's absence was bewildering and eventually frightening for the children left behind, depending on how long they were left alone. They were in the dark, dependent on others to take charge of them and inform them about what was occurring. Those who were able to speak with their mother found some comfort in hearing from her that she was all right and that she would soon be home. For instance, the concern that Perry expressed for his mother when she was arrested abated somewhat once he had spoken to her: "She said she'd be home soon, so I just waited for her to come back. I mean, it's [not] like I don't care about it, but I know I just have to focus on my work so I could get good grades. I knew eventually she would be home."

Figuring out how to find accommodations for the children was the most difficult for women who were living alone with their children. They asked the children's grandmothers, aunts, or, occasionally, fathers to get the children and find a place or places where they could stay temporarily, depending on how many children had to be accommodated. For some families with more than one child, this meant that the children had to be split up to stay in different places, because one relative could not house all of them. In addition, some of the arrangements made immediately following the arrest did not last and children were moved, sometimes more than once. As Shereece said in a letter to her mother: "My brother and I have been moved around like a charity case." She started off living with her grandmother following her mother's detention but, as she said, "it was tiring for my grandmother everyday." Her grandmother described a different scenario: she had thrown Shereece out of the house after Shereece attacked her physically. Shereece then stayed with her aunt for a short while, eventually ending up with her father and his fiancée.

For mothers who were sporadically engaged or absent, finding a place for their children to stay was considerably easier or even unnecessary. Their sporadic engagement meant that the child was being cared for by someone else, who provided the child with a home regardless of what happened to the mother. Crystal, for instance, was already living with her grandmother and thus simply went back to bed in her own home after the police left. Her sporadically engaged mother was spared the frantic scrambling to get someone to come for her child in the middle of the night, as occurred in Darlene's house. Furthermore, her mother's history of living apart from the family and being arrested in the past mitigated the impact of a new arrest on Crystal. The same was true for children whose mothers had been absent from the family for long periods. Some of them, in fact, did not even know that their mothers had been arrested. They didn't wonder at an absence of a day or two or even of several weeks, since their mother usually was not present anyway.

The anxiety of children whose mothers were released shortly after being arrested was short-lived but real, as reflected in Dequan's remarks about how he felt during the one night his mother spent in jail after her arrest:

JS: And did you speak to your mother?

DEQUAN: Yeah, I spoke to my mother from, like, from when she was in the lockup. She, I was speaking to her, I asked her how she doin', is she okay, she would respond, "Everything's okay."

JS: And how were you feeling while she was locked up?

DEQUAN: I felt like, I felt awful because, like, for me, like, she, for me she's my circle and I felt incomplete. For me, she's my half to my circle, she's my half to my whole. She's the number one lady in my life. I felt, I felt, just bad all over.

A mother's return from detention did not end the children's anxiety, which was frequently replaced by ongoing concern about what would happen when their mother went to court. Some children claimed not to know their mother was going to court, even though their mothers said they knew; others did not fully understand what going to court entailed or why their mother was going. Others misunderstood why their mother was going to court or had an exaggerated idea of the potential consequences of their mother's court appearance. Eight-year-old Roberto, for instance, feared what might happen to his mother when she went to court for a case in which she had cut someone in the arm with a knife. She was charged with aggravated assault, a felony that could result in a penalty of twenty years in prison. Such an outcome seemed unlikely, however, given the circumstances of the incident (in fact, in the end, his mother was sentenced to probation). Here is how Roberto related his concern:

JS: Do you know what could happen to her when she goes to court? [Roberto nods.] What?

ROBERTO: [*In a barely audible voice that conveys anxiety*] She could get locked up for life.

JS: No. She didn't do anything like that that would get her locked up for life.

ROBERTO: She could get locked up for a long time.

JS: What would happen if she got locked up?

ROBERTO: I would start crying.

JS: And what would you do? Where would you go?

ROBERTO: My dad's house.

Like Roberto, many of the children were anxious about the possibility of their mother being jailed. The women typically were required to make several court appearances before they were sentenced, having to attend an arraignment, a preliminary hearing, and possibly a trial and sentencing. Due to postponements caused by various parties (e.g., witnesses failing to appear), some women had to go to court several times before a particular hearing could take place. Each court date could create anxiety for the children, introducing the possibility that their mother would not come home. Margaret, the grandmother who had raised three grandchildren from infancy, recounted how her young grandson had been reacting to her arrest—her first—and her subsequent court appearances. The court date she referred to here was for her arraignment, a perfunctory hearing at which court dates for preliminary hearings are set.

MARGARET: And since I got locked up, he sits beside my bed.

JS: And he didn't used to do that?

MARGARET: No, he didn't used to do that. Remember you saw me in court last week?

JS: Yeah.

MARGARET: He wanted to follow me. I'm like, "You can't." He said, "What if you don't come back? What's going to happen to me?" So he packed his book-bag. I found his bookbag. He packed some stuff that he wanted to take. I came home and I said, "What's in your bookbag?" He said, "That's my stuff, in case you go away."

JS: Oh. He must be so scared.

MARGARET: They're scared. I understand, but I don't know what to do. I don't have nobody. They don't want to go to a foster home, so I don't know.

Margaret's grandson was justly concerned about what would happen to him and his siblings if Margaret was jailed, even if the likelihood of that out-come was remote. Recall that Margaret had raised the children from infancy because their father was in prison and their mother, a drug addict, had all but abandoned them; she had not seen them since Margaret took them home from the hospital, where they had been taken after their mother had left them alone in their apartment. With their grandfather dead and no other relatives willing to step up to help, the children indeed would have faced a very uncertain future had their grandmother been incarcerated. Margaret was among the few women who had a strong social network, but those connections did not trans-late to the assistance required to care for young and teenaged children, reflect-ing just how difficult it can be to find accommodations for children under such circumstances.

Even children more securely situated than Margaret's grandson felt uncer-tainty about where they would live and who would look after them if their mother was locked up. Jonathan, for instance, was eleven years old when his mother was charged with a drug offense. They were both living with his grand-mother and aunt, who had recently moved in with them after her release from a two-year stint in prison. Thus, if his mother had been jailed, he would have continued living with his relatives in his own home. Even though Jonathan was aware of this, he worried that he might be removed from the family and had made a contingency plan, albeit a nonspecific one:

JS: And so you don't know why your mom's going to court? Are you worried about her going to court?

JONATHAN: Uh-huh.

JS: Why?

JONATHAN: 'Cause if they lock her up, like, I ain't gonna have no one, like to buy me clothes, like the things that I want. 'Cause if I really want something, she'll get it for me. But if she goes to jail, then I ain't gonna get the things I want.

JS: Oh. So what do you think you would do if she went to jail?

JONATHAN: I'll stay in school.

JS: You'll stay in school? And who would stay with you?

JONATHAN: My grandma, and my aunt. If my mom was to go to jail and they'll take me away, I would run away.

JS: Where would you run?

JONATHAN: I would run anywhere, as long as they don't catch me.

Ten-year-old Melissa's more specific, if unrealistic, solution to the problem of what she would do if her mother were jailed reflected both her apprehension about being left alone and her fierce determination to show her devotion to her mother now that they had been reunited after Melissa's years in foster care:

MELISSA: But if she got to go to jail, I'm gonna tell 'em, then don't send her to jail because, the next time she gotta go to jail, I'm gonna say don't send her in jail, because she didn't do nothin'.

JS: So who would you say that to?

MELISSA: The police. If they gonna send my mom to jail, if they all gonna send my mom to jail, then they gonna have to send me to jail. That's the rule that goes around.

JS: Oh yeah? That if she goes, you go too? You wouldn't mind being in jail if she was there too?

MELISSA: I take up for my mom.

JS: Suppose she went to jail, and they told you you couldn't go to jail with her . . .

MELISSA: I would just go. I would just ask a cab to take me to the jail, take me to jail and send me and [unintelligible] up my mom.

JS: Well, suppose they tell you, "You can't stay here, little girl." Where do you think you would go stay?

MELISSA: In jail with my mom.

JS: Suppose your mom asked you not to go to jail with her.

MELISSA: I would still go.

In each of these cases, the children's anxiety stemmed from their uncertainty about what might happen to them if their mother were to be jailed. Children whose mothers were in fact already jailed pending their case's disposition had to deal with anxiety about their long-term fate, but they also had many other immediate concerns. For instance, many of the women detained in jail had limited options available for finding someone to care for their children and had to settle for less than ideal caretakers. The alternative—having OFS take the children—was abhorrent to most of the women. Danyelle expressed this antipathy quite clearly: "'Cause they give these kids to people that they think are good people, and them people wind up killing them kids. I don't want to deal with no

OFS as far as taking my kids. Oh, I don't want my kids in the system! I would give them to a friend or one of my relatives before I would let OFS get them! Believe me! Oh, no!" Her apprehensions about OFS led Danyelle to turn to her brother for help when she was detained in jail, asking him to move in and care for her four children. Her brother did not present himself as an ideal candidate for a caregiver for young children. He had been released from prison only recently after having served nearly fifteen years, and released prisoners often need significant support in order to reintegrate themselves into society. Furthermore, Danyelle reported that her brother had raped one of her sisters when she was a child. Nevertheless, she felt the children would be safe with him—or at least safer than in a foster family. Shortly after her release from jail, however, Danyelle discovered—when her brother dismantled her stove and stole her kitchen set—that he had been smoking crack. Although grateful that he had cared for the children during her absence, she decided his behavior could not be tolerated in her house and made him leave.

Danyelle's resort to her brother as temporary caregiver for her children reflects the limited options available to women who had narrow social networks populated by people with backgrounds similar to theirs. Patty, whose son Peter had revealed her whereabouts so the police could come arrest her, also left her son in the care of someone who did not turn out to be a suitable temporary guardian. Before her arrest, she and Peter had been sharing their house with a twenty-year-old friend of Patty who had recently been paroled from prison. While Patty was detained, the police raided the house because of a tip that her parolee friend was selling drugs there. In the process, they broke down the front door and ransacked the house. It fell to Peter to effect the repairs to the shattered door, with the result that his house was now protected from the elements by a door that let in rain and cold through a large gap between the top of the door and the doorframe. That too-small door seemed an apt symbol of so much that had gone wrong in his life: his father dead and his mother either in jail or spending her days on the street because of her addiction, Peter was trying to make do with the hand that had been dealt him, but as a youth who had been thrust far too early into an adult world, his efforts were falling short. His mother had tried to provide him with a measure of safety and security, but the gap her absence created—just like the gap over the front door—meant that Peter ultimately was unprotected from life's undesirable elements.[2]

With no income, Peter was unable to pay the rent and the parolee/caretaker was eventually arrested and jailed after carrying out a highly publicized armed robbery of a well-known retail establishment. (He had invited Peter to participate, but Peter had wisely declined, having recently been placed on probation himself because of a gun possession charge.) Peter moved back in with his grandmother, with whom he had lived off and on over the years because of his mother's drug use. Eventually, Patty was released from detention and sentenced to probation, but she did not return to live with Peter. After having filed the criminal complaint against Patty, Peter's grandmother had obtained a restraining order prohibiting Patty from contact with her or Peter.

Peter was not the only older child in this study who was placed in a difficult position as a result of his mother's pretrial detention. As Peter's circumstances suggest, mothers sometimes believed their older children could fend for themselves with minimal adult supervision. John, for instance, whom we have also met, was left on his own when his mother was detained. As he said, "This time she left me high and dry." John was not welcome at his older brother's house, perhaps because of the turmoil that had ensued the last time their mother had been jailed and John had stayed there. John was thirteen years old at that point, and he stopped attending school while his mother was in jail. OFS intervened, and John was placed in a group home. He ran away and returned home, but his older brother notified OFS, which then placed him with a neighborhood family with three adolescent girls. During his stay in the household, John was accused of raping the three girls but ultimately was adjudicated delinquent for a less serious noncontact sex offense. When his mother was arrested and jailed this time, she decided that, rather than risk having him enter the foster-care system again, it would be better for him to remain where they had been living together, which she described as an "abandominium," a room in a house that could barely pass as habitable. The young man who owned the house and to whom John paid weekly rent looked out for him after a fashion by allowing John to purchase some food with his welfare card and occasionally preparing a meal for him. By now, John was fifteen but again had stopped attending school. Instead, he was supporting himself as best he could by working in a factory or as a day laborer. Having recently broken up with his girlfriend, who was his son's mother, living in substandard housing and barely getting by, John keenly felt the loss of his mother to the criminal justice system, adrift without her as his anchor. He spoke the first time we met of how her detention was making him feel:

JOHN: That's why I'm depressed, because I wonder what is there to do for fun? Everything that I used to love doing, I don't care about anymore. I don't even remember what I used to love doing. Everything went so bad, what could happen. I'm trying to figure out what I can do to make me happy. There's nothing I can do to make me happy . . .

JS: You don't feel close to anyone? Who do you go to when you have a problem or something's bothering you?

JOHN: No one.

JS: Can you talk to a friend or anything about it?

JOHN: They can't do nothing for me. If I tell all my friends, what can they do for me? If I got my mother here or something, she can do something for me.

In this situation, we see the effects once again of the mother's social isolation: she had no family—not even her older son, who was tired of his mother's behavior (this was, after all, the nineteenth time she had been arrested)—and no friends to whom she could turn for help in a time of real need for her child. John's father had died in prison when he was very young, and his older half-brother, whom John had seen as a friendly figure he might turn to in need, had recently died after having been in and out of prison during almost all of John's life. Although John may have been carrying adult responsibilities—being a father, paying rent, trying to keep a job—he was not prepared for all that he was trying to manage. John attributed his misfortune to his mother's behavior: "I would be doing a lot better now if my mom didn't mess up big time." Nevertheless, she was still the only person in the world he thought could "do something" to help improve his circumstances.

John's fatherhood was a source of concern for him, largely centered on his desire to see his child more often because his ex-girlfriend's family allowed him to visit only once a week. The other teenage parents in this sample, however, all of whom were mothers, faced a different set of problems when their own mothers were held in jail until the disposition of their cases. The mothers of Ronice and Aleesha, two teenagers who had children, were jailed following their arrests. Despite the mothers' sporadic involvement with their lives before they were jailed, the girls wanted to be able to look to their mothers for assistance and advice, as many new mothers do. Their inability to rely on their mothers left them frustrated, angry, and sad. Aleesha was sharing responsibility with her grandmother for looking after not only her own child but also her sister, who was not much older than her baby. Although she was frustrated that her responsibilities as a mother constrained her from engaging in activities outside her home, her real resentment came from having to care for her sister. She looked forward to the day her mother would come home because "she'll take care of her daughter [Aleesha's sister]," freeing Aleesha to go out.

The consequences for Ronice of her mother's time in jail were particularly dire. Her mother had been detained in jail in the city after her arrest because she was wanted for a charge in another county. Her case in the city was dropped after a short while, but she was then transferred to jail in the other county to await disposition of that case. Although Ronice and her mother had lived apart more than they had lived together because of her mother's incarcerations and drug use (her mother had been locked up "probably like 75 percent of my life," according to Ronice), the two had enjoyed a brief period when they shared a house just before her mother's current arrest. The house was provided under Section 8, a public housing program. After her mother's arrest, Ronice remained in the house alone with her child until the manager of the housing program realized that a minor with a baby was living in a house without an adult present and threatened to evict them. Ronice moved to her aunt's house but returned with her baby to the house she had lived in with her mother for a few days every week to escape the clamor in her aunt's crowded household. It was important to her that the house remain in her mother's name, especially because losing this one could result in a long wait for another. Like John, Ronice had to shoulder adult responsibilities that few teenagers have to worry about. Here she discusses trying to hold onto the public housing:

RONICE: I go to her [a housing employee] for Section 8 and certification for housing.

JS: They certify that you're eligible for it?

RONICE: Yeah. No, certify that I still don't receive no income and my mom don't receive no income and they'll continue to pay the rent checks, the utility checks. They pay utility checks. But that's all right though.

JS: So do you have to take care of all that now?

RONICE: Uh-huh. It's stressful. They send termination letters. I gotta run down there to see what they talkin' about. 'Cause ain't nobody else gonna do it.

JS: Right. And you said it's stressful.

RONICE: Uh-huh.

JS: So what do you do to try to deal with the stress?

RONICE: Nothin'.

JS: Nothing? Is there somebody you can talk to about it?

RONICE: I talk to her, my aunt.

JS: Does she help you with any of the stuff you have to do?

RONICE: Uh-huh.

JS: What does she do to help?

RONICE: She takes me to get papers moved around and she helps me a lot.

JS: 'Cause it sounds like you have to negotiate with a lot of different systems like welfare and the food stamps and Section 8 and that kind of stuff and, and, um, and she's there to help you with all of that?

RONICE: Uh-huh.

JS: Do you know other kids your age who have to deal with those kinds of things?

RONICE: What? Yeah.

JS: Yeah? Why do they have to deal with it?

RONICE: My girlfriend knows that her mom is on drugs. She's not locked up but she on drugs, so she gotta take the housing responsibilities too and her welfare responsibilities 'cause she can't find a job or the child care for her kids.

JS: So you, the two of you, do you talk about it or help each other at all?

RONICE: No. I don't even talk about it. That's why I been cryin'.

Asked if she thought talking with other children in the same situation might help her, Ronice said she did not:

RONICE: Another child couldn't help me.

JS: No? Who could help you? Do you think anybody could?

RONICE: My mother.

JS: Your mother? Do you ever talk to her about that? No?

RONICE: [*Makes a sound indicating no*]

JS: How do you think she feels about it?

RONICE: She feel, she feels bad about it.

JS: Does she ever talk to you about it?

RONICE: About feelin' bad about it?

JS: Yeah.

RONICE: Yeah. She cry, but then it make me mad.

JS: That's she's crying? What about it makes you mad?

RONICE: 'Cause she can't do nothin' about it.

As John did, Ronice saw her mother as the one person who might help her, despite her frequent absence from Ronice's life, leaving it to other adults to help Ronice with whatever challenges she might have encountered. In addition, although the school near the house Ronice shared with her mother had a special program for teen parents, the one near her aunt's house did not. The result? Ronice stopped attending school.

Conclusion

Much of the attention to parental incarceration has focused on what happens to children while their parents are in prison. As this chapter shows, however, the period that starts with a parent's arrest and leads up to the incarceration may also present the child with traumatic episodes and anxiety-filled days. Many of the children witness their mother's arrest and some are firsthand observers of the crimes that precipitated the arrest. Some even become suspects themselves, simply by being around at the time of the crime. For those present at the arrest, the event is not only frightening to them but also degrading to their mother, who is taken away in handcuffs. No matter where the mothers are when arrested, however, they must grapple with the need to ensure that someone will look after the children until they return. The uncertainty over how long the mother's detention will last only exacerbates the anxiety both mother and child feel.

That the police would leave children alone in a house when they arrest a mother, or that they fail even to inquire whether the arrestee has children who will need assistance, may seem surprising or even shocking. However, such behavior by the city's law enforcement personnel is in keeping with the general practice of police departments nationwide.[3] Generally, the police adopt a willful blindness: they don't ask about the children, and even if the arrestee tells, the police would rather not know. Knowing might require them to take an action with which they would rather not become involved, such as deciding where a child should go to stay and with whom.

The issue of who should be responsible for the children of someone being taken into police custody presents dilemmas both legal and ethical. One of the greatest worries the women I met expressed during interviews and informal conversations was that their children would be turned over to child protective services. Not only did they worry about the quality of care the children would receive if they were placed in emergency foster care, but also they feared that the initial intervention would lead to a full-blown investigation of their family and possible longer-term foster-care placement. As a result, they decidedly did not want the police to alert the child protective services agency, thereby tacitly supporting the "don't ask, don't tell" approach the police favored. Instead, the mothers wanted to arrange for someone of their own choosing to take care of the children.[4] Even some child protection social workers are unsure whether they are the appropriate authorities to deal with these cases, because their agencies are set up to investigate cases of child abuse and neglect, not those where a parent is being taken away and the children may be left alone (Nolan 2003).

Police involvement in decisions about where the children will go poses a potential liability for law enforcement officers. Untrained in decision making about such matters and without explicit policies from their departments, individual officers are ill equipped to do the background checks needed to determine the suitability of temporary placements for children. Furthermore, from the arresting officer's point of view, such police involvement takes time and generates extra paperwork, disincentives for taking on the decision for what to do with a child. As one California police officer told researchers: "There are all kinds of pressures [for law enforcement] to not take the kids" (ibid., 16). The courts have given their tacit approval to police inaction, except in cases where a child's safety is of immediate concern.[5] The result is that children whose parents are arrested are "in danger of falling through the cracks," as the title of one report about parental arrest suggests (Nieto 2002).

The extent to which the children experienced their mother's arrest as a traumatic separation is conditioned by the household's composition before the arrest. Those who lived alone with their mother experienced the most disruption, because they usually had to move, perhaps even to be separated from their siblings and sent away from their neighborhood, school, and friends. In some cases, children stopped attending school because their caregivers were too overwhelmed with their temporary responsibilities to attend to enrolling them in their new school, especially since they did not know how long a child was liable to be staying with them. If their stay was to prove a short one, why go through the bureaucratic bother of enrollment?

For virtually all the children whose mothers were present before their arrest, the period between the moment their mother is taken into custody and her return home is a time of, at a minimum, concern and anxiety. Even children whose mothers were absent for mere hours experienced anxiety, but those whose mothers were detained faced the most difficult challenge. They had to live with worries about their mother and their own well-being for weeks and might be moved from one adult to another two, three, or more times. Here again we see the significance of socioeconomic status in shaping children's experiences of their mother's encounter with the criminal justice system. Although some women were detained in jail because of their status in the system at the time of their arrest (e.g., violating probation, having an outstanding arrest warrant), others simply could not pay even minimal bail. With greater financial means, they would have been able to pay their way out, thereby shortening their time in detention and hastening their return home, where they could reassure their children and alleviate their anxiety. Compounding the effect of their inadequate financial resources were their frayed relationships with others, associated with their social isolation. The mothers had few friends or family members to call on for assistance with paying their bail and helping them get home.

Children's worry about their mother's and their own situation may affect their school performance, their concern making it difficult to concentrate in class. Others externalize their feelings, becoming belligerent or even aggressive. Younger children, with an imperfect understanding of the situation in which their mothers are embroiled, can conjure dire outcomes that may increase their anxiety. Older children, however, may face even more daunting challenges, having adult responsibilities thrust upon them with few adults stepping in to support them. Their mother's prolonged absence after her arrest can result in significant unforeseen consequences. Being able to communicate with their mothers brings some reassurance, but it is a poor substitute for having their mother at home.

This period between arrest and case disposition, which often represents yet another disruption in the children's family life, is a preview of what is to come if a mother is incarcerated. Women facing the prospect of being incarcerated have to prepare for that eventuality and decide who will be willing and able to care for their children. Those who were fully engaged with their parental responsibilities realized how difficult this would be and recognized the limitations of a surrogate parent, even if that person was a loving relative. Jonathan's mother, Patricia, spoke of her concern:

JS: Well, if you did get sent to prison, what would you do about the kids?

PATRICIA: Well, my mom said that she would be there for them, but it's very rare that, you know what I mean, that they're gonna get the same love from my mom. You know, 'cause they, they're gonna need attention, you know? My mom's . . . (Her voice drifts off.) I know what it is to be a good mom, and what it is to be a bad mom. And I'm trying so hard not to be that, that negative mom that, you know what I mean?

JS: Right.

PATRICIA: And this [her arrest] pops up, you know what I mean?

JS: What's a bad mom?

PATRICIA: Bad mom's a person that does not take care of their kids, feed them. Unattended, you know what I mean? And just not there for them. To talk to them, to give them advice. You know, when they actually do, kids need somebody to talk to.

JS: Right.

PATRICIA: Someone, you know, who's not there for their kids at all.

JS: That's the bad mom.

PATRICIA: The bad mom.

JS: And you've seen . . .

PATRICIA: I've seen that before, man. They leave their kids unattended, they, you know, they go. And that's when I was living down that end. So I'm like, no, I don't want that for my kids.

The bad moms Patricia was describing were women so controlled by their drug habit that they neglected their children, even leaving them unattended. These were mothers who were "just not there" for their children. Drugs may have taken them away at one time, but as we will see next, prison was also a very effective means of ensuring that the mothers were not there for their children, even when they needed them.

5

They All Do the Time

Faith and Brittany, nine- and ten-year-old sisters, epitomize the meaning of adorable. They brim with exuberant energy, constantly sharing giggles and charming others with their smiles. However, their sunniness is eclipsed when talk turns to their parents, who are both in prison. The girls have lived with their beloved Granny since they were toddlers, when their mother and father began serving twenty-year sentences for robbery, and life for the girls is much different than they imagine it would have been if their parents had not been locked up. Granny, their paternal grandmother, is sixty-two years old and in poor health. She stopped working when the children came to live with her and now supports them through the Temporary Assistance for Needy Families program and disability insurance, supplemented by food and other donations from neighbors and others in the community. Granny gets little help from other relatives. The girls' maternal and paternal grandfathers were never part of their life, the former having died of a heroin overdose when their mother was still a child and the latter having been divorced from Granny years before the girls were born. Their maternal grandmother had recently started using heroin again after having stopped for eighteen years and is not only unreliable but also untrustworthy, so the girls almost never see her. When she promises to help out by visiting or taking them to her house for a weekend, she doesn't show up. Thus, she provides virtually no assistance at all, and Granny has learned not to count on her.

The girls and their grandmother live in mean surroundings: a small, low-ceilinged apartment with scant natural light in which the smell of smoke is so intense that it permeates a visitor's clothes and papers and lingers for days. The only relief from this grim backdrop comes from the girls' spirited vitality. However, their liveliness and laughter belie the suffering they experience due to their parents' absence. Both were placed in counseling when they were in kindergarten and still see a counselor every week because of their sadness and the emotional difficulties they continue to experience as they, their grandmother, and their parents count off the days of their separation.

Although Faith and Brittany's parents received long prison sentences, both made plea arrangements that enabled them to be paroled from prison after serving only several months. Neither returned to live with the girls. Their father went to a halfway house, and their mother moved in with her mother and stepfather. After a few months, both were sent back to prison for violating the conditions of their parole. This time, they were both sentenced to serve many years. Barring some intervention, Faith and Brittany will be well into their teens before either of their parents gets out of prison again, when they all can stop doing time.

Faith, Brittany, and their parents encapsulate many of the problems I encountered among the children and their mothers who were serving long prison sentences. Some of the issues raised by a parent's arrest and detention, such as emotional difficulties and communication problems, are amplified by incarceration. Most of the examples in this chapter are drawn from the sample of children whose mothers had been in prison at least a year, but some of the children interviewed while their mothers were in jail awaiting trial or had been incarcerated less than a year are included.

Temporary—and Not so Temporary—Living Arrangements

The children whose mothers had been in prison for at least a year were fortunate in their living arrangements during their mother's incarceration. All but one were living with relatives, and none were in foster care when I met them (see table 5.1). Most commonly, a child was living with a grandparent: seven of the seventeen children in this sample lived with a grandmother or with both grandmother and grandfather. One child was living with her great-grandmother, and three were living with an aunt or uncle. The one person who was not living with a relative was an eighteen-year-old who had spent most of her life moving from foster care to various relatives' homes until she was sixteen, at which point her relatives told her to leave, even though she had no place to go. She successfully prevailed upon a couple who lived near one of the relatives she had lived with earlier to let her live with them, although they received no financial assistance for doing so. Conspicuous by their absence were most of the children's fathers.

More Missing Dads

Only two children in the state sample were living with their fathers, although a woman's imprisonment would seem to be a circumstance when a father's presence is most urgently needed. Their absence might have been anticipated because, as we have seen, the majority of children whose mothers were involved

TABLE 5.1

Guardian during mother's incarceration

Guardian	% of children (N = 17)
Maternal grandmother	23.5
Paternal grandmother	17.6
Grandmother & grandfather	11.8
Aunt	11.8
Father	11.8
Grandfather & companion	5.9
Uncle	5.9
Nonrelative	5.9
Maternal great-grandmother	5.9

in the criminal justice system had fathers who were absent or barely involved in their lives. Where were the missing dads? Although two of the fifteen children not living with their fathers had fairly frequent contact with them, six others had no contact with theirs at all, and no one in the family seemed to make any effort either to find or get in touch with them. The fathers of three of the remaining seven children had died, a disproportionately high mortality rate for men in early adulthood, but the same rate found in the city sample. Finally, four of the fifteen children had dads in prison at the same time their mothers were incarcerated, a situation that for the children and their guardians doubled the challenges resulting from the mother's imprisonment.

For nearly all the children who were not living with their fathers, this absence was not a new situation, and they did not seem to expect their father to have changed just because their mother went to prison. One eighteen-year-old, Naja, whose father had lived with her during part of her childhood, was dismissive of his parenting role, especially because at the time of her mother's arrest when Naja was five, Naja and her siblings had been placed in foster care, which she believed her father had done nothing to prevent. Her mother had been incarcerated for most of Naja's life. I asked where her father was.

NAJA: Down there [in another neighborhood]. He might come through here or I might see him when my family was having something at my aunt's house like a dinner sometimes. But no, I don't really see him all the time.

JS: Why do you suppose that is? How do you feel about that?

NAJA: I gave up on that a long time ago. When I was living across the street [from where she now lived], he used to live over there too. But he was just living there. He was just there to pretty much tell me, "Oh, you can't do this," and "Be in the house at a certain time." He didn't care about taking care of us. He might as well have not been there. I been gave up on him. I hadn't gave up on my mother when I was coming up, but I had already gave up on him. She wrote me and everything and she sent us stuff.

JS: But you haven't given up on her? What made you give up on him?

NAJA: Because he was there, but he wasn't, like, there for me. He didn't never do nothing or stuff like that. He wasn't there and a father needs to be there. He can't be just living in the house because the mother [his mother] lives there. So I been gave up on him because I think he could have did something better than he was doing. He could of took care of my little brother and sister before they went back to [the state's child protective services]. He could have did more. He didn't have no record. My mother did. So . . . oh, well.

A striking aspect of Naja's narrative was the contrast of her faith in each of her parents. Although her mother had been imprisoned for most of Naja's life, the young Naja had not given up on her. Apparently, she had few expectations of her mother while she was in prison, understanding that she could not realistically count on her either to provide the everyday emotional nurture that children need or to fulfill normal daily parental responsibilities. Instead, Naja expected her father to come through in these areas because he was living with her. His failure to fulfill her notions of what a parent should do was even more disappointing to her than her mother's behavior during Naja's youth.

Although Naja expressed disappointment in her father and seemed resigned to his inadequacies as a parent, other children whose fathers were absent were resentful and angry about their failure to accept their parental responsibilities. Like Naja, Keith was eighteen years old, but he had not seen his father since he was four. He felt that his father had let him down, a state of affairs that was particularly hard for him because his mother was absent from his life more than she was present; he felt that neither parent was fulfilling their parental responsibilities.

KEITH: My dad's not a part of my life and it's like, I look at it like, how can you have a child and bring them on, bring them into this earth, and not have any connection with 'em?

JS: Mmm hmm. So your dad has no connection with you?

KEITH: No. I mean, I don't hate my dad, but it's just like, the last time I talked to my dad was about two years ago and I, now mind you, I haven't seen my dad. I might have been like four the last time I saw my dad.

JS: Really?

KEITH: Yeah. And he called me on the phone like two years, like a couple, like I—I think I was a freshman—he just started tellin' me all this stuff and sayin', you know, he still cares for me and, you know, he loves me and all this stuff but it's like then he started makin' like, sayin' like he bought me stuff for Christmas, makin' promises and then before I knew it, it was just lies. Like, "Oh, I'm comin' to spend the day with you," you know, whatever, and you know, I'd be home waitin' and he never showed up. Like, it's just, it would be things like that or either like he would tell me that, you know, he was around the area and he's gonna stop by but, you know, he just didn't. Like, to me, if you have a son and you're tryin' to make a connection with your son, why would you do those type o' things? Like, how hard is it for you to come down for one day and see your son? I mean, it's not that far. It's not like you live twenty hours away. I think he was sayin' to me at one time, well, you can have somebody bring you up here. But no. You're the father and I'm the son. You need to get to me. You're the one who hasn't been in my life. That's your, you know, that's your fault. And that's how I feel about it and I mean, I don't, like I said, I don't hate my dad. To this day I don't hate him, but I do have a lot of like, resen—, I guess, resentment towards him. Just 'cause of the fact that he wasn't in my life, it don't stop at that, he tried to get in my life and then did the same exact things he was doin' when he wasn't. So it's just like, what was the point? It was, you might as well just not called me because now we don't talk. He doesn't know how I'm doin' or what I'm goin' through. It's just like, what was the point? That's how I honestly look at it. What was the point?

Keith's description of his feelings reflects the profound impact that the absence of all these fathers can have on their children, especially with their mothers gone. Children have expectations of their parents, ideals of what parents should be like, based on their personal experiences and exposure to parenting models. Even though Keith's father had never been part of his life, Keith had a firm conviction that fathers have a responsibility to their children and that his father should have stepped up to fulfill his parental obligations in the absence of Keith's mother. The double abandonment that Keith experienced left him feeling bereft and betrayed.

Disruptions and Stability

Although I did not observe their family's home life before the mothers' incarceration, the way the mothers described their behavior when they were living on the outside made it likely that many of the children whose mothers were in prison had been exposed to styles of living similar to those the city children had seen. Courtney, a thirty-four-year-old mother of two children, had a serious crack habit and had been arrested dozens of times for crimes such as prostitution, burglary, and credit-card fraud, by her own account. She and her children had no regular residence, so they would all stay with an older man who had befriended Courtney. When she realized that she was regularly leaving her children for days while she went off to smoke crack, she recognized that her life had so degenerated that she hoped she would be sent to prison so she could get off the streets:

> I prayed to go to jail in January of '99, the night before I was arrested.
> I mean I stood on the corner and I prayed to God to go to jail. I asked the
> officers, I said, "Are you sure I don't have any warrants? I mean, I might.
> You might want to check." You know? I mean I wanted to go to jail.
> I couldn't do it anymore. I could see going home [to her mother's].
> I called my mom about going home, like, within that week and she said,
> you know, "If you come home, I promise I'll take you to [a psychiatric
> hospital]." If she would have said to me, "You can come home," I would
> have come home. I would have come home, you know. But you say to me you
> can come home but you have to go to the crazy house? No! No, I'm not
> coming home. No. But, um, that's not her fault. You know what I mean?
> I wouldn't want to live with me either at that time. You know, who would?

Often, children whose mothers' lives resembled Courtney's had not been living with them before their mother went to prison, just as we saw with children in the city sample whose mothers were sporadically engaged or disengaged. Custody arrangements had been made so that the children would not be exposed to their mothers' life, which could have put them at risk of inadequate care. In fact, twelve of the seventeen children had been living with other relatives before their mother's incarceration. Of those twelve, seven had moved in with another relative when they were six or younger. Their mother's incarceration therefore did not disrupt their everyday life in the same way it did for those living with their mother before she went to prison. Even children whose mothers had been able to care for them often were assisted by other family members. In fact, virtually all the children in the sample had at one time or another lived with other relatives, either alone or with their mother, before their mother's incarceration, as was typical when mothers were sporadically engaged in mothering.

The living arrangement of many of the children during their mother's incarceration appeared to give them greater stability and structure than was probably the case when they were living with their mother alone, based on what we already know about life before incarceration. In addition, a few of them seemed to be living in circumstances that were materially better than they would have been if they had been living with their mother. Thirteen-year-old Joseph lived with his grandparents in a recently built and well-maintained housing development in a middle-class suburban neighborhood. Driving into the development came as a shock to me after hearing Joseph's mother, Dawn, describe her preincarceration life and after seeing so many decaying neighborhoods in the city. Here I saw attractive homes with landscaped yards and two or three cars in each driveway. Joseph's house was immaculately clean and well maintained, with all the middle-class trappings, new furniture, and décor that could have come straight from the pages of an interior-decorating magazine. This must have been quite a contrast to the home in which Joseph began his life.

Joseph had been living with his grandparents since he was a baby. His mother's other children had been taken from her by the state's child protective service, due in part to the environment in which they were living when Dawn was heavily involved in drugs and her then boyfriend was both using and selling drugs from their home. Other drug users hung out at the house, which Dawn described as neglected and in disrepair. When Dawn gave birth to Joseph some years later, Joseph's paternal grandparents stepped in to prevent the state from taking their grandchild (the other children, who were taken by the state, were not their son's). By the time Joseph was born, Dawn not only was using drugs but also was heavily involved in many fraud schemes. Shortly before her current incarceration, she was a fugitive with an extensive arrest record. Once she was apprehended, she received a long prison sentence; she had been in prison for five years when she and Joseph entered the study. Joseph's father was also in prison, serving a ten-year sentence. Life with his mother and father would surely have been quite different from the suburban teenager's life Joseph had with his grandparents, which included summer camp, participation in school athletic teams, membership in the student government at his school, family trips and vacations, instant messaging friends from his home computer, and other activities in which middle-class children commonly take part. In other words, his life was a contrast to that of the underscheduled children described earlier.

Although other children might not have been living in residences equivalent to Joseph's during their mother's incarceration, their living situations were more settled and less disrupted than those described in earlier chapters. The guardians of some children gave them more supervision and provided a level of care the children were not receiving before coming to live with them. Eight-year-old Lamar had been living with his uncle Burton since his mother was incarcerated and, according to both mother and uncle, his behavior, academic performance, and health had all improved. For instance, his uncle took him to the dentist for the first time in his life. Lamar needed extensive dental work, including root canals, because his teeth had decayed significantly, the result, according to the uncle, of how much sugar his mother had allowed him to consume. Both his mother and his uncle reported that Lamar had been struggling in school when he was living with his mother; the school had even wanted to hold him back in kindergarten. When he moved in with his uncle, Lamar was enrolled in a new school, where he was placed in the first grade based on his testing. After a couple of months, however, he moved into the second grade, and his uncle explained why he thought that was the case:

JS: What do you attribute that to?

BURTON: Him getting good help and having someone around him that was able to be there when he needed the help, discipline.

JS: Was that you?

BURTON: Yeah. He's just—he just needed a good caregiver where, when it came time to do his homework, I would help him with it. Because, I mean, he basically understands his homework the majority of the time, but sometimes he doesn't. So I think he just needs to do it a little slower, that's all.

JS: And was there a sense that he wasn't getting the support when his mom was home?

BURTON: Yes, right.

JS: And why do you think it was that she wasn't doing it?

BURTON: She was too involved with his father.

Joseph's and Lamar's new environments were thus more conducive to healthy development than those their mothers could have provided. Nevertheless, even these stable households faced challenges resulting from taking in additional children. Most of the grandparents who were caring for their children—the largest category of guardians—lived on fixed incomes that were not calculated on the need to care for young children. For people like Faith's and Brittany's granny, a meager income made it a constant struggle to meet the children's needs and affected their ability to help the children maintain contact with their mothers. For Granny, for instance, paying for a couple of collect calls from prison could cost the equivalent of a winter jacket for one of the girls, a choice that she wished she did not have to make. Their situation was exacerbated by the fact that Faith's and Brittany's father was also in prison, and he persisted in calling the family nearly every day despite the financial toll on the family. The girls' mother, on the other hand, realized that Granny had to choose between phone calls and necessities for the girls and therefore called no more than once every other month, cutting off a vital link to her children.

Grandparents on fixed incomes were not alone in feeling an economic strain from the addition of the children to their households. Even the families whose material circumstances and employment indicated more affluence than the fixed-income families felt the pinch. As Joseph's grandmother, who had raised him from infancy, said: "Then there's the money thing, and that's a big thing too. It's very hard." Families with fewer financial resources struggled as well, especially if they already had their own children living with them, as Lamar's uncle did. None of the guardians were aware that the state provided financial subsidies to qualified families caring for a relative's children through a kinship foster-care program. Almost all would have benefited from that assistance.

"A Big Adjustment"

Finances were not the only source of strain on the children's families. For guardians and children alike, merging a child into a new household requires cooperation and patience as both attempt to adapt to their new situation. Children who were already living with someone other than their mother before her imprisonment did not have to make the same sort of adjustments as other children did, but the generational difference can be stressful for older guardians who thought they were finished raising children when their own became adults. Asked how it was to start being a parent all over again, Joseph's grandmother replied: "It's hard. Very, very hard. Especially being older. It's time consuming. You worry. I think you worry more as a grandparent than as a parent. Being older, I think you know more tricks in the book." Such situations are not eased when the guardian resents having to take care of the children, a feeling some guardians who refused to participate in the research expressed to me when I called to discuss the study with them. Conveying such attitudes to the children makes them feel unwanted and may generate bad feelings toward their mother, which in turn can make the task of reunification even more difficult once a mother is released.

In contrast to Joseph's family, whose stresses existed whether or not Dawn was in prison, families where the children had been living with their mother before her incarceration faced many challenges as they adapted to a new household. Not least of these was making the child feel welcome, loved, and at home. Keith, who felt so abandoned by his father, spoke about the struggle of adjusting to a new household, made necessary because his mother was not there to care for him. At the age of eighteen, he was staying with his uncle and his uncle's romantic partner, but he had spent nearly his entire life living with various relatives, with and without his mother. As he described her, his mother was sporadically engaged, perpetually in and out of his life, coming home to where he was staying for a short time—mere days at times—and then running off by herself or being sent to jail or prison. Keith moved from his grandmother's to his aunt's to his uncle's, a process he referred to as being "passed around." Here Keith struggled to describe the difficulties he encountered because of these changes in household:

KEITH: I went through a lot of different, like, just things, and it's like, I guess I . . .

JS: What kind of things?

KEITH: Like, just dealin' with like, the type of things as far as my mom and like
her not bein' there and just like, I don't know, like it just, it's just a whole
lot of things. Like, 'cause I never was really in one place. I was always bein'
moved back and forth from place to place. And it's just like not knowin' if
I was gonna stay there for this period of time or that period of time. Just,
like, you know, I don't know, I just, I, like, I think that, I don't know, I just
never felt like I belonged, I guess. Like, if I would stay here or I would stay
there or stay, it just, it was too much movin' around and, you know, bein' as
my mom wasn't there, I was confused about a lot of things, you know, you
know. Sometimes I took on, like, an attitude, like, you know what I mean,
like, you know, why isn't she here? You know, it's her responsibility and—I,
you know, basically that. But I just, I didn't know how, bein' young and bein'
a kid, you know, you don't know how to deal with things like this, you just
feel different emotions inside of you and it's just like you don't understand
why, you know, you're in this place. Because my mom would take up and
leave and do what she wanted to do or, you know, and leave the responsibility with somebody else and then it's like people have their responsibilities and it's like they're takin' more other responsibilities and it's just like,
as a child, you just have all these things goin' up in your head. Like, you
know, how long am I gonna be here? Is my mom comin' back? Why did she
do what she did? It's just like, and it's like you, you have to get attached to
the person you're livin' with. You have to feel some [unintelligible] com-
fortableness about stayin' with that person 'cause I mean, for me, for you to
just up and stay with somebody, even if it's a family member, if you've never
stayed with them, that's a big adjustment. You know, I mean, you eat there,
you have to sleep there, you have to live there. So it's like, you know, you
have to feel comfortable with that placement, and I mean it's not always
easy to get comfortable with people. Sometimes it takes a while so, you
know what I mean, it's just a whole big process of dealin' with that.

"Just a whole big process of dealin' with that," indeed. As Keith points out,
children have to adapt to a whole new family: moving in with them disrupts
their routines and knocks the emotional underpinnings out from under them.
Children who spent their lives with their mothers until incarceration separated
them from each other find this adaptation especially challenging, particularly
because the person to whom they are probably most attached in the world and
on whom they depend is not there to help them through this transition. They
have no say in whom they will live with, and if they are unhappy in their temporary living situation, there is little they can do about it. Those who have been
separated from their mother before her incarceration, by contrast, may not
experience her departure to prison as such a wrenching event. Keith's need to
adjust to a new family life, as was the case for many of the children, arose not

only from his mother's incarceration but also from her sporadic engagement with her children and her peripatetic lifestyle, which regularly sent her off to the streets in search of drugs. In other words, disruption to his household and family life began well before his mother ever went to prison, and Keith's need to adapt was the same regardless of the cause of the separation from his mother.

Adapting to a new family could also be difficult if children were separated from their siblings when their mother went to prison. In this sample, fifteen children had sisters or brothers; five were living with at least one of their siblings, although two of the five had another sibling from whom they were separated. The remaining ten children were living apart from their siblings, but 60 percent of them had been living in different households long before their mother went to prison, yet another family disruption characteristic of these families. Joseph, for example, had three half-siblings, one of whom lived with her own father. The other two had been adopted after the child protective services agency intervened following allegations of child abuse, which effectively cut off the opportunity for him to develop a relationship with those siblings. Fear that Joseph would likewise face adoption was in fact what motivated his grandparents to take custody of him at birth. Other children, however, had been raised apart from their siblings under less dire circumstances. As was the case for Joseph, it was not their mother's incarceration that wrenched them from their siblings but the family situation that preceded it. In the two cases where the mother's incarceration did indeed lead to siblings being separated, the children were living close enough to each other that they were able to get together often. In both cases, the families had decided to have them live in different households not because of a lack of room but because they thought it in the best interest of the child, such as keeping a youth in the same school he had been attending before his mother was imprisoned.

No doubt other children of incarcerated parents are not as lucky as the children I met and end up living apart from a beloved sibling while their parent serves time. In addition to not having to cope with such separations, nearly all the children in this sample were also fortunate enough to have had safe and secure environments in which to live while their mothers were in prison. Nevertheless, their mothers' incarceration had consequences for all the children.

The Toll of Parental Incarceration

"Like You Have a Space in Your Heart Missing"

Everything about Rasheeda spoke of discomfort the first time I met her. She fidgeted throughout the interview, constantly rubbing the table at which we were sitting or picking at the layer of grime on it, whooshing her hands over the surface. She squirmed in her chair, rolled her head around, and rolled and crossed her eyes while looking up. At one point she pulled her T-shirt over her

head and spoke to me from within her flimsy fortress. It was difficult to assess
whether this was her normal behavior or the result of the unhappiness she was
feeling about her situation at that moment. And who wouldn't be unhappy
under the circumstances? Rasheeda was in a group foster home that housed one
hundred children, improbably set in a grim industrial wasteland amidst ware-
houses and old factories with tractor trailers parked nearby. Railroad tracks no
longer in use crisscrossed the streets. This was the last place anyone would want
to call home, and the enormous old building housing the children was decidedly
unhomelike. The day I visited Rasheeda underscored the setting's bleakness:
overcast skies, barren vegetation, patches of dirty snow alternating with soggy-
looking ground. A child would have to possess an especially sunny disposition
to feel happy after being taken from her home and dropped into these surroundings on such a day. Rasheeda did not, but it was small wonder, considering her family situation.

One of five children in her family, Rasheeda normally lived with her
father, who worked nights and weekends, leaving the children—including his
one-year-old—home alone most of the time. Her mother, Belinda, had recently
been arrested for the twelfth or thirteenth time by her own estimation. Belinda
was a heavy crack user who saw her children only occasionally, depending on her
husband and other relatives to care for them. When Belinda did come around to
the house where her husband and children lived, it often was to steal from the
household, an activity in which she enlisted Rasheeda's aid. Her other means of
earning money was through prostitution. Not long after Belinda's most recent
arrest, which led to her being jailed before trial and eventually sentenced to two
years in prison, child protective services (CPS) removed all the children from
their home. The reason? Belinda's one-year-old child sustained a life-threatening
injury when left at home unsupervised and was taken to the hospital, where CPS
was called in to investigate. When CPS went to the house, they concluded that it
was unsafe for habitation and sent the children into foster care. In Rasheeda's
case, that meant the group home where I first met her.

Despite the fact that Rasheeda and Belinda spent long periods of time living apart, Rasheeda keenly felt the loss of her mother when she was incarcerated. When I asked her how she would describe what it's like to have a mother
in jail, she replied: "It's not fun. It doesn't feel good. [long pause] It's like you have
a space in your heart missing." Whatever Belinda's shortcomings as a parent,
she was still Rasheeda's mother and no one else fulfilled that role for her. In fact,
both Rasheeda and Belinda said there were no other adults to whom Rasheeda
felt close, with her mother offering this explanation: "She isolates herself. I don't
know what would happen if she opened up and let people know how much she
participated in crimes for me. I know secrets ruin lives. She's had to stuff so
much of my shit inside. A lot of little things have had a great big disastrous
effect on my children."[1]

Rasheeda's sense of loss and of being alone epitomized the most notable impact of incarceration on the children I met: the emotional toll their mother's absence took on them. Although the children's feelings may have been more complex than they were able or willing to communicate, nearly all of them reported that they felt sad that their mothers were locked up and that they could not be with her. Eleven-year-old Jessica, for example, said she felt "miserable" while her mother was in prison, even though she had not lived with her mother for years before her incarceration. Some children felt abandoned and alone, while other youths' sadness was mixed with anger, disappointment, and resentment because of their mother's behavior. Twelve-year-old Danielle had been raised by an elderly relative because, as her mother admitted, her alcoholism had made her an "unfit mother." Danielle's mother, Virginia, had been in prison for more than nine years by the time Danielle was twelve and, even though mother and daughter had spent little time together, Danielle found having her mother in prison hard, not just because she could not see Virginia but also because it set her apart from other children: "My friends always talking about their mothers. I can't say nothing positive about my mother."

The emotions the children expressed varied noticeably as a function of their age. Younger children, no matter how difficult their circumstances when they were living with their mother, always wanted to be with her. Mothers mean security, warmth, and love that children are unable to duplicate elsewhere. As Jessica, who had lived with her aunt most of her life, said: "It's not the same, having parents and having a aunt. It's different to me." Young children were much more forgiving of their mothers than older children were, not angry and disillusioned. Younger children's sadness stemmed from an ongoing yearning for their mother's mere presence—her touch, her smile, her laugh. In the following excerpt, nine-year-old Takanna described her longing and her mother's haunting presence:

JS: How is it [her mother's incarceration] hard on you?

TAKANNA: Because sometimes I miss her or sometimes when I'm thinking about her, I think she's next to me but—And sometimes I look up at the clouds and I get, and I get, um, and I miss her. 'Cause I see different stuff.

JS: You see what?

TAKANNA: I see stuff like that reminds me of her, so . . .

JS: Like what would remind you of her?

TAKANNA: Like, um, she had picked some flowers one day, she put them on the table, and she said that they're pretty, just like me. She said that and then, um, I think, like um, it was like a flower and I, I started crying.

JS: Did the cloud look like a flower?

TAKANNA: Yeah.

JS: And that made you think about the time she picked the flowers and she said that?

TAKANNA: Yeah.

JS: Okay. And you said that sometimes you think she's next to you, right?

TAKANNA: Yeah.

JS: When does that happen?

TAKANNA: When I'm watching TV. 'Cause sometimes, um, when we're watching TV, we used to watch the cooking channel and sometimes we used to watch *America's Funniest Home Videos.* When I laugh, I say, "Look, Mommy, look!" And she's not there.

The sadness some children felt became so troubling that they were sent to counseling. Brittany and Faith had been seeing a counselor since they were in kindergarten, and Keith was being treated for depression. Fourteen-year-old Valencia was another youth who had difficulty coping with her mother's absence. Like Brittany and Faith, Valencia lived with her grandmother during her mother's incarceration and, like them, was extremely attached to her:

> I love my mother. If I had a choice . . . I love my grandmother and I love to be here with her but I miss my mom so much. I just want to be with my mother. I grew up with my grandmother, you know. I was eleven years old when I came down here [to her grandmother's]. I never got to be a teenager with my mother. I never really got that experience. I miss her so much. I just want her home already. It's really bad 'cause when things happen, I want to tell her about it and I really can't because she's not here and I really want her to really be here. I wanted her to be here for my fifteenth birthday. I want her to be here when I graduate. I want her to be here for my prom. I want her to be here for so many things, but she might not be here and I hate that. I want her to be here so bad. I love my mother. She is a very good mother. She's awesome.[2]

Marilyn, Valencia's mother, had never been arrested before this incident, when she agreed to transport drugs for a man and was apprehended with them. Before she was sentenced, the prosecutor claimed to be seeking a sentence of forty to eighty years, a prospect that frightened Valencia so much that she threatened to kill herself and was hospitalized for a week. Following her discharge, she was under psychiatric care and also saw a counselor at school, but she eventually stopped all treatment, believing that, as she said: "I'm fine. I am a regular, healthy, outgoing teenager and I don't need to be in this program that tells me that I am depressed when I am not."

Valencia's lament for the fact that her mother would not be there to share important moments was not uncommon. In contrast to the younger children, adolescents are more independent of their mothers, especially as they accumulate evidence over time of their ability to survive without Mom. Their sadness is flavored with more bitterness, a greater awareness of what might have been but is irretrievably lost. As they mature and begin to realize that childhood is receding and adulthood looming ever closer, they must resign themselves to the notion that their mother will never have the opportunity to share with them all the milestones of youth: graduations, school successes and failures, proms, first crushes, science projects, a daughter shaving her legs for the first time, making the team, not making the team. The list is long, and while few mothers will miss all of these events, most women in prison will miss at least some—and most of the children will miss having their mother there for that special moment, as well as the myriad ordinary moments of daily life: being hustled out the door in the morning for school, watching TV together, playing in the park, going to the movies, shopping, and simply being together, however tenuous that togetherness might be for some children and their mothers. Keith discussed the irrevocable nature of the loss of these special moments:

> By her not bein' there, she like, she really doesn't know anything about us. Like, she knows us because we're her children but it's just like, she doesn't realize, like, they're, I mean, those moments, like, when I won prom king, I couldn't come home and say, "Mom, I won prom king." Or she, you know, when I went to prom that night, she couldn't take pictures of me. She wasn't here. When you miss those kind of moments and those things in a kid's life, that stuff doesn't go away. She wasn't at my graduation when I graduated from high school. Those things can't come back.

"That stuff doesn't go away," and, over time, both resentment and resignation can lead children to try to divorce themselves emotionally from their mother. In the following excerpts from a letter to a mother who had been incarcerated for several years, a teenager reveals the magnitude of the toll taken by the loss of such shared experiences and time together:

> Your presence in my life is no longer possible and for the past year I have agonized over this decision. I have received all the things that you have sent and with each one I ended up more confused than before. You are my mother and that fact will never change, but due to the events years ago your title as mom has slowly disappeared. I can no longer classify you as a mom because you are not here to play that part. A mom and a mother are two totally separate things. In letters that you write you say that I am beautiful and to keep smiling, but while reading the letters the fact that you have not seen me in years is so strong and it makes me

miserable. You no longer have the rite [sic] to complicate my life or try to be a part of it; it is my life now and only mine. This is my year to figure out where I want to go and what I want to do and I refuse to let you burden me with a past that is no more and a future that does not exist. Think back of the last thing you remember that I wanted to be when I grow up, the car that I really liked and wanted, and the birthday that we shared together. I promise you none of those facts are the same as they used to be and many birthdays have passed and I have grown older, but you would not know. You have no idea what I love and enjoy and where my dreams lie in this world. You have no idea how high my goals are set. . . . You can only imagine these facts with so many others about my life. The image in your head of what I look like and the person that I am are most likely from the childhood in which you raised me. But now it is time for me to be whom I want to be and time for you to cherish what we had and not try to create a life with/for me. We are separate now and have been for years, that is the truth. . . . You will spend more time where you are now and during that same time I will be growing older and creating a life for myself. . . . I will love you always for who you once were and I will never forget the memories that I have of you.

Although one of the tasks of human development is to create an identity separate from that of one's parents, doing so normally entails realigning the parent-child relationship, not renouncing it. What this teenager is proposing in her letter goes far beyond establishing her own identity. In a sense, she has decided that in order to do so, she needs to abandon the hope of sharing her life with her mother. When she wrote this letter, she stood at a threshold; she decided to turn and wave goodbye to her mother as she moved on with her own life.

The older youths in this study were more clear-eyed about the behaviors that got their mothers in trouble with the law and therefore were more likely than younger children to be resentful, angry, or disappointed, often feeling that the separation they had endured could have been avoided but for their mother's actions. These feelings were especially pronounced in instances where mothers had been in jail or prison more than once. Naja's family had been especially hard hit by her mother's incarceration, with all the siblings separated from each other. Some were in foster care or adopted, while others, like Naja, lived with various relatives after having spent some time in foster care. When Naja was a young teen, her mother, Aimee, was released from prison for a brief period after serving nearly ten years, and the two lived together for a couple of months. After Aimee violated the conditions of her parole, she was reincarcerated but eventually paroled again. Upon this second release, the two did not live together, but Aimee was free for only a short time before she was arrested on a new charge and sent back to prison again. Naja spoke of what it had been like to have her mother in prison:

NAJA: Now it's easier. Like now it's nothing. When I was younger, if somebody would ask me where my mother is I'd say down South or something. I would tell nobody that my mother was in prison. But now that I'm older, it's just like, "She in prison." Now it's not as hard as it used to be. Sometime it is. That's why I say if she write me I take it hard. Like I'll read the letters and then I'll be crying. But now that she in prison it's not hard on me because I went through all this time. So it's just like another day. And I can't, like, depend on her to come out. Now I just quit hoping. If she come out, she come out. If she don't, she don't.

JS: So you don't have any expectations?

NAJA: No, I don't expect her to come out here or think she'll come out and change. I used to think she would change her ways but my sister and brother didn't. My sister had no hope in her. She was like, oh, you believe this and you believe that, you think she really going to change. But that's just me. I'm just kindhearted like that. When she came home the first time, I did expect her to change. Like I expected her to have a job and everything and she did. But then, to me, my mother's fall was her boyfriend.

JS: Why? What did he do?

NAJA: He didn't have no job or nothing, and he was just a downfall for my mother. Because before she had met him she was going to work, coming home and everything. She would sit here and talk to me and everything. Then when she met him and then he moved in, and it was just like it was her downfall. You can't be working and he not be working and staying in the house all day. She would never come in the room and talk to me no more. She just went in her room and closed the door. That's why I, like, never really stayed home. I was gone myself. But I think that was her biggest downfall. Her boyfriend. She just stopped working and everything. She was doing good at first. After she went back to jail that time, I just ain't have no hopes no more. No hope.

JS: So you had hoped that she would stay out of jail.

NAJA: Uh huh. After the first time she did all them years. I was thinking, well, she'll come home and change and everything. And then she had found a job and she used to buy us stuff. We went places. But her boyfriend was her downfall.

Here again, children's expectations of their parents influence their feelings about them. Recall that Naja had given up on her father, no longer expecting him to fulfill his parental role, but that she had given her mother a pass, so to speak, while she was in prison. Naja's siblings may have thought her faith in her mother's ability to step into her role as mother was naïve, but Naja clearly held fast to the hope that Aimee would return from prison able to take on the responsibilities she expected of her mother. That Aimee did this for a short while—providing for the children, going places and doing things with them—made her fall from grace all the more bitter a betrayal to Naja. Perhaps Naja's siblings experienced less disappointment because their expectations were so much lower.

Like Naja, Keith had experience with a mother who had been in and out of prison; in his case, the stints in prison were shorter but more frequent than those of Naja's mother. His mother, Janilla, had a serious drug problem and admitted to having been arrested numerous times and convicted nearly 20 times. In the following excerpt, Keith begins by explaining that Janilla's behavior has tried the patience of family members:

KEITH: My grandparents, they ended up takin' me but I was stayin' with a friend of my aunt's because it was just a whole big situation because my grandparents are basically fed up with it too, 'cause my, 'cause my, this is not the first time my mom has been locked up. This has happened, she has gotten locked up numerous times before, and it's just, they look at it like, you know, Janilla's an adult. She knows what she's doin'. She knows she has kids. She has a responsibility. By you bein' an adult, you cannot keep doin' what you want to do and leave the responsibility on other people. That's just not right, regardless of whatever she was goin' through with the drugs and, you know, she can't control it or whatever. You have to do, even if she doesn't want to stop, she needs to do it for her kids. You know what I'm sayin'?

JS: Mmm hmm.

KEITH: Because it's not fair. Why? Why is it fair for somebody else who hasn't had three kids and have their own life, take on somebody else's responsibility when they weren't asked? You know what I'm sayin'? And that's, I mean, that's why a lot of times, I don't really feel sorry for my mom and I'm not tryin' to say it to be mean because even though I understand, you know, drugs are chem—, they are an addiction and you can become addicted to it, you have, I mean, you have kids. She has four kids and it's like, I can't even, I mean, I'm her child but I'm, it's not even so much about me anymore 'cause I'm an adult now but my brothers and sisters are the ones who want to feel, feel what I felt because of her not being here. If she was here, it would be a whole lot different and it's just like, for me, why would you let drugs, to me like, why would you let drugs take you away from your family? You know what I mean? You have two, three sons and one daughter and it's like, you're gonna miss out on their life before you know it, they're gonna be older, and who knows if they even want to spend time with you? They might feel like, well, you didn't want to spend time with me, apparently, 'cause you wanted to do drugs and do what you wanted to do, so why should I spend time with you now that I'm older? You know what I mean? And kids become very like, like I don't want to say, like, resentful but they, like, they, they have the attitude like, well, I don't want to be bothered.

At times, expressing their resentment and anger created internal conflict for Keith and other adolescents. Peter, the sixteen-year-old who was living in the house raided by the police while his mother was in jail, had decidedly mixed emotions about her incarceration. He saw the potential damage that could result from a mother's incarceration: if "your mom's locked up, you just, you just get worse." Why? "Because you don't got no one there for you. So you do your own thing." Yet Peter thought that his situation might have been worse if his mother had not been locked up. He felt good about having alerted the police to his mother's whereabouts, as we have seen, believing that her arrest would result in his mother getting some help. Here, Peter had first explained that his criminal behavior began when his mother was using drugs heavily and not looking after him; he continued:

PETER: She got locked up and I just kept on goin' and goin' and I just kept turnin' for the worse.

JS: So you think that it's because she was locked up. But do you think if she had not been locked up your life would have been different?

PETER: I think she, if she wasn't locked up, she'd be dead. Couldn't stop her from doin' heroin. She was doin' bad.

JS: But how about your life? Do you think your life would have been different if she hadn't been locked up?

PETER: Uh, if she wasn't? Yeah. If she wasn't locked up all the shit outta my house would have been sold to all these people round here and I'd end up fightin' and shootin' at 'em or, I don't know, shit would be a lot crazier.

In other words, his mother would have sold their possessions to support her heroin habit. He went on to explain that had she been home, he would have been exposed to her heroin use.

JS: So you think that actually would have been worse for you than if she had been in jail?

PETER: It would be the same shit.

JS: So you think either way . . .

PETER: Her being in jail was the best thing for her.

JS: How about for you, though?

PETER: Ah, that was different. I don't know. Both ways is bad. Because I had a taste on my own where I could do whatever I want and my mom was gettin' high, do whatever I want regardless. So basically, for a couple years, I was doin' what I want. So I didn't really care . . .

JS: Either way . . .

PETER: Yeah, I ain't really care about anything or anybody. I didn't give a crap.

Peter found himself with two equally poor alternatives, both of which offered him the prospect of a life in which he had to hustle to survive and protect himself. What would have served him would have been to have his mother home and drug-free, but that seemed unlikely at the time. Her continued drug use and her incarceration led Peter to be harshly judgmental of her—"She's an asshole"—and to resent her behavior for resulting in the type of life he was living. Unlike the younger children, Peter did not speak of missing his mother, possibly because of his resentment of her but also because she had been absent so often from his life. Nevertheless, he still loved and cared deeply about her. One day, Peter talked about his tattoos and his plans for future images. He showed me the spot on his arm reserved for his "Living a life of crime and loving it" credo and then showed me a tattoo in memory of his father. He planned to recognize his mother by having her name tattooed around his neck. This design seemed an apt symbol of the complicated feelings he shared with other children whose mothers were in prison: although he was angry at her because her behavior had such a deleterious effect on him and the life they had shared, she had an emotional stranglehold on him because he loved her. She was, after all, his mother.

"Turning for the Worse"?

Among the children in this study, how common was behavior that was "turnin' for the worse," as Peter felt his had? Because the degeneration in Peter's behavior seemed to be merely a progression along a trajectory on which he had embarked early in his life, it would be difficult to attribute his current actions solely to his mother's incarceration. His father, up until his death, had been incarcerated for much of Peter's life, and he had been exposed from a very young age to his mother's drug abuse, which resulted in periodic homelessness for him, exposure to and participation in his mother's drug lifestyle, and separation from her because of incarceration and other events. Furthermore, Peter grew up in a low-income urban environment where crime was common, so environmental conditions influenced him as well. In other words, Peter's life, like those of many of the children introduced in earlier chapters, included numerous risk factors that could account for his antisocial behavior. His mother's current incarceration was not the starting point for his deviance.

None of the children whose mothers had been in prison for more than a year exhibited the kinds of behavior that Peter did, nor did they or their family members report the sort of behavioral problems documented by research based on parental or other reports. Emotional difficulties were far more prevalent among the children in this study than were occurrences of misbehavior. For instance, unlike the teenagers in the city sample, more than half of whom had been arrested, none of the adolescents whose mothers were in state prison had ever been arrested. Few of them had the sort of academic problems seen in the city sample, although a few had disciplinary problems in school. However, it is important to remember that the children whose mothers had been in prison for extended periods differed from the children in the city sample in some significant ways that could have affected the likelihood of engaging in deviant behavior. Only five of the seventeen children lived in an urban environment; the rest lived in suburban or exurban communities where environmental influences were considerably different from those to which the children in the city sample were exposed. Furthermore, many of these children had experienced less exposure to violence, drugs, or criminal behavior compared to those in the city sample, having spent a considerable amount of time living with relatives who were not involved in such activities. Seeing their mother's behavior and feeling the effects of its consequences were enough to convince some children that they should rigorously avoid involvement in similar acts.

Although the extensive antisocial behavior Peter engaged in was not found among the children in the state sample, some of them did have behavioral issues. Phenomena such as school suspensions and school failures, however, were rare, and fighting was far less common than among the first group. There were exceptions, of course, such as Shamika, a sixteen-year-old who had stopped going to school after she became pregnant. The baby's father, who was awaiting the birth not only of Shamika's baby but also of a child by another adolescent, was in a juvenile detention facility, and Shamika herself had been picked up by the police several times, although never formally arrested or charged. Before dropping out of school, Shamika was often truant and had begun running away frequently. Her friends were involved with a gang, and she still engaged in some serious fighting, even early in her pregnancy. Her misbehavior had begun when she was about fourteen, when several events converged that might have had a considerable impact on her life.

Shamika had lived most of her life with her mother and grandmother, who presented significantly different role models for her. By her own account, Shamika's mother, Ebony, was the exceptional child in her family, whose members were mostly professionals with long-term careers. Ebony became pregnant at fifteen and dropped out of school, went on to have two more children by two other men, and never got her GED. Despite these events that stereotypically presage a life on welfare, Ebony had held the same job for several years and had been married for ten years. However, she was also a heroin user who was sporadically absent from the household for extended periods and had been arrested several times. By contrast, Shamika's grandmother hewed close to the family model. She was a college-educated woman who had worked in a professional capacity for the same employer for more than twenty years. Divorced after a relatively short marriage, she had then lived with a man for ten years, until Shamika was thirteen, at which time the couple split up and Shamika's world began to unravel. She and her grandmother moved from the city where Shamika had grown up to a nicely furnished apartment in a leafy suburban complex on the city's outskirts. Thus, Shamika lost her grandfather figure and her home and left her school and friends behind, virtually all at the same time. The real blow for Shamika came a year later, when her mother moved away to be with her husband, Shamika's stepfather (Shamika's own father was dead). It was at this point that Shamika began skipping school so she could go back to her old neighborhood, where she started hanging out with a group of gang-involved guys and getting picked up by the police. Later that year, her mother was incarcerated and Shamika began running away from home, returning to the city to spend time with her friends. After serving nearly a year in prison, Ebony returned home for six months before she was arrested for a new offense and reincarcerated. Despite her mother's presence, Shamika continued acting out to such an extent that there was talk of sending her to a boot camp. Her pregnancy prevented that course of action, but it also led to her decision to drop out of school. Since then, Shamika had spent most of her days hanging out at home, waiting for the baby's birth.

Of course, an intact family is not an inoculation against the unpredictable course of adolescence and, as many parents of teenagers can attest, a playful and obedient child can develop into a sulky and rebellious adolescent even when living with both parents. With a parent in prison, distinguishing between "what is" and "what might have been" is well nigh impossible. Jessica, for instance, is eleven years old, poised on the brink of adolescence, hanging on to her doll with one hand and reaching for more sophisticated pastimes with the other, suddenly spending hours on the phone with her friends and wanting to go to their houses all the time. Jessica has lived with her aunt for most of her life because her mother's drug abuse and mental illness made it difficult for her to care for Jessica. Her mother was serving a four-year sentence for an assault with a knife and her father was incarcerated as well, with a history of several earlier incarcerations. Jessica's aunt, Barbara, reported that Jessica was not as kind as she used to be and had started exhibiting anger problems, even throwing things around, as her mother had done in the past. She had also recently gotten in trouble with her teacher, and Barbara had been summoned to school by the principal. Barbara had even begun to worry that Jessica might be following in her mother's footsteps. Had her mother been around, would Jessica have been acting differently, less moody and kinder than she had been lately? Her aunt attributes her behavioral changes to the effects of puberty, not her mother's absence. As she said, Jessica was "trying to find her way 'cause she's caught in between puberty and a whole new world of next stages. . . . She's caught in between worlds right now, you know, 'cause she still plays with her dollies, you know, and then the other one's trying to be grown at the same time."

It may be difficult to quantify the degree to which a child's behavioral problems are attributable to a parent's imprisonment, but the case is strong for ascribing emotional issues to this circumstance. Although a child might have otherwise had emotional or mental health problems, the feelings that these children expressed and had to manage, such as sadness or resentment, arose specifically in reaction to their mothers' incarceration. The rocky emotional terrain the children had to negotiate was for many exacerbated by the stigma associated with having a parent in prison.

"Where's Your Momma?"

Children separated from their parents for whatever reason—military service, illness, employment assignments, divorce—no doubt miss them as fiercely as the children in this study missed theirs. However, one aspect of parental incarceration that sets the experience apart from other reasons for parent-child separation is the stigma associated with it. A child whose parent is stationed in a combat zone may miss the parent and feel tremendous anxiety about the parent's well-being, but the child at least does not normally feel the need to hide the parent's whereabouts from others; indeed, those children can feel proud that their parent is serving the country. Prisoners' children, by contrast, know that there is no honor associated with serving a prison sentence. When asked if they knew why people were in jail, the young children routinely replied with a statement along the lines of "that's where they put bad people" or "that's where you go when you do something bad." The children therefore must contend with finding a way to accept the notion that the mother they love might have done something that society condemns. Accepting that their mother has done something "bad" may make younger children sad, and they may even recognize that their mother's incarceration is not something that should be shared with other people in general. As we have seen, older children's sadness may well be colored by anger and resentment if they believe that their mother is responsible for the behavior that led to her imprisonment, especially if they think that she could or should have taken steps to prevent herself from involvement in criminal behavior.

Children also must decide how to explain their mother's prolonged absence and manage the public aspect of the situation, a task made especially difficult in these cases precisely because it was their mother who was incarcerated. In the world many of them inhabit, expectations of fathers are few.

Expectations of mothers, however, are high. Mothers are the anchors of the family, and every child is supposed to have a mother. In addition, having a mother in prison is a relative rarity, whereas having a father in prison is far more common and therefore less shameful. One eight-year-old child whose father had been in prison for four of his eight years frequently told others that his father was in jail, apparently with little sense of shame. However, after one of his mother's arrests, he asked if they "send girls to jail." Part of his uncertainty stemmed from never having been told where his mother was when she was in jail; he thought she was at college. In his mind, jail was a place for boys, not girls.

The stigma accompanying a mother's incarceration stems not only from the shame of having a mother who has acted in ways that defy conventional standards of motherhood and expectations of women more generally, but also from the profound sense of being outside the norm for children and their families. In an excerpt earlier in this chapter, Naja said she used to tell others that her mother was down South. Here she elaborates on her reasons for doing so and discusses the difference between having a mother and father in prison:

JS: So you would tell people that she was down South or something. Why was that?

NAJA: Because I was embarrassed. Everybody was living with they mothers and I was living with my aunt and my grandmother. They would say, "Where's your mother at?" She wasn't dead or nothing so I didn't say that. I would just say that she lived down South and I didn't live with her. But after I became friends with them and we got older, everybody knew where she was at. My sister, she never really hid it.

JS: Did you know any other kids when you were growing up whose moms were in prison?

NAJA: When I was little and we went to the programs [for prisoners' children], we would go to outside stuff. They would pay for us to go to classes at [a community college], like art class. All of them, they moms was in prison. And by the time we got older we would see some of them on the street. Yeah, I started knowing people whose mothers was in prison.

JS: Did you know anybody outside of that program whose mother was in prison?

NAJA: Un huh. I probably met some. But people couldn't talk about it.

JS: How about anyone whose dad was in prison?

NAJA: A lot of people's dads was in prison. A lot of people's fathers is in prison.

JS: So they talk about that?

NAJA: Yeah. Your father being in prison is not as bad as your mother being in prison.

JS: Why is that?

NAJA: I guess because your mother have an image to hold, like to take care of you and everything. Most people's fathers be in since they was babies, for killing somebody or doing this or selling drugs. So it's not a big deal. So when your mother be in prison for something like my mother was in prison for, it's even worse. A mother being in prison is worse, period, than a father. Because most of the time a father don't never take part in the kid's life anyway.

Most children felt the stigma of having a mother in prison, knowing that this marked them and their family as different. The discomfiture they felt about others knowing about their mothers' situation was clear, and children commonly said that they told anyone who asked where their mother was that it was none of their business. Others made up cover stories, as Naja had done in the first years of her mother's incarceration. Nine-year-old Takanna told others that her mother was on vacation if they asked where she was, but her story was created not just because of a desire to conceal her mother's whereabouts but also because of her sensitivity to the difference between her family and others:

JS: So nobody, none of your friends, know where she is? How come you don't tell them?

TAKANNA: Because I don't want them to, um, treat me another way.

JS: Do you think they would if they knew?

TAKANNA: I think so.

JS: Why?

TAKANNA: Because, um, they have, um, 'cause they live with their mom and dad. They're happy and stuff. And, um, they don't get mad or anything. They don't, but in my family, it's different.

JS: Yeah? How is it different?

TAKANNA: Because my mom is in that place and I miss her a lot. And that, I wish she'd come home.

At times, a carefully constructed façade could be destroyed, with significant distress resulting. This was the case with Jessica, the eleven-year-old who had lived with her maternal aunt since she was five. Jessica's mother had been incarcerated for two years in the women's prison, her first "state time," but she had also been in and out of local jails for several years. Barbara, Jessica's aunt, had never revealed to the authorities that Jessica was her niece, not her daughter, because she did not want anyone at school to know that Jessica's mother was in prison. One day not long before I spoke with Jessica, a classmate was sitting in front of a computer in their fifth-grade classroom and asked Jessica what her mother's name was. Unbeknownst to Jessica, he was searching the state's

Department of Corrections Web site, which includes an inmate locator feature. When she told him her mother's name, he entered it. Suddenly, Jessica's real mother's face filled the screen for all her classmates to see. Jessica ran crying from the classroom, but of course her cover was blown: everybody now knew that her mother was in prison. It is likely that many of the children, or at least their parents, already knew that Jessica's mother was in prison because her crime—a violent one in which the victim was an adolescent—had been on the local news and in the newspapers. Jessica took this publicly humiliating experience hard. The onset of her recent change in behavior, which worried her aunt, as discussed earlier, coincided with this event. Although Barbara worried that this behavior might indicate signs of Jessica's mother emerging in Jessica, the timing of this rough spell seemed suspiciously coincidental with Jessica's public humiliation.

Staying Connected

Valencia was thrilled. Her mother, Marilyn, had managed to get transferred to a state prison located a mere forty-five-minute car ride away from Valencia's grandparents' house. Valencia had moved there after her mother's incarceration, which put her some six hundred miles away from the prison where her mother had served three years until this transfer. Valencia had not been able to visit her mother because the costs associated with the trip were beyond the family's means. Now, however, seeing her would be a snap. Or would it? Valencia and her grandmother would have liked to visit Marilyn often now that she was so close to their home, but the family's financial situation still constrained them from doing so. Valencia's grandparents were straining to make ends meet even before Valencia and her sister moved in with them, living in a public housing project on a fixed income supplemented by food stamps. The family's old car was unreliable and a breakdown would be costly. Then there was the cost for gas and a babysitter for the grandparents' great-grandchild, who was living with them as well. All together, these "little things," as Valencia referred to them, prevented them from visiting as often as they would have liked. What's more, the family's phone had recently been disconnected because of past-due bills, which removed another way for Valencia and Marilyn to stay connected. Nevertheless, Valencia was in some ways luckier than most children, who saw their mothers far less often.

One of the most daunting challenges of parental imprisonment is maintaining the parent-child relationship during the separation. The challenges children and their mothers have to address vary based on the nature of the relationship before incarceration, the ties between the mother and the child's current caregiver, the child's age, and factors such as family income and location of the child's residence. Even under the best of all possible conditions and even when the individuals are determined to stay in contact, as Valencia and

Marilyn were, sustaining a relationship between a child and a parent in prison is difficult. Compared to cell phones, text messaging, and online communication, which enable instant connection with anyone, anywhere, the methods for communicating with prisoners seem antiquated. Cell phones and Internet access as a rule are strictly forbidden in virtually all prisons, although some prisoners have occasional online access. Visits, letters, and phone calls are generally the only means available to children to remain in contact with their incarcerated mothers and thereby maintain and nurture their relationship, but children have unequal access to even these limited methods of contact and varying degrees of desire to use them.

Life without Phones?

For children raised in the age of cell phones, which have enabled them to reach others seemingly whenever and as often as they wish, the inability to use a cell phone to call their mother would in all likelihood be incredibly frustrating. Imagine then a situation where not only could you not call your mother whenever you wanted to with the certainty that you could either reach her or expect an immediate call back, but you could not call her at all. Inmates do not have private phones in their cells and must share a public pay phone, available to them only during certain times of day, and they can only place calls, not receive them. Thus, children are entirely dependent on their mother's ability to call them. They cannot pick up the phone and share their happiness when they've received a good grade on a test. They cannot reach out for comfort when someone has hurt their feelings.

The phone would certainly seem to be the easiest means to share day-to-day events, helping to normalize the child's relationship with the mother, but daily calls were out of the question for the children in this study. All calls from prison are collect calls, and companies that provide phone service for inmates have negotiated agreements with state correctional agencies that permit them to append high surcharges to each minute of use. Even a relatively short phone call can be unaffordable for families on limited incomes. For instance, a fifteen-minute call might cost as much as thirty to forty-five dollars, an amount that makes these phone calls an extravagance for most families on a tight budget. Furthermore, when a mother calls her children, she also wants to speak with the adult who is caring for them, consuming more precious phone minutes. A fifteen-minute call to a household with two children and one guardian might allow each child only three or four minutes to talk with his or her mother.

Financial limitations were a significant part of the reason why the children in this sample spoke to their mothers so infrequently. Faith and Brittany, whose mother generally abstained from calling them because she realized what a financial hardship it imposed on Granny and the girls, were certainly not alone among the children who rarely spoke with their mother. Four of the seventeen children (24 percent) said they never spoke to their mothers at all, and another eight (47 percent) spoke to their mothers less than once a month. In other words, seven in ten children rarely or never talked with their mothers by phone, and only one child spoke to his mother weekly. He was luckier than his three-year-old half-brother, Matthew, who lived with his paternal great-aunt; she not only disapproved of the boy's mother and father—a drug dealer also incarcerated during most of Matthew's short life—but also resented having to care for a young child when she was seventy years old. She had refused to accept calls from Matthew's mother, Courtney, except on one occasion. That time, Courtney recounted, the great-aunt told her that she accepted the call because Matthew had been asking for her all week. "I don't believe it," the great-aunt said. "He just started saying, 'Mommy, Mommy, Mommy.'" In this case, then, phone communication was cut off because of the poor relationship between Matthew's mother and his guardian.

The infrequency with which children spoke with their mothers could make conversations awkward, and it was clear that with the passage of time, their importance began to fade for the children. Brittany, for instance, did not seem to care too much if she spoke to her mother or not. Her father called almost daily from prison, and the financial burden this placed on Granny was the reason her mother rarely called. Yet, asked if she would be willing to talk to her father less often if it meant that she could talk to her mother more than once every two months, Brittany said no. Granny, of course, wanted to stay in touch with her son during his incarceration, but the result was that Brittany and Faith had rarely talked to their mother since they were toddlers, and their mother-child relationship was now tenuous. Keith explained how awkward attempts at approximating a normal parent-child relationship could be when mother and child have been apart for a significant time. Here he described their infrequent phone conversations:

> I've talked to my mom on the phone a few times and, I mean, the times that I talked to her on the phone, I mean, we had short conversations. She'll ask me how I'm doing or something. And that's basically about it. But, I mean, we don't have anything to talk about because, like, I just don't know what to say. I don't know what to tell her. It's like I said: even if she was to come back and come out of jail, it would take a lot for us to develop a relationship as mother and son because she hasn't been around my life, she doesn't know things that have gone on with me, and it's like I can't just come out and tell her like this, this, this, and all this detail and . . . I can't tell her things because that comfortableness that I felt from her when I was younger I don't feel anymore, so I can't just sit up there and talk to her like I normally could. Like it's going to take a while for me to even do that.

It is not hard to envision a teenaged Brittany saying much the same thing when she is Keith's age. Their experiences underscore both the difficulty and the importance of removing barriers to communication between a parent in prison and her children if their relationship is to be sustained and nurtured.

Back to Snail Mail

Given the difficulty of communicating by phone, a logical alternative would be for mother and child to write letters to each other, provided the child is old enough to write. Even this simple solution, however, was surprisingly under-utilized. Although nearly all the mothers liked to write to their children, the children for the most part did not reciprocate. It was common for mothers to say—and children and guardians to confirm—that they wrote to their children regularly. Often, they included drawings or handmade items as gifts. Some mothers also sent along items such as achievement certificates they had earned for taking part in training programs or volunteer activities. But even if a mother wrote to her child often, most of the children did not write back. Of the seventeen children whose mothers were in prison for at least a year, only four said they wrote to their mother, whereas almost all the mothers said they wrote to their children regularly. The exceptions were mothers who had been incarcerated for years and whose children never wrote back to them. In those cases, mothers eventually cut back significantly on the number of letters they sent.

What might account for this disparity between the children's and mothers' correspondence? The children, especially, had few other options for communicating with their mother. They could visit only if someone took them to the prison and, as we have seen, could speak on the phone only if the mother called and their guardian was willing and able to pay for the call. The explanation lies in the different worlds the two parties in this potential correspondence inhabited. The mother had hours and hours available to write daily if she wished; the child had a life filled with the usual activities that make up children's days and occupy their time. The children may have missed their mothers, but most of them had developed attachments and relationships that helped fill the void, whereas the mothers had no substitute children. Maintaining contact with their children therefore had more emotional urgency for them. Furthermore, the mother's writing a letter or sending drawings and gifts to a child could reinforce her sense of motherhood and represented a concrete means of reminding her children that she was still their mother and therefore irreplaceable.

For some mothers, sending letters and mementoes of their life helped assuage the guilt they felt because of their separation from their children. Courtney, who had prayed to go to prison, felt remorse for how her behavior has affected her eleven-year-old son's life. Although they lived together during his early years, Courtney was incarcerated when her son Josh was three and has been in and out of prison since, due to her drug use and crimes related to it. By the time Josh was six, Courtney realized that her drug habit was controlling her life to such a degree that she was unable to care for him. She herself called the state's child protection agency and asked them to take Josh and place him with her mother, who had been reluctant to have him live with her because she did not understand the extent of Courtney's drug problem. Since then, Josh had been living with his grandparents, and Courtney's drug problem had persisted up until her most recent incarceration. Courtney wrote to Josh regularly and also sent him photos and any certificates she received for participating in programs, which she viewed as a way of letting him know that she was trying to give some meaning to their separation: "I just keep them [the certificates] and send them to him and let him know that I'm, you know, doing something myself, you know, and not just sitting here wasting time. That's not why Mom's not with you, you know. I want him to know that I'm doing the best I can with what I—you know, I'm away from you, but I'm doing the best I can with the time I have." Her correspondence with Josh was her way of trying to persuade him that, although they were separated, she was trying to take steps to improve herself with the objective of staying out of prison in the future.

From the child's perspective, writing letters to a mother far away must seem an inadequate and artificial substitute for a face-to-face conversation, since it is a monologue without immediate feedback from the person to whom the letter is addressed. The lag between letters is surely frustrating to children grown accustomed to instant messaging, texting, and tweeting. Thus, it is not particularly surprising that children in general were not good at holding up their end of the correspondence with their mothers. As Jessica explained: "I just don't feel like writing down all night. I don't like to express myself on a piece of paper." Instead, she said, she wanted to talk in order to communicate her feelings. Writing to a mother far away was not emotionally satisfying for the children, when what they wanted was to see and be with her. Asked at the end of an interview if there was anything else he wanted to say, Peter, whose mother was in jail for several months and was suffering from both depression and a chronic, life-threatening disease, perhaps expressed best how many of the children felt about writing letters:

PETER: Actually, I want to talk to my mom. I just want to go see her.

JS: Have you thought about writing her a letter also?

PETER: I don't like that shit.

JS: No? Why not?

PETER: I don't feel like it. I really don't want to call her. I just want to straight up see her and talk to her. I don't want to play that. Talking to her on the phone or writing letters and stuff don't mean anything to my mom.

JS: Well, you might make her feel good if you wrote her a letter.

PETER: Probably, but it don't make me feel any better.

Peter's lack of sympathy for his mother's situation was understandable, especially considering how difficult Peter's life had been as a result of his mother's drug addiction, their numerous separations from each other, and her involvement in the justice system. Yet he still wanted to see her so they could talk, but even that simple wish, shared by Jessica and so many other children, was often difficult to fulfill due to the issues surrounding visits to their mothers.

Visiting Mom

Visiting a correctional facility is not a simple process. The primary concern of correctional administrators is maintaining safety and security in their institution and doing so entails strict routines and rules. A visitor does not simply show up at a prison door and announce that he or she would like to visit inmate #73562. Each prisoner has a list of approved visitors, who are permitted to visit only at specified times on specific days. As a general rule, children must be accompanied by an adult. As a result, children visiting their mothers share their time with the adult who brought them, which can mean that the child and mother spend very little time just talking or interacting with each other. Everyone entering the prison is subject to search. Institutions vary in the physical layout of their visiting areas, so children may be able to touch and hug their mother or they may have to sit behind glass that separates them from their parent. Nationwide, separate visitation areas for parents and children are available in about one-third of women's prisons and in fewer than 10 percent of prisons for males, according to a recent survey (Hoffmann, Byrd, and Adams 2007). Clearly, prisons are not the most inviting places to bring children, and some parents and children simply prefer that the children not visit.[3]

The state prison where the mothers in this study were incarcerated was headed at the time by an administrator who was genuinely concerned about the prisoners' relationships with their families and did what was possible to encourage visitation. The visiting area contained games, toys, and activities for the children and mothers to play together. Prisoners housed in the minimum-security area of the facility were able to spend time with their children outdoors on the prison's grounds, a pleasant park-like setting. A national youth organization was allowed to operate a program in the prison that brought children there to engage in organized activities and projects together with their mother. Finally, the prison offered a van service that provided transportation to the prison approximately once every six weeks from ten different points in the state. Children boarded the van at one of these locations and were driven to and from the prison for visits. They were permitted to travel without an adult companion to enable them to visit with their mothers without an adult competing for the mother's attention. In many ways, therefore, this prison was far more advanced than other institutions in its attempts to facilitate and encourage mother-child visitation and engagement during the visits, especially compared to an institution like the city's jail. There, children could visit only if accompanied by a parent or adult bearing the child's birth certificate or other evidence of their relationship, and visits were permitted only during normal working hours on weekdays. This combination made it unlikely that children whose mothers were jailed there could visit, even though their mothers might be serving a sentence of as long as twenty-three months.

Despite the state prison's well-intentioned accommodations to the needs of the inmates and their families, the children in this study did not visit their mothers frequently. In fact, seven of the seventeen children whose mothers were in prison long-term never visited her, and the remaining ten visited less than once a month. The reasons for the infrequency of visits were related to transportation issues, as well as the mother's, child's, or guardian's feelings about visiting.

Even with the van program, the prison was difficult to reach because it was located in a rural community in the northern section of the state, far removed from almost all the metropolitan areas that were home to a majority of the prisoners before they were sent to prison. As one mother said: "This place is in the middle of nowhere." The closest major metropolitan area was about forty-five minutes away by car; driving to the facility from other parts of the state could take hours each way.

The van program was intended in part to address the difficulty associated with getting to the prison, but it was not a perfect solution. Although it operated from ten different places, many areas were still far from the pickup points. One child, for instance, lived more than an hour away from the nearest stop, which meant that his aunt or grandmother would have to drive him there in time to catch the van in the morning. If the adult chose not to accompany the child to the prison, she would either have to wait several hours for the van to return or drive home and come back later in the day to pick the child up—more than four hours of driving back and forth. The child, in the meantime, would have spent about six hours being driven, because the prison was nearly two hours from the pickup point. Furthermore, the van operated only during the week, which meant that the child had to miss a day of school and the adult who took him to the van might have to miss a day of work if she was employed. These disincentives to traveling by the van meant that relatively few of the children made use of the service. Only four of the ten children who had visited their mother took the van; two of the four had used it only once or twice. Those who used it reported that few children ever were in the van, except at Christmastime, when gifts for the children were distributed at the prison.

For the children, the alternative to the van was to take public transportation or be driven by a family member or friend. There is scant direct public transportation to the town where the prison is located and none that goes directly to the prison. Getting there from almost any major metropolitan area typically required taking a train to one city and then a bus to a park-and-ride lot, where visitors would have to call a taxi to get to the prison. As a result, children typically relied on their families for transport. Families complained about the cost of driving to the prison in view not only of the cost of gas but also of the wear and tear on their cars, which were often one breakdown away from being unusable, as was true for Valencia's family. Furthermore, some families who were caring for other children not related to the mother in prison had to pay for a babysitter while they were gone, a significant expense for families on limited incomes. Taken together, the expenses could mount, and some guardians thus decided not to go at all. As Jessica's aunt said: "I refuse to go all the way down there to see her."

Some guardians refused to take the children because they felt that prison was no place for a child to see his or her mother, and because they remained angry about the mother's actions that resulted in her imprisonment, requiring them to travel long distances for visits. Josh's grandmother expressed a sentiment shared by other guardians when she explained why she refused to take Josh to see Courtney in state prison, although she had taken him to visit his mother on several occasions when she was in the local county jail: "When she's local I would take him, 'cause for a while when she was in county, I would take him over there during visiting times. And then she moves to a further away one, I just, I won't do it. I don't think he should go, and when she calls she says, 'Why didn't you bring Josh?' I said, 'Why don't you stay out of jail?' You know? If you want to see your son, here's the way to do it, and it doesn't involve me driving for hours."

Other guardians were on bad terms with the mother and did not want to become embroiled in disagreements during the visit. Billy, for instance, was a nine-year-old who lived with his father while his mother was incarcerated. His parents were divorced, and the last time his father, Ted, had taken Billy and his brother for a visit, their mother had been argumentative and insulting to her ex-husband. Ted no longer wanted to be subjected to that type of treatment and had decided not to take the children anymore, especially because the trip was long, requiring the children to get up at five in the morning, and neither child was particularly happy to be going. As Ted said: "I have a tough time gettin' 'em up there. I gotta, I gotta fight to get them up there anyway, because I felt that it's important for them to see her, and they fight me all the time. Oh, yeah, they, they don't necessarily jump for joy to go."

Despite how much they missed their mothers, older children did not seem motivated to make the effort to visit them, either because they had grown bitter and disillusioned about their mother or because they had built their own lives and were unwilling or uninterested in spending an entire day driving to and from the prison to spend a little time talking with her. As one child said: "It's kinda far, and I'm always busy." Even some of the women in prison, such as Keith's mother, understood why their children might not want to visit:

> My son is consumed with his own life. Now I mean, if somebody said, "Well look, I'll take you up there," then he wouldn't have a problem coming, but this is three hours away from where I live and so it would take a whole day, 'cause there would be traveling time here and back, and I don't expect anybody to consume a whole day to come up here. I mean, their lives don't stop just because I'm incarcerated. I would expect nobody to put their life on hold. My son is eighteen years old. He's in the prime of his life. You know, he's working and dating and doing things that kids do. I wouldn't expect him to take and try to find a means, or a way to get up here to see me 'cause I'm incarcerated in a place like this. I wouldn't want him to have that picture of me in a place like this. It would be different if I was in a halfway house, in that type of setting. I, no, I don't want him up here. I mean, I've seen him at the county jail and that's been unpleasant too because you don't have contact visits. You know, you have to visit through the telephone and the glass and all that kind of stuff, and that's very unpleasant and children shouldn't even be exposed to all that kind of stuff.

Like other ways of communicating, visits had their limitations. Although the youngest children said they had fun when they visited their mothers, the experience of leaving the prison without their mother could cause tears and sadness that might persist for a day or two. Seeing one's mother for an hour or two inside a prison is hardly an adequate substitute for having her near every day, sharing in one's life.

Conclusion

Numerous risk factors are present in the lives of offenders' children before a parent is incarcerated, as we have seen, but their parent's imprisonment introduces a new set of challenges. Children clearly have much to cope with as they do time along with their mother. Many not only have to deal with the loss of their mother, but also must adapt to a new family situation and possible separation from their siblings. As Keith described it, this adaptation can be hard emotionally, with the children never really feeling wanted as they move from one household to another. Coping can be more difficult if their mother's absence is perceived as a problem that cannot be shared with others because of the stigma associated with imprisonment, which was true for virtually all the children I talked with, particularly because it was their mother, not their father, who was in prison. A mother's imprisonment was a particularly galling betrayal of gender stereotypes, running counter to the idealized image of what a mother should be.

The ease with which a child adjusts to a mother's absence due to incarceration varies as a consequence of a number of factors, of which the earlier relationship is among the most important. For instance, children whose mothers were sporadically engaged or disengaged before going to prison may be more resigned to the idea of separation and more accustomed to living without their mother's involvement. Consequently, they may feel the need to see or speak with their mother less acutely than do children who have spent all their lives with their mother and feel her absence intensely. Children whose mothers were only sporadically involved or largely absent from their lives may still feel sorrowful about their mother's absence. Jessica, for instance, had lived most of her life with her aunt because of her mother's frequent absences and concerns about her mother's violent temper, mental illness, and drug use. Nevertheless, Jessica described herself as feeling "miserable" every day while her mother was in prison. Her misery, however, was born not only of her mother's incarceration but also of the separation that preceded it, the fact that her father was in jail and had been for most of her life, and the sense that her family was different from other children's families. She deeply felt the loss of a "real" family and understood that her parents were not involved in her life in the same way that other children's are. As a result, she longed to be connected with her mother.

Jessica's feelings highlight the need to examine children's lives from a life-course perspective and understand their situation as part of their life history (Graue and Walsh 1998). Jessica spent her earliest years living with her mother, forming a deep attachment to her in the process, as children do in their early years (Bowlby 1979). Despite Jessica's having lived most of her life with her aunt, her bond with her mother remained intact, along with the elusive image of an idealized family she had never had. That her mother had cared for her during her earliest years underscores the importance of examining children's lives and development in context with a parent's life course as well, recognizing how individuals' lives are inextricably linked with others' (Elder 1994). For example, having a child may deflect a woman from a trajectory that included involvement in criminal activity. Even if that deflection is only temporary, it may enable the woman to care for her children during their earliest years, establishing an unbreakable bond between them. That bond can subsequently affect the child years later, even if the mother-child relationship has altered in the interim.

A father's life history should also be a part of any attempt to understand a child's life. Jessica's father was absent almost her entire life, mostly because of his own incarceration. In other children's cases, however, the fathers had turned their backs on their parental responsibilities. The children's emotional struggles resulting from their mother's incarceration were a clear indicator of their need for support during a difficult time. Those who criticize mothers who end up in prison should question what responsibility fathers have for their children and ask why so few take on that responsibility at a time of the child's greatest need.

For most children, coping entailed trying to maintain their relationship with their mother, but the obstacles associated with doing so were significant. Relationships require regular communication if they are to grow and can weaken without such exchanges. The amount of communication that takes place between mother and child during incarceration is determined in part by the child's age and structural factors such as family income and geographic location. For instance, the very youngest children who have not even developed language are entirely reliant on an adult to determine the frequency with which they can see and connect with their mothers. Infants who do not have an opportunity to spend significant amounts of time with their mothers will in all likelihood develop a primary attachment to the adult who cares for them. As they age, such children may feel less need to talk to or visit their mother than do older children whose mothers were an integral part of their life while growing up. These older children may be highly motivated and desirous of staying in touch with their mothers. Even those whose wish to remain connected is strong, however, may find it difficult to achieve this goal if their family's financial situation constrains their ability to do so or if they are located at a distance from the prison where their mother is incarcerated. As was true in the other spheres of the children's lives, low-income families had a harder time maintaining contact with the imprisoned mother, significantly limiting visits and phone calls.

The links between the mother and the children's guardian also affect the children's ability to maintain contact with their mother. Guardians like Valencia's grandmother who enjoy a good relationship with the imprisoned mother can do much to help sustain and nurture the child's bond with her by encouraging and facilitating communication between the two and acknowledging the mother's rights to be involved in decisions about the child, thereby reinforcing the mother's position as parent. By contrast, guardians who are on bad terms with a parent or who simply do not put effort into ensuring that the child and parent stay connected can undermine the relationship between parent and child. Faith's and Brittany's granny, for instance, ensured that the girls remained in frequent contact with their father but did little to nurture their relationship with their mother. Already, the importance the two girls attached to that relationship was fading.

The potential damage that can be inflicted by guardians who resented or disliked the mother of the children in their care was aptly illustrated by people who declined to participate in this research. Some women I met at the prison had consented to take part along with their children, but they had very little communication with the child's current caregiver, or the temporary guardian was so angry about the situation that she refused to take part or allow the children to do so. One paternal grandmother who was caring for a prisoner's four children expressed extreme anger and hostility toward their mother when I called to confirm her willingness to have one of the children participate. She delivered an invective about the children's mother in an extremely loud voice, cursing and insulting her in vulgar terms. She also displayed hardheartedness about the children's emotional needs, saying that she refused to either take them to visit their mother or allow anyone else to do so, acknowledging that she did not care how much the children wanted to see their mother. There was little doubt that the children could hear what she was shouting. Not only were they hearing terrible things about their mother, but they also were finding out—possibly not for the first time—how unwanted they were in their grandmother's home. Needless to say, the grandmother refused to participate, so none of the children in the family were interviewed. However, it was easy to imagine that life for these children was far more difficult than for children like Lamar and Joseph, whose guardians welcomed and supported them. The angry grandmother effectively cut her grandchildren and their mother off from each other by refusing to take them to visit, and her vitriolic words, painting their mother in such negative terms, risked sabotaging the children's relationship with her.[4]

Although the interview comments reflected how emotionally detrimental parental incarceration can be, the children, mothers, and guardians reported far fewer behavioral or academic problems than one would expect on the basis either of earlier research or of my interviews with the children in the city sample. This difference may have been attributable in part to the contrast in settings and to the stability of the households where the children lived with their guardians. In fact, this sample may have overrepresented children living in particularly stable situations. Their mothers had a good enough relationship with the children's guardians that they were able to communicate with them, and the guardians themselves were cordial and receptive to participation in the research. How typical such situations are for children of incarcerated parents awaits further investigation. The emotional heat generated by the angry grandmother who refused to participate is an indicator of just how difficult it can be for the relatives caring for prisoners' children, so we must hope that situations like that are not the norm.

Parental incarceration exacts a considerable emotional toll on all children, whether because it disrupts the strong attachment they have with their mother or because it makes more manifest the gulf that separates some children from having the family and mother-child relationship they yearn for but have not experienced. As children age, they move on with their own lives, but the experience of having a parent in prison surely marks an important turning point in each child's life course.

6

What Lies Ahead

Terence's start in life was not promising. Here's how his mother, Cynthia, described herself and what happened the day he was born:

> I was a heavy drug user. Though I had already had two children, my two children were in turn with my grandmother and my mother, off and on. I mean I used drugs real heavy, and I can't express it enough, I mean real heavy. I never used needles, like that. I never used needles, I always used a pipe, and I was in love with that pipe and I thought that pipe was more than life itself. When I got pregnant, I did try to stop using drugs. When I got pregnant with Terence, I was devastated by the hurt of Terence's father leaving me—you know, um, just not being there for me. He was a big-time drug dealer. I used to steal his drugs. Worst thing a person could ever do is get a free high, 'cause in turn that free high got me nowhere.
>
> I was having contractions and, um, I had first made a phone call to top my drugs, and then I had a few contractions. So I called my drug dealer, but I also called the ambulance. The drug dealer got there before the ambulance got there, so, basically, the drug dealer got there before the ambulance got there. I, I opened my door, which I have this, this security door. I was home by myself, in my bed smoking my pipe, with all these drugs, and then I'm in hard labor, I mean my labor, my contractions, is coming real fast, my water broke. I kept getting high in the room by myself, and um, the pain was so great that I couldn't bear it anymore, so I laid down in my bed once more, and I knew the baby was coming, but I, but I didn't even care because what I did was, I put some more in that pipe and I kept puffing, and I think that I could've killed myself and this child, and I kept smoking, and I kept smoking. And I heard the door rattling, but by that time it was too late, 'cause now I'm laying on the

floor with my legs far apart, eating sugar, with a bottle of Popov [vodka] on the floor. I lifted Terence out up off the floor and laid him on top of my stomach, with a towel and covered him, and kept smoking, and kept smoking. Shit.

I call Terence my God-blessed child, because the poor kid could've died. Now, that's not the end of the story, because, being as how I was the drug addict that I was, when the, uh, ambulance driver came through my window, I was laying on my floor. I had the pipe in my hand. I had just took a hit. They were trying to put an IV on me and make sure that the baby was okay. I didn't care, 'cause I never asked, "Is the kid okay?" Um, I carried my pipe and drugs and took it to the hospital with me. Shit, [unintelligible] shit. And I was at the hospital, smoking the pipe. My kid could've died. I could've died, I lost so much blood.

Had his birth been the only inauspicious event in Terence's life, perhaps the concern it raised would have been less. But Terence's introduction to the world was followed by other circumstances and disruptions that did not improve his lot. Cynthia's delivery was not an epiphany that made her resolve to give up drugs. Instead, she kept using, relying on her grandmother, who had raised her from the age of ten because her own mother was abusing her, to care for Terence. Eventually, the law caught up with Cynthia: when Terence was three, she was convicted of a drug offense and spent a couple of years in state prison, hundreds of miles from Terence and his sisters. Terence continued living with his grandmother during his mother's incarceration. His father was never part of Terence's life and certainly did not step up to fulfill his parental responsibilities while Cynthia did time.

Cynthia's imprisonment accomplished what her harrowing delivery did not: it made her give up drugs. However, she still felt the need to get high, so after returning home she began drinking heavily. At the age of five, Terence reunited with a mother who no longer had a drug habit but quickly became an alcoholic. And so she remained until Terence was about ten years old. Along the way, Cynthia was arrested a few more times for theft-related offenses, spending short periods of time in jail. Once she stopped drinking, however, Cynthia was able to introduce more stability into her life. She found steady employment in a factory and was able to create a home for her children without having to rely on her grandmother to care for them, although her encounters with the law never ended.

When I met Terence, he was sixteen years old and the consequences of his turbulent life were evident. Terence was struggling in school. Although he was in tenth grade, he was reading at a fifth-grade level, which Cynthia speculated was the result of her drug use during her pregnancy. Whatever the cause, school was not a happy experience for Terence and his grades were poor. He was so unhappy with school that he avoided going as much as he could, becoming a chronic truant. When a child repeatedly skips school, the city's truancy policy calls for the school district to engage with the family in efforts to ensure that the child attends classes. Increasingly formal measures are taken if families and children do not cooperate in crafting a solution. Ultimately, a family can be referred to family court if less formal measures fail to stop the truancy. Fines can be imposed and, in the most extreme cases, the court can order a parent jailed for five days for not complying with the school district's and court's efforts. Cynthia apparently had ignored previous warnings about Terence's truancy from the school and court and was fined, because that is precisely why she was locked up when I met her, according to her own account.

Terence's academic challenges were not the only difficulties he was having at school. Terence was a fighter. He easily took offense at remarks other students made and quickly resorted to violence in response to perceived wrongs. His frequent fighting led to numerous suspensions from school, which did little to improve Terence's relationship with educational institutions. His antipathy toward school was so great that he was hoping he might be forced to leave altogether and join Job Corps, a national residential program that enables youths like Terence to finish their high school education while also acquiring vocational skills.

Terence's fighting was so frequent and severe that an arrest was probably inevitable, and indeed that was exactly what had occurred not long before we met. This arrest, however, was Terence's second; his first was on a stolen-car charge, but Terence said he had beaten that case. His second arrest was for assault, but even before the case was heard in a formal delinquency proceeding, the court had ordered Terence to attend a program for at-risk youth every day after school. There he received academic support that enabled him to bring his grades up for a short while, although they subsequently fell. Despite the benefits the program provided him, Terence was trying to find a job, because being employed would earn him a release from the program. If he succeeded in getting a job, however, it seemed likely that his academic work would suffer, especially because he would no longer be able to avail himself of the after-school program's support.

When I met Terence, he was living with his older sister, her husband, and their baby because Cynthia was still in jail. Her five-day confinement for failing to cooperate with the school district had turned into eight months: once she was turned over to the criminal justice system for the truancy issue, the authorities determined that she had unresolved cases from the past and detained her until the court disposed of them. Even though Terence liked living with his sister and her family, he missed Cynthia terribly. Her absence had made him feel uncomfortable and unstable, and his one wish was that she would come home soon.

For children like Terence and others, childhood is far from the idealized notion of a time of innocence and wonder. Instead, their childhoods are mined with hazards that put them at risk of experiencing the sort of problems with which Terence was struggling. Like the other children I met during the course of this research, his mother's incarceration was just one of several circumstances that had shaped his current trajectory. His mother's drug abuse, alcoholism, and criminal behavior; the family's lack of financial resources; the disruptions to their family life; and his absent father—all helped mold the person that Terence had become. Although incarceration was exacting a significant emotional toll on Terence and the other children I met, my research revealed that many of the reasons children like Terence who have a parent in prison may be worthy candidates for the nation's "most at-risk children" lie in the family and community environments of the children before that incarceration.

Disrupted Families and Disadvantaged Communities

My interviews and home visits with the children in the city sample provided an opportunity to learn about the antecedent conditions that might affect how a child responds to his or her mother's incarceration. They showed how important it is to place significant childhood events, like a parent's imprisonment, in context with a broader view of a child's life (Graue and Walsh 1998), recognizing how linked children's and parent's lives are from a life-course perspective (Elder 1994). My research also revealed that, like Terence, many children were struggling in the very areas identified as ones where children exhibit problems following a parent's incarceration and that the problems confronting these children before the prison doors close on their parents need to be addressed if troubling outcomes are to be prevented. Academic problems were common; many children lagged behind in achievement or had trouble at school because of disruptive or other types of antisocial behavior. A majority of the adolescents had already been in trouble with the law themselves, and younger and older children alike often were involved in fighting. In the emotional domain, many struggled as they experienced confusion about their mother's behavior and had to cope with upheavals resulting from disruptions to their family, usually precipitated by their mother's drug problem. Incarceration was not the reason for their struggles. Instead, their home and community environments presented several risk factors that contributed cumulatively to the odds that these children would be disadvantaged,

Many of the difficulties the children encountered were related to their economic circumstances. Consistent with the overrepresentation of low-income individuals in the criminal justice system, nearly all of the children's families were poor, which was not surprising given that the great majority were single-parent households headed by women employed in low-level jobs, when they were working at all. As in Cynthia's case, few of the mothers received any support from the children's fathers. The children clearly felt the strain of living in households where money was so limited, recognizing that they were missing out on what other children had. Given one wish, children whose mothers were still at home nearly always wished for something that would improve their economic situation. They wished that their mothers would be rich or that they "had all the money in the world," for instance. Often, they wanted to have a lot of money so that they could buy a bigger house and pay the family's bills, obviously uncomfortable with their shared sleeping quarters and sparse furnishings.

Poverty brings with it many adverse conditions that children must surmount in order to rise above society's lowest rungs. The schools the children attended lacked resources and were not places of safety and security for the children. Perhaps not surprisingly, then, many children were struggling academically, although the schools were not the only reason for their poor performance. Their home environments, frequently overcrowded and characterized by conditions not conducive to concentration, too often did not lend themselves to their doing schoolwork at home. The children also lacked other opportunities for cultural and intellectual enrichment that might have helped them, and social capital was in short supply as well, which meant that the children had diminished sources of social support and positive role models that might counterbalance the negative influences in their lives. Unlike children of more affluent means, the children I met in the course of this research were not being assiduously groomed for an effortless entrée into the middle-class world.

The children's low-income status also meant that they typically were exposed to violence in their neighborhoods and thus made vulnerable to all the potentially deleterious effects associated with such exposure (Aisenberg and Herrenkohl 2008; Buka et al. 2001; Margolin and Gordis 2000). Many children's wish to get a nice house was no doubt motivated in part by the desire to leave their neighborhood behind, given that so many characterized them in negative terms, referring to the shooting, fighting, and open-air drug dealing that they saw and heard in their streets. Unfortunately, the streets of their communities were not the only setting in which children were confronted with violence. All too often, children witnessed violence perpetrated against their mothers and at times saw their mothers use violence against romantic partners and others. Children were well schooled at home in the belief that violence was an acceptable and even expected way to respond to provocation, and many had absorbed the lesson, engaging in frequent fighting at school and in their neighborhood. By the time they reached adolescence, this physically aggressive behavior was one of the reasons a majority of the teenagers in the city sample had been arrested.

In addition to the violence the children experienced at home, the exposure to their mother's criminal offending—which in some cases introduced the children to criminal lifestyles at a very early age—presented the risk that the child would learn attitudes and beliefs conducive to their own offending, as postulated in social-learning theories (Akers et al. 1979; Bandura 1973; Sutherland, Cressey, and Luckenbill 1992). Their mothers, however, were not the only ones in their family who might have served as negative role models: the extent of criminal behavior among their fathers, indicated by their high rate of incarceration, was notable. As a result, many of the children in the city sample turned out to be children of an incarcerated parent, even though many of their mothers ultimately did not have to go to prison for the offense with which they had been charged. Some of the adverse conditions in these children's environments and even some of the children's behavioral, academic, and emotional problems might have been related to paternal incarceration. Nevertheless, a father's absence due to incarceration did not seem to be the reason for the children's living conditions. Most children whose fathers were or had been in prison had little contact with them either before or during their incarceration. No mother and no child in this study ever spoke longingly of a different way of life before Dad went to prison, although some imagined that life might have been better if their dad had been part of their life. Instead, little distinction was made between incarcerated fathers and those who were absent for other reasons. Most of the fathers who were missing were dismissed as unreliable or undesirable and were typically men with whom the mothers wanted little to do. As a consequence, the children had few opportunities for interaction with them and had attenuated bonds to them. How much salience their father's incarceration had to their life would be difficult to gauge without longitudinal studies that follow the children over time. What is indisputable is that the children's mothers were the primary parent figure in their lives, and that the children's separation from them—for whatever reason—had far more significant consequences for their daily lives than their father's absence did.

A key challenge facing the children was their mother's substance abuse and her criminal behavior related to it. Families where mothers had serious drug-abuse problems were the most likely to experience disruptions to the family unit, either because the mother was off running the streets or was locked up following an arrest. Her absences, combined with her need to support her drug habit, had financial consequences for the family, further straining already meager resources and sometimes leading the children to feel the need to help provide for the family. In the case of some children, their mother's substance abuse was so all-consuming that the child and mother rarely lived together, sometimes separated from each other for years. These separations were a mixed blessing for the children: on the one hand, they were removed from potentially harmful environments and placed in homes with relatives who offered greater stability and security, but on the other they suffered from the loss of a family life that included their mother. This disruption to the mother-child bond could have profound emotional consequences for the children, especially if a long-absent woman tried to reclaim her position as mother, thereby straining the child's loyalty and affection toward his or her surrogate parent. Even though not all drug-addicted women engaged in this sporadic style of mothering, all of those who did had a serious drug problem. The undesirable consequences associated with this sporadic engagement underscore the necessity to address the needs of addicted mothers.

Reading this litany of adversities the children encountered, it would be easy to overlook the children's enjoyment of the same pleasures children not similarly burdened enjoy. Younger children liked to play games, ride their bikes, and take part in sports, while the older youth also enjoyed going to the movies, talking on the phone with friends, going to parties, and just spending time with their peers. Almost all the children had strong emotional attachments to their mothers and loved their families. A mother's absence, therefore, could—and did—have significant emotional consequences.

More Disruption: Mom Gets Busted

A high-ranking police official once told me: "There's no good way to take a parent away from their children." Indeed, descriptions of what occurred at the time of a mother's arrest demonstrate that the police paid scant attention to her children. Although there was no evidence that a very young child was ever left on his or her own when a mother was taken into custody, the mothers' accounts of how the police dealt with the issue of their children were remarkably uniform. If the children were present at the time the woman was arrested, the police sometimes allowed the mother to call someone to come take the children. At other times, however, the presence of an older child was apparently sufficient to assure the police that the children would be looked after, and so they were left alone to fend for themselves. More often than not, however, the mothers were arrested when they were away from their children, and in those instances the children were literally out of sight and thus out of mind.

How police are to deal with the children of the adults they arrest presents ethical, legal, and practical challenges. Nevertheless, the trauma of a parent's arrest, which has been found to linger long after the incident (Jose-Kampfner 1995), underscores the importance of resolving such issues and instituting new practices. Several states have begun to recognize the need for police departments to have written policies and procedures that can minimize this trauma and provide professional intervention that ensures child safety without over-reliance on foster care. Accomplishing this objective requires commitment and collaboration on the part of various agencies, including law enforcement, child welfare, and community service providers, but some jurisdictions, such as San Francisco, Los Angeles, and other municipalities, have shown that this can be accomplished. Their approaches include educating police officers about the effects of parental arrest on children, and identifying children in need of help and ensuring that child welfare professionals are available in a timely manner when needed to assess children and find a place for them to stay, preferably with a family member (Puddefoot and Foster 2007). Such programs can serve as models for law enforcement agencies throughout the nation interested in the welfare of children whose parents are in trouble with the law.

The extent to which child welfare authorities should be involved with arrestees' families also poses ethical questions. As we have seen, children whose mothers are involved in the criminal justice system were in jeopardy of negative life outcomes even if their parent had never been arrested, and other researchers have noted that offenders' children need attention well before a parent is incarcerated due to all the other risk factors they face (Johnston 2006). A parent's arrest therefore could be conceived of as an alarm, signaling that a child may be in jeopardy and that some intervention would be in order beyond merely ensuring a safe placement for the child. Of course, intervention in the family life of a person merely accused or even convicted of a crime can be an unwelcome and unjustified intrusion, as well as a burden on those charged with the responsibility of intervening. Indeed, some social workers interviewed as part of a California study of policies regarding children and parental arrest expressed reservations about involving child protective services, which is set up to deal with cases of child abuse and neglect, although most felt that a parent's arrest did call for some action by authorities (Nolan 2003). Therefore, the question of whether to intervene with arrestees' children—and if so, how and when—merits thoughtful discussion and careful consideration among interested parties and policy makers before any steps are taken.

For all the mothers who were living with their children when they were arrested, the hours following their arrest were typically marked by frantic worry about their children if they were not sure that someone had taken charge of them. Even those who had been able to contact someone to take responsibility for the children's welfare were sometimes uncertain about where the children were staying. If they had not been able to call someone before being taken into custody, they had to wait until they were allowed to make a call and then had to hope they found someone who would find someplace for the children to stay until they returned home. In some cases, that return ended up being weeks or even months later, and this protracted detention could have unexpectedly serious short-term consequences. For instance, as days turned into weeks, a relative or friend who had agreed to take the children for a brief stay might decide that caring for them for so long was too burdensome and therefore passed the children off to someone else. Some children were separated from their siblings. Some had to switch schools. Although a rare occurrence, some children were taken out of school altogether because the temporary caregiver either would or could not travel the long distance to school and did not bother to register the child at a school close by.

Being locked up had other practical consequences for the women and their families, most notably in the maintenance of their homes. Being in jail meant that rent—or, in one instance, a mortgage—likely was not being paid, which in turn put the family at risk of losing their home, a particularly frightening prospect for those living in subsidized housing who had waited years to get into such accommodation. Young children seemed unaware of this possibility, but some adolescents, like Peter and Ronice, felt responsible for trying to hang onto the family home, adding to their anxieties and burdening them with adult responsibilities. Thus, the children faced not only short-term disruption to their home but also the possibility that their family would lose its home altogether.

For the children who were living with their mother at the time of her arrest, the period following that event was marked by anxiety and bewilderment for hours, days, or weeks. Nearly all were frightened by the experience, both by seeing their mother taken into custody if they were present at her arrest and by the uncertainty about the future that her removal precipitated. When would she be back? What would happen to them in the meantime? Would their mother be all right? Why were they taking her away? All these questions arose for the children, and the incomprehensibility of this unfamiliar aspect of the adult world settled over them like an obscuring fog. Speaking to her on the phone once the mother was permitted to call offered the children a measure of reassurance, but until she returned, their dual anxiety about their own fate and their mother's left the children fearful, worried, and confused.

Children whose mothers were detained in jail before trial were most profoundly affected by the separation, which could be protracted. Repeated delays in the processing of their mother's cases and detainers that resulted in her transfer to other facilities meant that she could be in jail for months. For the children, the distinction between being locked up to serve a sentence and locked up to await trial mattered little. Their lives were disrupted, they were displaced from their homes, and they were living with a great deal of uncertainty about when their mother would return. Speaking to their mother by phone while she was in jail presented the same difficulties children whose mothers were in state prison encountered, even if the calls were more affordable. Although the county jail was closer to the children in the city sample than the state prison was to the state sample children, the barriers to visitation were nearly as formidable. Visiting hours were incompatible with the schedules of the children and their caregivers; children had to be accompanied by a parent or guardian with proof of their relationship, such as the child's birth certificate; and getting to the jail without a car could be challenging and time consuming. As a result, children's visits to their mothers while they were in the county jail were rare and children could go months without seeing their mother.

The children in the city sample were not equally affected by their mother's arrest or ensuing detention. Most notably, those living with other relatives before their mother's arrest were far less likely to experience any disruption to their lives or to feel the same degree of anxiety about their future. Their mothers were not regularly engaged in caring for them and their absence thus did not signal a change in circumstances for them. Some children, in fact, were unaware that their mothers had been arrested. In these cases, then, the earlier disruption to their family life mitigated the effect of what was, for many other children, a traumatic event.

Incarceration: A Disruption Like No Other

State prisons are intended for long-term incarceration, so a parent's departure for such an institution signals that the children face a protracted separation from the parent that brings with it disruption to their regular life, difficulty communicating with the imprisoned parent and the possible concomitant erosion of the parent-child relationship, and the stigma of having a parent in prison. Given all the negative aspects of parental incarceration, it is easy to understand why people assume that children will suffer emotional consequences and that some of the difficulties they experience could manifest in troublesome behaviors. One of the striking findings in this study, however, was the relative lack of such behavior among the children in the state sample. Although numerous reports of problems among children of incarcerated parents appear in the literature, other reports indicate that the effects of parental incarceration may not be as dire as anticipated, especially the research that relied on examining children themselves instead of on adult reports. Thomas Hanlon and his colleagues, for example, anticipated finding "children abandoned and in dire need of rehabilitation resources and professional intervention" because of the voids in their lives due to family disruption (2005, 80). They also expected that the children would be particularly vulnerable to deleterious outcomes because of the neglect they assumed the children experienced due to their mother's drug abuse. However, that was frequently not the case, principally because the mothers, before they were imprisoned, were not the primary caregivers of the children; other mother (and father) figures cared for them. However, the children in that study were young and might well change as they moved into adolescence, particularly because many had associations with delinquent peers. As some studies have shown with respect to delinquency and adult crime, children of incarcerated parents face a life-long elevated risk of these behaviors, which perhaps will be manifest in the children Hanlon and his colleagues studied as they grow older (Huebner and Gustafson 2007; Murray and Farrington 2005).[1] Nevertheless, the lesson to be drawn from Hanlon's work (2005) is that a counterbalancing force can mitigate the potentially corrosive effects of maternal absence, whether due to drug abuse or incarceration, as it did for the children in the state sample.

Although the children I interviewed whose mothers were in state prison were living in safe and secure environments during their mothers' incarceration, many other children may experience more adverse conditions than they did, and such conditions may contribute to the negative consequences reported elsewhere in the literature. Psychiatrist Stewart Gabel, for instance, noted in the early 1990s that, based on his clinical observations, other factors were at least as important as the separation in determining antisocial behavior among children of incarcerated parents, specifically, family dysfunction and poor parenting on the part of the caretaker parent (Gabel 1992, 1993). Further research with larger samples is required to test the validity of this hypothesis and determine what is more important in explaining the troubling problems identified in other studies—a child's exposure to potential risk factors in his or her living situation during a parent's incarceration, the antecedent conditions he or she experienced before parental incarceration, or a combination of the two.

The biggest impact of incarceration on the children I interviewed was its emotional effect. However, looking at children's lives before their mothers were even sentenced made clear that this impact was conditioned by the children's earlier living arrangements. For children from intact families in which mother and child lived together before the mother went to prison, the disruption ensuing from long-term incarceration tore at the emotional core of the family, even if the children's new living arrangement provided them with greater stability. As one child said, having a mother who was imprisoned was "like a space in your heart." By comparison, those who were already living with another relative before their mother went to prison felt the effects less acutely, although they too experienced complicated emotional reactions to their mother's absence.

The emotional impact their mother's incarceration exacted on these children cannot be overstated. The most common emotion was sadness, pure and simple, especially among the youngest children. A counterweight for them, however, was the deep attachment most had formed with those who were caring for them, although that bond did not erase their yearning for their mother. Sadness among the older children was often tinged with bitterness and anger born of years of broken promises and disappointment in their mother. As the adolescents approached adulthood, they increasingly recognized that the opportunity to share their childhood with their mother had passed them by.

Resolving the emotional difficulties the children experienced and finding ways to nurture their attachment to their mothers was made more difficult by the numerous barriers to communication put in their way. Family and economic factors were key determinants of the extent to which the child and mother could communicate with each other. The relationship between the child's guardian and the incarcerated mother could make all the difference in whether and how often a child was able to see or talk to his or her mother, since the power of access to the mother rested with the guardians. Women like Valencia's grandmother, who made every effort within her limited financial means to ensure that Valencia would see or speak often with her mother, helped children stay connected and optimistic about their future relationship with their mother. Others did almost nothing to foster a close mother-child relationship, like the angry grandmother whose extreme hostility toward the mother led her to refuse to help her grandchildren remain in contact with her.[2] Some guardians who were angry with the mothers or disapproved of the behavior that led to her incarceration might draw the line at allowing the children to visit but would permit them to speak with their mother by phone, as Josh's grandmother did.

A guardian's financial situation was fundamental in determining how and how often a mother and child communicated. Since children almost universally eschewed writing letters regularly, the only means of communication was by phone calls or visits. The outlandishly high rates charged for calls from the prison meant that for some families they were either unaffordable or had to be rationed with great care. Precious and expensive minutes on the phone had to be shared with others in the household as well. Although far better than not talking at all, these occasional and limited phone conversations were meager substitutes for a mother's daily involvement in a child's life.

Visits to the prison were infrequent in the state sample. The prison was so far from most children's homes that getting there was a challenge, particularly if a family was dependent on public transportation. The prison's geographic location was in part an artifact of history and in part a function of the demographics of the prison population. In most states, the female prison population is small enough to house in one facility, as is the case in this state. Historically, women in trouble with the law were sent to the countryside so that they could be reformed, away from the vices and temptations of the big cities, which accounts for the rural setting of this prison. Changing times and new penal philosophies have not led to a change in the sites of many women's prisons, and so the mothers sit off in the country, far from their children. Even a program like the bus service the prison provided for the children every few weeks was underutilized, in part because the roundtrip was so long—and the visit so short.

The difficulty in communicating with their mothers was another reminder to the children of how different their family was from other children's. Most of the children recognized that their mother's absence was due to something shameful, and the stigma associated with their mother's situation led most to keep it a closely guarded secret. Cognizant of the difference that set them apart from their peers, many children wished they just had a "normal" family, a concept hard to articulate but one that could be achieved simply by having their mother home, as twelve-year-old Shaquil said:

JS: How do you think life would be different for you if she would be here?

SHAQUIL: It'd be normal.

JS: And right now it's not? It's not normal?

SHAQUIL: Yes.

JS: What would be normal?

SHAQUIL: It would be me, my mom, and my sister. We can just be our little family and be all together.

The idea that just having mom at home would coalesce the family once again and make life "normal" is beguilingly simple. In reality, however, a mother's return from prison did not guarantee either that the family would be reconstituted and normalcy would prevail or that the process would be trouble free.

Mommy's Coming Home!

All too often, a mother's return from prison did not instantly erase the difficulties of the past but introduced a new set of challenges, some resulting from the differing expectations mother and child brought to the process, some from the numerous barriers imposed on people returning from prison, and still others from the mother failing to change the behavior that led to her legal problems in the first place. The convergence of these factors can lead to disappointment and bitterness for the child. Instead of the hoped-for joy and normalcy that would accompany their mother's return from prison, both Keith and Naja, for example, watched their mothers return to drug use and criminal behavior, struggling unsuccessfully to find a place in society that would have kept them on a pathway away from prison, which is where both their mothers ultimately returned (see chapter 5).

Although some children expected to continue living with their guardian after their mother's release, others, especially young children, expected to be reunited with their mothers and anticipated that everything then would be fine. Even some older children, less jaded by their previous experiences than were Keith and Naja, looked forward to a better life once reunited with their mother. John, from the city sample, talked about how he envisioned things would be after his mother returned home from serving her sentence in state prison:

JOHN: So. I feel like, whenever she gets put away, I have that awkward feeling, you know. Empty feeling when she's not home. And when she comes home,

I feel better, you know. Everything is better. You know, no matter how hard I could work right now, everything's not going to get the way it was. When my mom's home, I really ain't gotta work, and everything's just the way it was, so . . . [*voice trails off*]

JS: When she's home, how are things different?

JOHN: I don't know, it's just like, buy a nice house—no matter what, I always get a nice house, the whole house is always fixed up nice, always clean, no bugs, no nothing. And it's like, she's there, you know, she's the person I could ask questions about, you know. You know, I really don't [ask questions] anymore but, you know, it's the point that it's my mom.[3]

When John's mother was released from prison, she did get them a nice house in which to live—a far cry from the "abandominium" where the two had been living before her incarceration and where John had continued living by himself after her arrest. She found employment and the two lived together, although John felt restricted by her after having been on his own for more than a year and did not like her telling him what to do. Despite the promise of the initial months following her return, however, Linda was arrested again two years after her release.

The imprisoned mothers I spoke with had much more modest expectations than the children; few expected to be reunited with their children immediately after release. They seemed to harbor fewer illusions about the difficulties of a reunion after years of separation during which their children had formed attachments to others. Vanessa had been in prison for nine years when she was released on parole and went home, although she was subsequently reincarcerated. Here she talks about the difficulties of reuniting with her daughters, one of whom she barely knew:

When I went home, I think Danielle was real angry with me. I didn't sit down with her and ask her how she felt. I was thinking, "I'm your mother; when I get out, everything will be fine," but it's not like that. Lakesha and I had a little shouting match. "You can't tell me what to do; you ain't been here in a long time." It breaks your heart to hear your child say that to you. It's easier to talk to Lakesha than Danielle because we had a semi-bond before I was locked up. Danielle was only three months old when I got locked up. She met me in prison, when she was five months old.[4]

Children like Danielle who had little opportunity to form an attachment to their mother during a long incarceration may have developed a strong bond with their guardian instead. These children can feel tremendous conflict and experience difficulty separating from their guardian if their mother returns from prison and expects to put on the mantle of motherhood again. Raheem, for instance, was an eleven-year-old who had lived with his maternal grandmother during his mother's incarceration, which began when he was two years old. When he was eight, his mother, Malita, returned from prison and moved in with Raheem and his grandmother. When, two years later, Malita moved in with a friend and took Raheem with her, he saw his grandmother only on weekends, but his yearning to be with her was clear: during the week, he would cross off the days on the calendar until Friday came around and he would be able to go to his grandmother's to stay with her. He did not count the days until he would return to his mother's. In addition to the emotional bond Raheem had to his grandmother, his life at her house was quite different than it was with his mother: all his toys were at his grandmother's house, he had several friends in her neighborhood, and he was allowed to go outside to play. At Malita's, he had to stay indoors and just watched television for entertainment or occasionally played video games with Malita.

Bridging the emotional gap between mother and child after a long separation or mending the tattered parent-child relationship created by repeated disappointments were not the only obstacles to a happy reunification. The mothers faced significant impediments in trying to establish a household where they could care for their children. Typically, people leaving prison exit with very few financial resources or sources of assistance on the outside (Petersilia 2003). Setting up a household means at a minimum obtaining housing and adequate furnishings and finding a source of income. Women might move in with a family member, but in some cases, they either are not welcome or the family's own situation is so strained that they cannot take in a woman—and her children (Roman and Travis 2006). Women convicted of drug offenses face special challenges. The change in welfare policy enacted during the Clinton administration allows states to deny public housing to people convicted of drug offenses, even if they just want to stay in someone else's public housing. Thus, if a returning prisoner convicted of a drug offense wants to stay with a relative who lives in a public housing apartment, her relative risks losing the apartment if authorities learn that she is staying there. Even apart from these government-imposed restrictions, financial constraints can make it difficult for former inmates to obtain housing for their children and themselves. The combination of low education level, limited employment history, few job skills, criminal convictions, and possibly problems such as substance abuse or mental illness, coupled with employers' reluctance to hire former prisoners, can make it difficult for them to find employment (Solomon et al. 2004; Visher and Travis 2003). Without a job, the women have the choice of depending on someone else for support, earning money from illegal sources, or going on welfare. The welfare policy changes that allowed states to ban people convicted of drug offenses from public housing imposed a lifetime ban on welfare benefits and food stamps for parents convicted of felony drug offenses via the Personal

Responsibility and Work Opportunity Reconciliation Act of 1996, unless a state enacts a law opting out of or limiting the ban.

Past as Prologue?

What does the future hold for these children? In light of the difficulties that most of them face—poverty, frequent disruptions to their family life, violence, distressed schools, limited social networks—one might predict troubled adulthoods. Interacting with many of these bright, laughing, energetic young children, it was hard for me to imagine that they might someday become criminals, the fate that many people fear awaits prisoners' children. It was difficult to imagine even that they might soon become the type of adolescents who were part of this study. The future seemed bleak for far too many of the teens I met in the city, with many using drugs, engaging in violence, and struggling in school or dropping out altogether. Most of these teenagers had already accrued arrest records, and some had already become parents. Since I first met the older adolescents in the city, most of them have turned eighteen—adults in the eyes of the law. The city's criminal records reveal that all those who were arrested as juveniles have also been arrested as adults. One is currently serving a five- to ten-year sentence in state prison, a disappointing but not entirely surprising outcome, given how she appeared when I met her. The field notes I recorded at that time reflected the concern I felt about her: "She's a kid who's on her way to some serious trouble if something pretty radical doesn't happen that would cause her life to turn around."

The mothers themselves present a cautionary tale about the future for some of these children. Several mothers were children of prisoners when they were growing up, and their recollections of childhood are eerily similar to the lives that are unfolding today for the children in the study. Here, for example, is how Sandy talked about life with her mother when she was growing up. As an adult, Sandy had been arrested with her boyfriend, with whom she had lived since she was fourteen years old. At the time she was interviewed, she had served seven years of a ten-year sentence.

JS: What did your parents say about you living with him at fourteen?

SANDY: Um, I was somewhat incorrigible, because of the way I grew up. My mom was an addict. So then she got clean and she was in recovery and she tried to be like supermom and I couldn't take it. So I just went and lived with him.

JS: How old were you when she got clean?

SANDY: Fourteen.

JS: What was she addicted to?

SANDY: Everything. Heroin, speed, pills.

JS: Would she use in front of you?

SANDY: I really—not intentionally. But I had made it my business to run up in the room and I've seen a lot.

JS: Did you understand what was going on?

SANDY: Yeah.

JS: And was your dad around?

SANDY: My father died from heroin when I was five. But my stepdad, yeah. I have a couple stepdads.

JS: Were your stepdads users?

SANDY: Um, yeah.

JS: So at the age of fourteen, you decided . . .

SANDY: I was out.

JS: 'Cause suddenly your mother got clean.

SANDY: Oh God, yeah. And anything I asked she said no, and I said why, and she said, "Because I said so." It was just—okay, I been doing what I wanted to do for a long time now, and now you're coming and telling me what I can and can't do? I wasn't used to it and I wasn't ready for it. And I used to tell her— I was real grown up for my age, you know, I raised a lot of kids 'cause my aunts and stuff were on drugs, so my cousins stayed with us—and I used to tell my mom: "Just 'cause you got help and you changed doesn't mean that it changed me. I'm still the way I was." So I had to go live with the father of my kids.

Later, Sandy talked about her mother being in and out of jail throughout Sandy's childhood.

SANDY: My mom's been in jail many times. She's just never made it to prison.

JS: What was the longest time she was locked up?

SANDY: I never knew how long she was locked up 'cause she never came right home. After she got out when she was locked up, she would go running and then she came home. One time she was in jail, and she came—I didn't even see her—she came, she got dressed, she had to go to court. Then she—I don't know where she went, but she didn't come home for a long time, and my stepdad didn't know where she was and when we found her she had got raped. And when she came home, her nose was broken, both her eyes were black, her leg was broke, they cut her nipple. I remember that like it was yesterday.

JS: How old were you?

SANDY: Um, about eight. Seven or eight. After that she went crazy. I remember a lot of things. A lot of bad things happened to me and I've seen a lot of bad things happen to her throughout her addiction.

The "bad things" that happened to Sandy included sexual abuse by both an older male relative and one of her mother's boyfriends, as well as physical abuse by her mother:

SANDY: My mom beat the shit out of me, so . . .

JS: Really?

SANDY: Oh, yeah, 'cause I used to go through her stuff and try to find her drugs so I could flush them. I would break her needles. And I knew I was gonna get beat for it, but I didn't care. She broke my jaw. Oh yeah, my mom *beat* me.

JS: She broke your jaw? How old were you when she did that?

SANDY: Thirteen.

JS: And when you went to school with a broken jaw, did anybody—

SANDY: I had to go live with my uncle.

JS: For how long?

SANDY: I stayed with him for like a couple months. I went back home. I didn't tell him my mom did it.

JS: So how come you had to go live with your uncle?

SANDY: Because I didn't want to live with my mom. Like she was afraid that I was gonna say something, so I just moved in with my uncle to stay away from her. I went back.

JS: And she would beat on you.

SANDY: She used to strangle me, I mean, like she was fighting me, like I was her enemy or something. I used to think that she hated me. Still to this day, I just don't think that she cares. Like she doesn't remember my childhood, she doesn't remember raising me. It's like she really doesn't have a bond with me, anyway.

Like the children I interviewed whose social worlds were narrowed by their circumstances, Sandy had few resources to draw upon for help. She did not even have many relatives to turn to. Her father, as noted, had died when she was five but until then had been in prison for most of her life. Her mother lived with another man whom Sandy considered her dad, but he was imprisoned and left the family when she was still young. Sandy's aunts were drug addicts. Moving in with her boyfriend ultimately offered little in the way of a safe haven. She became pregnant at sixteen and, she said, "I had two kids by the time I was eighteen and he beat the crap out of me the whole time." Sandy's life thus had parallels with those of several children in this study whose mothers were serious drug abusers: the sense that they should try to look after their mother, the exposure to violence, the frequent disruptions to their family life, teenage parenthood, and through it all, a deep emotional attachment to their mother, like Sandy's to her own mother: "I love her dearly, with all my heart, no matter what she's done." Sandy's greatest worry as a mother is that her daughters might follow in her footsteps, not just with respect to her behavior but also with regard to how she felt toward her mother:

JS: And what's your biggest worry about your children?

SANDY: That this cycle in my family, that they'll be a part of it, and I don't want them to be. I just hope that they—I can't say learn from my mistakes, but I should have learned from everybody else. But I just hope that they're stronger than I was. I just want to be able to get out there to show them another way to help that cycle stop. That's my biggest fear. I just want them to do the best they can do. They can be whatever they want to be.

JS: And what impact do you think being locked up has had on them?

SANDY: I've been where they're at, being a child of a mother that . . . Now I'm in my mom's shoes. I feel their pain. I've been there; I know what they're feeling. And I know what my mom was feeling now and I know what she felt. It's like I can't be mad at my mom, I can't hold a grudge against my mom. I did, and I hope that they don't have to go through anything like I went through, to be able to look past that and understand it.

Can children reasonably be asked to understand and look past a parent's circumstances, particularly when the parent's actions can have such far-reaching and consequential effects on their children? The younger children I met in the course of this research were certainly more accepting and less likely to see their mother in a negative light than were the older ones, who did express resentment at how their lives had deviated from their dreams because of their family situation. Some, however, exhibited an unusual degree of understanding of how their mother's own past was inextricably linked to the direction their own lives had taken. John, the young father who was living on his own during much of his mother's incarceration, saw with remarkable clarity how his mother's history had funneled him into his difficult circumstances.

At the end of his interview, asked what he would wish for if given just one wish, John said he needed more than one: "I would wish that my mother would straighten out. I would wish my girlfriend would get her head straight. I wish I could live happily ever after." We continued talking and, a short while later, he said: "You know what I would really wish for? I wish that my mom had had a great life when she was a kid. I wish she had went to school, graduated. I wish she had went to college, and I wish that she never touched drugs. That would be so great on me. If she had done all that, my life would be ten times better."

John's insight into the connection between his mother's past and his present was striking. He knows that the past cannot be undone, but he recognizes that his mother's upbringing placed her on a trajectory as a child that John was in some ways repeating, just as Sandy feared would happen to her children. In fact, John was one of the adolescents with a juvenile record who had been arrested as an adult since turning eighteen. Yet a story like Sandy's or John's are not inevitable for all children. Individuals' pathways through life have turning points at which they can be deflected from the trajectory they are on (Sampson and Laub 1993). Thus, we can hope that some of the adolescents who seemed headed for lives patterned after their mother's or father's might be influenced by opportunities to develop more productive and healthier alternatives for them and their own offspring. We can take inspiration and hope from young adults like Naja and Keith, whose early years suggested they would not fare well in the future. What is especially striking about the remarkably similar course of their lives was that they managed to rise above the numerous disruptions to their family life, defying the odds. Neither one could point to a specific person, program, or belief system that helped them, but something enabled them to dodge the pitfalls that led toward a difficult future, as seemed to be the case for John, Peter, and so many of the other adolescents I met. Keith and Naja were remarkably resilient and, at the threshold of adulthood, seemed poised to move forward in a positive direction, even if they still had to deal with the emotional residue of their mothers' lives and their separation from them.

Like Keith and Naja, most children were not able to articulate what helped them cope with their mother's incarceration and beat the odds. For some, the length of time that their mother was incarcerated and their long experience of not having her there to rely on meant that they had to build a life independent of her. Others were sustained by the surrogate families who cared for and nurtured them while their mothers were in prison or otherwise absent from the family. Maintaining contact with their mothers also helped some children, giving them hope that they could survive the separation and reconstitute the life they had shared once the prison doors opened and released their mother. The powerful reassurance children could derive simply by seeing their mothers was aptly expressed by Valencia, who responded this way when asked what helped her cope with her mother being away: "When I saw her for the first time last summer. That's the first time that I realized that it's going to be okay. It made me feel so much better when I saw her for the first time. Just seeing her, just looking at her, I felt so good."

Scholars who have studied resiliency in children have identified several factors that help them successfully cope with traumatic events and noxious environments that can easily overwhelm children and produce negative consequences. Protective factors are found at the individual, family, and community levels. Among the most important are an adaptable and positive personality; a supportive family environment that is cohesive, warm, involved, and consistent, with clear rules; a support network, either in the form of an external social agency or other family, friends, or adults; academic achievement; good schools with helpful teachers and peers at school; and prosocial role models (Garmezy 1983, 1991; Waller 2001; Werner and Smith 1992). No doubt these same factors help some children of incarcerated parents overcome not only their parent's incarceration, but also the pre-incarceration conditions that classify these children as at risk. Unfortunately, many of these protective factors were lacking in the children's lives. More research, particularly longitudinal studies, may help explain how some prisoners' children overcome the odds while others engage in risky behaviors, struggle with problems in school, or suffer serious psychological consequences.

Moving Forward

Although children of incarcerated parents have been characterized as some of the most at-risk children in the United States, it is appropriate to ask whether this characterization is fair. If it is, is parental incarceration itself what puts children at risk or is it a proxy for other aspects of children's lives that elevate the odds of undesirable outcomes for them? The lives portrayed here revealed that, indeed, most children were living in environments that would qualify them as at risk by nearly any measure. However, these risks were present well before the mothers went to prison. The extent to which a mother's incarceration jeopardizes children's well-being must be viewed in context with the other facets of their lives. Waiting to intervene until a parent is incarcerated is to wait too long, because the factors that put these children at risk typically present themselves well before a parent goes off to prison. That is not to deny that parental incarceration introduces additional serious issues for the children that should be addressed as well. Rather, the conclusion here is that children whose parents become involved in the criminal justice system are often dealing with a variety of issues with which they need help. Research has established that parents' criminality, apart from incarceration, is a predictor of delinquency in their offspring (Farrington et al. 2001; Lipsey and Derzon 1998; Loeber and Dishion 1983; Robins, West, and Herjanic 1975), but this study suggests that children whose parents are in trouble with the law—even if not incarcerated—may be at risk of other undesirable outcomes, such as academic difficulties, behavioral problems, and teenage parenthood.

Given the daunting odds so many of the children face, one might be forgiven for thinking that the problems are too numerous and too entrenched to address. Certainly, some of the most significant challenges in the children's lives stem from their family's poverty with its concomitant ills, such as under-resourced schools, dangerous neighborhoods, and reduced opportunities for cultural or intellectual enrichment or participation in recreational activities or sports. Although poverty does not condemn children to negative outcomes, that it elevates such risks has been well documented (Bradley and Corwyn 2002; Brooks-Gunn and Duncan 1997). The risks associated with poverty are compounded for poor children whose parents are in trouble with the law, because of the links between low socioeconomic status and harsh treatment by the criminal justice system. Members of minorities, who have far higher poverty rates than whites, as well as poorly educated people, are far more likely to be incarcerated than are members of other demographic groups (Bonczar 2003; Pettit and Western 2004), which in turn significantly elevates the likelihood that some groups of children—especially African American youths—will experience parental incarceration (Wildeman 2009). Thus, poverty has a double impact on children whose parents are involved in the criminal justice system: not only does it directly affect their health, well-being, and development but also it makes them more likely to have a parent go to jail or prison, compared to children of higher socioeconomic status whose parents commit crime.

This book offers no plan for combating poverty, but the examples of the children in this study should be added to the considerable evidence about poverty's effects on children and underscore the pressing need to address this social problem. Many programs have shown that investment in high-quality care early in a child's life, along with enhanced learning experiences, can produce significant benefits at far less expense than the social costs if a child is not deflected from a negative trajectory. What is needed are effective public policies that support evidence-based programs and practices that enhance the life chances of the most disadvantaged youth in our society.

Besides poverty, parental drug addiction was an enormous part of the problem for many children in this study. In addition to causing disruptions in the children's lives long before incarceration could threaten their families' unity, the mothers' substance abuse exposed the children to criminal behavior and placed them at times in dangerous environments. In cases where a mother's drug use left her unable to care for her children, family intervention was required, and other relatives assumed the role of guardian for the children.

The many problems associated with drug addiction have been well documented, including those of substance abusers' children. But unlike poverty, which is a complex structural phenomenon, addiction is a health problem that can be effectively addressed through appropriate treatment. It is not news, however, to note that both the demand and the need for more treatment far exceed its availability (Peugh and Belenko 1999). The decision to treat some addictions through the criminal justice system rather than the public health system has contributed to the increase in our prison population over the last three decades, especially among women (Mauer, Potler, and Wolf 1999). Imprisoning addicts without treating them has not been shown to end drug use, so the drug-related problems that plague these families will not be magically resolved by locking Mom up. Addicted parents in prison who are denied treatment are at risk of resuming their habit upon release, thrusting their families back into the situation that led to the incarceration in the first place, as Naja and Keith attested. Even addicts who receive treatment while in prison require support after release, because recovery and abstention from drug abuse is an ongoing process. Thus, in addition to therapy in prison, addicted parents need relapse-prevention support after their release. Greater service availability is also needed in the community both for those who return from prison without having received treatment and for those who have not gone to prison but want to end their drug use. Programs for drug-addicted mothers that include a component focusing on mother-child attachment have shown promising results for women in jail diversion or rehabilitation programs (Dallaire 2007). However, drug programs are not a magic bullet for these families: many substance abusers do not want to go into treatment, and many who do will fail or relapse later. Nevertheless, if increased availability of treatment helps only a portion of those who receive it to reestablish their ties with their children and ameliorates some of the conditions in their children's lives, is that not sufficient reason to invest in such services?

The increase in the likelihood of imprisonment for women convicted for drug offenses is related to the country's laws and policies that favor treating drug use as a criminal rather than a public health matter. The likelihood that this philosophy soon will change seems remote, so it is the criminal justice system we must look to for a response to those convicted of drug offenses that is less destructive of family ties. One solution is to make more community-based alternatives to incarceration available for nonviolent offenders. Such programs, which can be either residential or nonresidential, cost the public far less than locking people away in prison cells. They can provide supportive services while keeping offenders under close supervision and enable them to maintain some community and family ties more easily than they could from prison. Community-based programs also present less risk of the detrimental psychological consequences associated with incarceration that make prisoners' reintegration into the community more difficult. For instance, the prison environment encourages prisoners to become both dependent and distrustful (Haney 2003), qualities that undermine their ability to resume their roles as parents. Alternatives to incarceration can help avoid the inculcation of these undesirable concomitants of imprisonment.

Community-based alternatives could also address a persistent problem: the difficulties for children of visiting their incarcerated parents. Although reliable statistics on how often children get to see their parents do not exist, we know that many mothers in prison rarely receive visits from their children, and nearly six in ten mothers in state prison report never seeing them during their entire prison term (Glaze and Maruschak 2008). The major obstacle for anyone who wishes to visit a prisoner is typically the distance to the prison and the difficulty of getting there. Children face an additional impediment: being dependent on adults either to take them to the prison or, in the case of the state sample, to get them to the bus that took children to see their mothers. Commendable as the idea behind that institution's van program is, its logistics and the limited number of pickup spots made it a viable option for only a few of the children I interviewed. Nevertheless, this state facility's program went far beyond the efforts for prisoners' children of many other states. A recent survey of 387 prisons nationwide found that less than a third (29 percent) of female facilities provided subsidized transportation for family members and only 14 percent of them were paid for by the state's department of corrections. The rest were financed by local charities or faith groups, often with some assistance from the state. Only 13 percent of the facilities for women (six institutions) reported that public transit to their facility was available, so a car was a virtual necessity for those wishing to visit (Hoffmann, Byrd, and Adams 2007).[5] The lack of transportation coupled with long hours of travel that visits often entail, visitation hours that may not work well for all who would like to visit, and sometimes frustrating experiences at the prison makes clear why so many mothers rarely see their children.

Prison authorities of course cannot control the circumstances or interpersonal dynamics that may prevent mother-child visits, such as the absence of an adult willing to take the child to prison or a child who does not want to go, but a broader effort to provide transportation could help mothers and children remain in contact if families wish to have children visit mothers in prison. Some families oppose the idea of allowing such visits, fearing that they may normalize parental incarceration or be too upsetting for the children (Hairston 2007), as was the case with some of the children and their caregivers in this study. Nevertheless, most of the children wanted to see their mothers and regretted not being able to visit more frequently, and mother-child visits may help children cope better with the profound emotional strain parental incarceration can impose on them. In addition, research has shown that frequent visitation during incarceration has helped women stay connected as mothers. Incarcerated women who were deemed "connected mothers" at one time period were much more likely to have reestablished a relationship with their children five years later and to have remained connected even if they were still in prison during the intervening years (Martin 1997). Finally, visitation that encourages mother-child relationships may improve the prospects for family support when a woman leaves prison, which would in turn enhance the reentry process and diminish the likelihood that she will reoffend, as research on the role of family in the reentry process has found (Arditti and Few 2006; Hairston 1988; Homer 1979; Sharp and Marcus-Mendoza 2001; Visher and Travis 2003).

Although visitation can benefit both children and parents, visits will not occur daily or even weekly, even with more available transportation. Thus, other means of maintaining contact between mother and child are needed. As my research made plain, mothers try hard to remain in touch with their children by writing to them often, but this correspondence is more often than not a one-way affair. Most of the children did not like writing to their mothers. Instead, they wanted to be able to talk to them, if not in person then at least by phone. The onerous surcharges imposed on calls from prison often make phone calls such a financial burden for those caring for the children that calls are rare or, in some cases, prohibited altogether. If prisons are unwilling to end these arrangements that favor phone company profits over parent-child relationships, then legislatures should end them, as New York State did in 2007 (Confessore 2007). But for some poor families, long-distance calls even without surcharges may be too expensive to permit frequent contact, so prisons should explore creative methods for facilitating phone calls between a mother and her children. Some prisons have collaborated with other agencies to provide a site where children can come and have a "virtual visit" via a video monitor. Today's voice-over Internet protocol (VOIP) services, such as Skype, permit users equipped with a Webcam and microphone attached to their computer to see the person they are calling at no cost. Cameras equipped with mikes are available for under a hundred dollars, a small investment that prisons could make that would do much to enable children to maintain their relationship with their mother. On the other end, institutions like community centers, libraries, schools, or churches might be able to make these setups available, recognizing that some discretion would be required to avoid having the service publicly identified as the "prison cam," thereby adding to the stigma many children of incarcerated parents feel. A facility close to home where older youths could go on their own in order to see and share with their parent news about their daily lives would benefit most children and their parents.

The emotional difficulties associated with separation can be mitigated by visits and communication between parent and child, but even regular visitation will not eradicate the sadness that pervades so many children's emotional landscapes. Children also need support from caring adults and even from other children whose parents are in prison. The shame and stigma associated with having a parent who is incarcerated renders many children mute on the subject of their parent's whereabouts, but programs such as local support groups give them a chance to share activities or reveal their emotions without having to worry about being different from other children. Although such programs sound promising, scant empirical evidence about their benefits exists (Hairston 2007). One exception is the program Girl Scouts Beyond Bars: in addition to taking part in scouting in their community, twice a month girls participating in this program go to the prison where their mothers are incarcerated. There they engage in scouting projects together with their mothers, enabling them to share in activities in a way that a visit in the regular visiting area does not. Evaluations of the program show benefits for both daughters and mothers and an improved relationship between them compared to nonparticipants (Block and Potthast 1998). Mentoring is another approach to providing support for these children; it has received considerable financing from the federal government. Mentoring programs have been established around the country with these funds; many are run by faith-based organizations, modeled on Amachi, a program that was established in Philadelphia. Although mentoring programs targeted at children of incarcerated parents likewise have not been rigorously evaluated (DuBois and Rhodes 2006), there is evidence that mentoring programs in general confer modest benefits in the academic, behavioral, and social domains (DuBois et al. 2002), and there is reason to hope that children of incarcerated parents would receive similar benefits. Furthermore, the presence of a concerned adult who can offer advice or a sympathetic ear would be welcomed by many of these children. Mentors can also provide some respite for those who are taking care of the children during the parent's incarceration. For children whose mothers are in prison, this will most commonly be the child's grandparent (Glaze and Maruschak 2008). Grandparents and other relatives who have taken on the responsibility for another person's child can certainly feel stressed by the experience, and any assistance and support would likely be welcome and might help reduce their stress, thereby improving the family environment for the children as well.

The notion that programs beneficial to caregivers and parents can have ancillary benefits for the children is important to bear in mind. As helpful as a mentor or a child-focused program can be, no external, occasional intervention can completely counteract the potential harms that can arise in families characterized by stress and its concomitant tensions. Upon their release from prison, mothers face considerable obstacles in rebuilding their lives. Like all prisoners, they must deal with the psychological readjustment associated with their return from custody, where their daily activities were strictly controlled by others and their survival meant adopting an attitude of wariness and distrust (Haney 2003). The adjustments required for successful adaptation to prison are inimical to success in the world outside, where adults are expected to be independent and self-directed and where healthy interpersonal relationships are built on trust. A parent planning to reunite with her children thus must manage not only the challenges associated with rebuilding a parent-child relationship, but also those arising from the transition from captive to free person.

In addition, a mother must confront the behavioral issues that led to her incarceration and find ways to house and support herself and her children if she wants to reunite with them. As noted earlier, these tasks present their own sets of challenges. Without sufficient support for these fragile families, life may quickly overwhelm them. One woman in prison who was a chronic thief reflected how precarious she anticipated her return home was liable to be: she said that she felt she literally would need someone by her side at all times to prevent her from lapsing into her customary behavior patterns. Thus, programs are needed that help ex-inmates navigate the rocky shoals of reentry, thereby enhancing their likelihood of being able to resume their parental responsibilities.

Some may question the wisdom of reuniting children with parents they might view as bad mothers, believing them morally unworthy of or unequal to the task of being a parent, but the children yearn for this reunion. Intervention is required when children have been in jeopardy, as was the case when Peter was left alone in an apartment for days at a time when he was a preschooler. Few children lived in situations like Peter's, however. More commonly, if mothers were unable to carry out their parental responsibilities, like several in this study, other family members stepped in to care for the children temporarily, for instance, when the mothers were on the streets. Despite the intermittent nature of some children's contacts with their mother, almost all the children felt deeply connected to them. Whatever the inadequacies of some of these mothers' parenting, the children loved them as deeply as any other children love their mothers.

Taking the children's perspective into account is vitally important when considering how best to deal with the many issues that arise when a parent is incarcerated, and some movement toward that end is underway. Notably, advocates for prisoners' children have been promoting the adoption of a bill of rights for children of incarcerated parents nationwide. Created by San Francisco Partners for Incarcerated Parents, the bill of rights addresses the many obstacles discussed in this book and calls for children to be protected and have their voices heard at the various stages of the process that begins with a parent's arrest and continues through incarceration. Instituting some aspects of the bill would require modifications in police, court, and prison policies and procedures, but as this book has shown, change is warranted if the criminal justice system is to do its part to minimize the harm inflicted on children when a parent goes to prison.

Conclusion

Many questions about children of incarcerated parents remain to be answered. This study has shown that a central question that must be addressed is how much parental incarceration contributes to negative consequences among the children once other relevant risk factors are taken into account. This question can best be answered through longitudinal studies of prisoners' children and appropriate comparison groups that assess the children both before and after a parent is imprisoned. Such studies would enable us to address other important questions, such as the effect of a child's age at the time of parental incarceration on the child's development and on the impact of the separation, or whether boys and girls react differently to parental incarceration. The studies could explore what aspects of the child's caregiving arrangement during parental incarceration contribute to the child's adaptation to the absence of the parent, or how varied levels of contact during incarceration affect a child's adaptation and the relationship between parent and child following release. A critical area of investigation as well is identifying what factors contribute to resiliency among children affected by parental incarceration.

Ford Maddox Ford's famous novel *The Good Soldier* opens: "This is the saddest story I have ever heard" (1955, 3). Competition for the saddest story is stiff, especially when it comes to tales involving children—sick and dying children, children caught in the throes of war, abused and neglected children, children who lose a parent through death or abandonment, survivors and nonsurvivors of natural disasters, and the list goes on. Surely the stories of prisoners' children are contenders for the title. Hearing such stories evokes our compassion and sympathy, but most of us soon turn to issues of more immediate salience to our lives. Unless you are the child of a prisoner, the parent who is in prison, or another family member, you may well forget the stories of the children profiled in this book. I hope you do not. Prisoners' children have become the innocent victims of our nation's mass incarceration policies; they and their parents' plight deserve our attention. The decks are stacked against these children. They need every hand we can stretch out to help them surmount the obstacles in their way.

APPENDIX A

DOING RESEARCH WITH CHILDREN OF INCARCERATED PARENTS

Very little research has been carried out that involves children of prisoners. No doubt one of the reasons is that working with this population presents at least three challenges: identifying the appropriate population, gaining access to the children, and obtaining permission from the various people (parents, guardians, and children) and institutions (prisons, courts, possibly child protective services) involved. This appendix explains how participants in this research were identified, recruited, and interviewed.

Researchers interested in children of incarcerated parents have commented on the difficulty of identifying and contacting the children: no systematic records are kept that would enable their easy identification. The same is true of children whose parents have been arrested but not convicted. No government agency or school records information about the children of those arrested or imprisoned. Selecting children from a community would require a very large sample in order to identify a sufficient number of prisoners' children or children whose mothers were awaiting trial. The best way to find the children, I concluded, was to work through the mothers to request that they and their children participate. However, I needed different strategies for recruiting children whose mothers were still living at home and those whose mothers were incarcerated.

Since a primary objective was to talk with the children before the mother's trial, I needed to identify some mothers soon after their arrest but before their cases were concluded in court and they were sentenced. One logical place to try seemed to be the courthouse, where women would come for preliminary court appearances. To determine how best to approach the women in that setting and obtain their agreement to participate, I held a focus group with women who had been in prison or jail but were then residing in a halfway house in the city where the research was conducted. During the focus group, we discussed potential ways to approach the women, how to recruit them and their children, and how to talk with the children. The participants felt that women might distrust someone they did not know and suspect me of being from the local child protective services agency, which would represent an obvious threat to a family worried about the possibility of children being taken into foster care. The discussion led to the conclusion that the best way to gain the women's cooperation was to be introduced to them through their attorney, possibly the only person involved in their case whom the women were likely to trust.

The city's public defender office represents 85 percent of all criminal cases brought to the courts there. I requested its assistance in introducing me to women defendants, telling them that I wished to speak with them and briefly explaining the reason why. The defender's office recommended recruiting women during the arraignment, a hearing a few days after their arrest at which defendants are given a trial date. The defender identified all the women scheduled for an arraignment on a given day and attempted to speak with each one before the hearing to ascertain if she had children and would be willing to meet me to hear about the project. If a woman agreed, she and I would meet in a private room next to the courtroom, where I could determine that she had at least one child of the target age of eight to eighteen, explain the study to her, answer her questions, and request that she and her child participate. If a woman was interested in participating, I asked her to talk with her son or daughter to see if the child would be willing to take part as well. Follow-up calls were then made to determine whether the child had agreed; if so, arrangements were made to interview the mother and child at their home.

After the initial interview, I would call the mother after her next hearing to learn what the outcome was. Usually, this was a preliminary hearing, a sort of minitrial at which the prosecution presents its evidence so a judge can determine whether it is sufficient to warrant going forward with the case against the defendant. If so, a trial date is assigned. Given the vagaries of the criminal justice system, almost all the women's cases experienced some delay that resulted in the preliminary hearing being rescheduled, sometimes as many as three or four times, almost always on a date at least six weeks after their appearance. Thus, cases could be continued for months before they reached the trial stage. Once the case outcome was determined, I would return to interview the child again a few months after the sentencing. Along the way, however, I lost contact with some families because telephones were disconnected or people moved. In other instances, cases were dropped and thus no sentencing occurred. When this happened, the child was not interviewed a second time.

During this process, it became clear that virtually all the defendants who were sentenced were receiving probation. Although the study design anticipated that some of the women would be on probation, women sentenced to prison were also needed for the sample. When I discussed this with the public defender's office, I was told that women who were the most likely to be sentenced to prison were being held in jail before their trial and were not brought to the courthouse for their arraignment. I therefore needed a new system for recruiting women being held in pretrial detention at the county jail.

The county's prison system and the warden of the jail where the women were held pending trial granted me permission to go to the jail to recruit women with the public defenders when they went to interview the women for case preparation. Together, we would go to the designated official visitors' area, where the defenders met their clients in private while I waited in an adjacent room. Just as in the courtroom, the defenders would tell the women about the study and ask them to stop in my room if they were interested in hearing more about it. I explained the study to those who came in to see me and, if they were interested, asked them to talk to their child about it to see if he or she would be willing to participate. If the child agreed, the mother also was to ask whoever was caring for the child if it would be all right for me to come to the house to interview the child.

Recruiting participants in this way proved a time-consuming and sometimes frustrating process, but using their best estimates of how long it would take to place a call, the women would tell me when they expected to speak to the child, and I would return to the jail shortly after that date and request a visit with the woman to find out whether the child had agreed. This process could repeat itself several times before the mother finally succeeded in speaking with her child about the study. Once the child consented to take part, I would then call the household where the child was staying to arrange an interview. (On occasion, the child's guardian said she knew nothing about the study or the child's agreement to participate, despite the mother's assurance that she had obtained both the guardian's and the child's agreement.) If the child and guardian were in agreement, I would then return to the jail to arrange an interview with the mother before interviewing her child.

In addition to seeing how children fared in the period immediately following their mother's incarceration, I wanted to speak with children whose mothers had been incarcerated for longer periods of time. To do so, I turned to the state prison for women in a neighboring state. The prison's superintendent, who was very concerned about the issue of prisoners' children, agreed to assist me in recruiting the women. Once I obtained permission to conduct research in the prison from the state commissioner of corrections, the facility agreed to have prison staff distribute to the women a flyer giving some information and answers to common questions about the study. Two information sessions were held in the facility's gym so that interested women could learn more about the study and sign up to participate. Women who agreed to participate were asked to contact their children and the children's guardian to see if they would be interested in participating. Guardian participation was not required, but the guardian did have to give permission for the child to participate if the child wanted to do so. The women in prison were given a reply form where they could indicate whether the child and/or guardian had declined or accepted and provide contact information for the child if he or she had agreed to take part. A stamped envelope addressed to me was also included. Women who did not reply received up to three follow-up letters, each of which included another reply form and stamped, pre-addressed envelope, requesting that they let me know the outcome of their request of their child and the child's guardian.

Of the forty-seven women who expressed interest following the information sessions, sixteen failed to return the forms, eight had children or guardians who declined to participate, and seventeen agreed to participate. The rest could not be reached despite repeated attempts. Of those who agreed to participate and said that their child and the guardian had agreed as well, two guardians would not permit me to interview the children after the interviews with the mothers had already taken place, so those children were not part of the sample.

WHO PARTICIPATED?

Women defendants in the city and the prisoners at the state prison who reported having a child between the ages of eight and eighteen were eligible for participation in the research. In addition, the state prisoners had to have been incarcerated at least one year at the time of the interview. One child per family (the index child) was chosen for the study. If a woman had more than one child between the eligible ages, then the child whose birthday was next in chronological order was chosen as the index child. (There were two exceptions to the rule of interviewing only one child per family, and both occurred with families of women in state prison with two children. When I arrived at each house, both children were expecting to be interviewed and in order not to disappoint them, I spoke with both. The final sample includes both children from these two families.) Over time, as the data were being collected and analyzed on an ongoing basis, the sampling became purposive, with the objective of including more teenagers in order to ensure sufficient data about how adolescents view their mothers' criminal justice involvement.

In total I interviewed sixty-seven children, seventy-four mothers, and eighteen guardians. (As explained earlier, in some cases, the child was unavailable for interviewing after the mother was interviewed, despite both individuals' initial agreement to participate.) Among the mothers I interviewed, thirty-five were awaiting trial and were not in jail at the time of the initial interview, twenty-two were in pretrial detention in jail, and seventeen were in state prison. Twelve of the guardians were caring for children whose mothers were in state prison, five were caring for children whose mothers were in pretrial detention, and one was a woman with whom a child actually lived, although her mother was not imprisoned.

HOW THE STUDY WAS CONDUCTED

For all the families, the first interviews were held with the mothers. This was done in part to determine how much the child knew about the mother's situation; if the child was unaware of her actual whereabouts or her criminal justice involvement—which was the case for two children—I wanted to be sure that my questions did not inadvertently inform the child of a situation the family had chosen to keep secret. If a child was living with a guardian, then the guardian was also interviewed before the child.

As noted, in the city, the original intent of the study was to interview children before and after the mother's trial, in order to achieve the objective of learning what life was like for children before the mother was incarcerated and how that changed as result of her imprisonment. However, in nearly every case where the mother was living at home with her child before her trial, she either was sentenced to probation or had her case dismissed. The children whose mothers were sentenced to prison were not living with them during the pretrial period because their mothers were in jail before the trial. As a result, only a sample of children was interviewed both before and after their mother's trial.

Informed consent was obtained from the adult participants for their own participation. In addition, mothers and guardians signed separate consent forms in which they agreed to allow the child to take part in the study. Children signed assent forms after I informed them orally of the study's purpose, what their participation involved, and the risks and benefits associated with it. Mothers and guardians were paid ten dollars for their participation and children were given ten-dollar gift cards for a toy or clothing store each time they were interviewed. I told the children explicitly and emphatically that they would receive the gift card even if they chose not to answer some questions, in the hope that they would not feel obligated to talk about topics they did not want to discuss. All interviews were tape recorded and transcribed except for some that took place with mothers in jail and those conducted with mothers in the maximum-security unit of the women's prison. In those cases, respondents' answers were recorded by hand. I have noted where quotes in the book came from hand-transcribed interviews, acknowledging that the words may not have been exactly as the women spoke them. They do, however, accurately reflect the substance of what they said. All other quotes are verbatim, based on the audio recordings.

In addition to the interviews, field notes were recorded contemporaneously during the research and questions were adapted or added as themes began to emerge from the interviews. The interviews and field notes were analyzed through a process of repeated readings to identify themes in the children's lives.

APPENDIX B

A PORTRAIT OF THE CHILDREN AND THEIR MOTHERS

This appendix contains descriptive statistics highlighting some demographic information about the mothers and children who took part in the study, as well as information on the mothers' criminal histories.

DEMOGRAPHIC CHARACTERISTICS

Selected demographic characteristics of the mothers in the sample overall, as well as within each of the three recruitment sites, are shown in table B.1. The women ranged in age from 23 to 52, with an average age of 34.1. Nearly three-quarters of the mothers were black, while the rest were white. Although African Americans represented a larger percentage of women in the nonincarcerated sample (86.5 percent) than in the two groups of incarcerated women (60 percent in jail, 64.7 percent in prison), they were no less likely, statistically, to have been in detention or prison than were white women. Six women (8 percent) were of Hispanic ethnicity. Although Hispanic women were overrepresented in the jail sample (15 percent of that sample, compared to only 8 percent of the overall sample), there was no statistically significant relationship between a woman's ethnicity and her likelihood of being incarcerated. However, white women were slightly overrepresented in both the jail and the prison samples compared to the overall population in those facilities. This may have been because inmates from racial or ethnic minority groups and their families were more fearful that a white woman like me was a wolf in sheep's clothing, so to speak, who might call child protection authorities for some reason, putting their children at risk of being placed in the foster-care system.[1] A few women in the city jail did talk about their concern that the local authorities would step in, but that was a general anxiety that seemed unrelated to the research. Only one woman—who happened to be white—explicitly worried that I would call the authorities because her son was living on his own while she was in jail.

On average, the mothers had 3.3 children. Some had as many as ten children; nine had one child each. For women who had more than one child, it was very likely that their children had different fathers. For instance, in

TABLE B.I

Demographic characteristics of mothers (means and percentages)

	Total Sample (N = 74)	No pretrial detention (N = 37)	In pretrial detention (jail) (N = 20)	In prison (N = 17)
Age	34.1 (6.01)[a]	34.59 (6.57)	32.95 (5.59)	34.53 (5.33)
Race/ethnicity (%)				
African American	74.3	86.5	60.0	64.7
White	25.7	13.5	40.0	35.3
Latina ethnicity	8.0	5.4	15.0	5.9
Number of children	3.3 (1.80)	3.4 (1.80)	3.1 (1.55)	3.24 (2.11)
Marital status (%)				
Married/common law	27.0	32.4	15.0	29.4
Separated/divorced/widowed	20.3	21.6	25.0	11.8
Single	52.7	45.9	60.0	58.8
Years of education	11.07 (1.43)	11.25 (1.16)	10.55 (1.43)	11.31 (1.85)

[a] Numbers in parentheses are standard deviations.

families where the mother had two children, 90 percent of the children had different fathers. Of the sixty-five families with more than one child, only four (6 percent) comprised children who all had the same father. Most of the women were not married, with 52.7 percent never having married and another 20.3 percent reporting they were separated, divorced, or widowed. Women who were married (14.9 percent) or living in a common-law marriage (12.2 percent) were no less likely than the other women to have had children fathered by different men.

As might be expected from a sample drawn from individuals involved in the criminal justice system, the women generally came from a low socioeconomic stratum. Most mothers were not employed, relying on state aid to support their families. Of those who were not incarcerated when initially interviewed, twenty-six (70.3 percent) were not employed. Of these, three said they were looking for work. Eight (21.6 percent) of the women interviewed at home were working full-time and another three (8.1 percent) had part-time jobs. Few of the women had a history of stable, long-term employment. Several had no history of employment in legal occupations. Their lack of work experience is probably tied to their educational background. As shown in table B.1, the mothers generally had less than a high school education: six in ten had left school before the twelfth grade ($M = 11.07$), while 25.7 percent had completed high school, a rate of educational attainment notably below average compared to women in the general population (U. S. Census Bureau 2004). Nine women (12.2 percent) had one or two years of postsecondary education, and two women did not provide information on their educational background. Perhaps not surprisingly given their level of education, almost all of those who did work were employed in low-skill, low-wage occupations such as home health aides, housekeepers, or factory workers.

As for the children, although there was nearly an equal number of boys (n = 33) and girls (n = 34) in the sample overall, boys represented two-thirds of the sample of children whose mothers were in jail awaiting trial (table B.2). Their average age was about twelve, although they ranged in age from eight to eighteen, as intended. Although not a statistically significant difference, the age distribution of the three groups of children did differ: nearly half (46.7 percent) the children whose mothers were in jail awaiting trial were teenagers, compared to only 28.6 percent of those whose mothers were home and 35.3 percent of the children whose mothers were in prison. Part of the reason for this was that I purposefully attempted to interview teenagers once I started recruiting women in the jail because they were underrepresented among the children whose mothers were home awaiting trial.

Like the mothers, most of the children were black (73.1 percent), the rest white (25.4 percent) or biracial (1.5 percent). As with age, the racial distribution in the three groups differed, although not statistically significantly. A greater percentage of the children whose mothers were in jail (40.0 percent) and in prison (41.2 percent) were white, compared to the percentage of white children whose mothers were home (11.4 percent), which was generally consistent with the racial makeup of the mothers interviewed.

The grade distribution for the total sample and for each group of children shows that the children whose mothers were in jail were more likely to be in high school than the other children, a result of the difference in age among the groups (table B.2). One notable finding with respect to their educational status was the number of children who had stopped attending school among those in the jail group. While teenagers whose mothers were in jail awaiting trial represented only 41 percent of the teens in the city sample, they accounted for 75 percent of those who had stopped attending school.

TABLE B.2

Demographic characteristics of children (means and percentages)

	Total Sample (N = 67)	Mother at home pending trial (N = 35)	Mother in pretrial detention (jail) (N = 15)	Mother in prison (N = 17)
Age	12.7	11.3	12.7	12.1
	(8.4)[a]	(2.6)	(2.9)	(3.1)
Sex (%)				
Males	49.3	42.9	66.7	47.1
Race/ethnicity (%)				
African American	73.1	85.7	60.0	58.8
White	25.4	11.4	40.0	41.2
Biracial	1.5	2.9	0	0
Latina/o ethnicity	6.0	5.7	6.7	5.9
Grade in school				
2	10.4%	17.1%	6.7%	0.0%
3	10.4	11.4	6.7	11.8
4	11.9	8.6	6.7	23.5
5	16.4	20.0	20.0	5.9
6	4.5	2.9	0.0	11.8
7	10.4	11.4	13.3	5.9
8	14.9	17.1	13.3	11.8
9	4.5	2.9	0.0	11.8
10	4.5	2.9	13.3	0.0
11	1.5	2.9	0.0	0.0
Graduated HS	3.0	0.0	0.0	11.8
Stopped attending	7.5	2.9	20.0	5.9

[a] Numbers in parentheses are standard deviations.

CRIMINAL HISTORY

Information about the mothers' criminal history was gleaned from their interviews and is shown in table B.3. The women generally reported having been arrested on multiple occasions, ranging from one to forty times. Overall, they

TABLE B.3

Mothers' Self-Reported Criminal History

	Total Sample (N = 74)	No pretrial detention (N = 37)	In pretrial detention (jail) (N = 20)	In prison (N = 17)
Mean number of arrests	7.3 (13.2)[a]	5.3 (16.2)	10.2 (6.9)	8.3 (11.1)
	(N = 66)	(N = 35)	(N = 16)	(N = 15)
Mean number of incarcerations	1.4 (1.5)	.5[b] (.9)	2.8 (1.7)	2.1 (1.2)

[a] Numbers in parentheses are standard deviations.

[b] Statistically significant difference between this group and those in jail or prison (p < .001)

had an average of 7.3 arrests, although the three groups of mothers varied in their arrest histories: women awaiting trial in the city jail had been arrested on average nearly twice as many times as the women awaiting trial at home (10.2 arrests vs. 5.3). The state sample prisoners had an average of 8.3 arrests. Averages can be skewed because of a few extreme cases, such as one woman who said she had been arrested forty times, but the median number of arrests reflects the same relative distribution, with the city detainees having the highest median number and the women at home the lowest (9.5 arrests vs. 2.0). The median number of arrests for the state sample was 3.0.

These differences in arrest histories are not surprising. People are typically not sentenced to prison the first time they are arrested, so people serving time in state prisons would be expected to have a record of prior arrests. The higher arrest rates for the women in the county jail are likewise understandable. Bail is usually set higher for individuals who have extensive records of previous arrests, making it more difficult for them to get out of jail before trial. Furthermore, many women who were in jail were already on probation at the time of their arrest due to a prior conviction. When that happens, the probation department will typically request that the probationer be held until the outcome of the new case is known, at which time a decision about the continuation of their probation can be made. For these reasons, women in jail and prison typically have longer arrest records than those released following an arrest.

As might be expected from the difference in the number of prior arrests among the groups, the women's incarceration history also varied. Some women were unable to specify how many times they had been incarcerated in jail or prison; "I've been in and out, in and out" was a typical response to that question. This usually meant that the woman had been jailed in county facilities for short periods of time, followed by a period on parole or probation. Upon release, she would be arrested and convicted again, which in turn would constitute a violation of her supervision, resulting in her being jailed again for the violation, if not for the new offense. At times, such women would also spend some time in state prison. Although not every woman was able to specify the number of times she had been incarcerated, 62.2 percent of them did report having spent some time in jail or prison in the past. In this case, statistically significant and substantive differences existed among the three groups of women. Nine out of ten (90.0 percent) women in pretrial detention had histories of incarceration compared to only three in ten (30.6 percent) of the women at home awaiting trial. All the state-sample prisoners had been previously incarcerated. As would be expected from these rates, the average number of times the women had been imprisoned also differed significantly, with the women at home awaiting trial having significantly fewer prior incarcerations (.5) than either of the other two groups. As with arrests, the pretrial detainees (2.8 incarcerations) reported more incarcerations than either the women at home or those in state prison (2.1).

Table B.4 shows the most serious current charge for which the women were either serving time in state prison or had been arrested in the city. A drug charge was the most common offense for women in jail or prison, whereas assault was the most frequent charge among those at home awaiting trial. In fact, a larger percentage of the women not in custody (44.1 percent) were charged with a violent crime (assault or robbery) than those either in pretrial detention (15.8 percent) or in prison (37.5 percent, including homicide/manslaughter). A sizable percentage (36.9 percent) of women in jail awaiting trial were charged with shoplifting, theft, or theft-related offenses (forgery, motor vehicle theft). Many of them had committed these offenses to support their drug habit.

The assaults with which the women at home were charged typically involved a fight with someone they knew, such as a neighbor, an intimate partner, or a relative. Many were fairly minor fights but some were more serious in nature, such as hitting someone in the head with a hammer or stabbing someone in the abdomen. Why were they not in jail, while those who were in detention were charged more often with nonviolent offenses? Women who were not in detention but had been charged with assault either were able to provide bail or were released from custody on their own recognizance. The women in jail, however, either could not pay their bail or fell into the category of women being

TABLE B.4
Mothers' Most Serious Current Charge

	Total Sample (N = 69)	No pretrial detention (N = 34)	In pretrial detention (jail) (N = 19)	In prison (N = 16)
Drug possession/distribution	24.6%	17.6%	36.8%	25.0%
Assault	24.6	38.2	10.5	12.5
Theft/shoplifting	10.1	2.9	26.3	12.5
Robbery	7.2	5.9	5.3	12.5
Fraud	5.8	8.8	0.0	6.3
Forgery	5.8	8.8	5.3	0.0
Homicide/manslaughter	4.3	0.0	0.0	12.5
Motor vehicle theft	2.9	2.9	5.3	0.0
Prostitution	1.4	0.0	5.3	0.0
Other	13.0	14.7	5.3	18.7

held because they were already on probation or parole at the time their offense occurred. The inability to pay even a modest amount (e.g., $100) of bail reflected the precarious financial situation in which many of the women found themselves. Furthermore, they knew no one who would come forward to bail them out, either due to their acquaintances' lack of financial resources or the absence of individuals in their social networks they could rely on for this type of assistance.

NOTES

INTRODUCTION

1. Hispanics, who constituted an estimated 15 percent of the general population in 2007, accounted for 20.8 percent of prison inmates. The disproportion among African Americans was even more pronounced: making up only 13.5 percent of the general population in 2007, they nevertheless accounted for 38.2 percent of prison inmates (H. C. West and Sabol 2008).

2. Although the rate at which women are being imprisoned has increased much more rapidly than men's in the last several years, the inmate population remains overwhelmingly male: in 2007, men represented 93.1 percent of the nation's prison population (H. C. West and Sabol 2008) and 87.1 percent of the jail population (Sabol and Minton 2008).

3. In 2001, the Annie E. Casey Foundation and Women's Prison Association estimated that ten million children had "parents who have been imprisoned at some point during the children's lives" (2001, 8).

4. Given the unique characteristics of separation caused by incarceration, it would be important to know whether such separations affect children differently than separations for other causes. Unfortunately, little research has been done that compares prisoners' offspring with children separated from their parents for other reasons, and results from what has been done are far from conclusive. Although an early study found that prisoners' children did not differ significantly from children separated from their fathers due to divorce in terms of their self-concept, relationships with their parents, or their sense of locus of control (Moerk 1973), a more recent study found that children separated from their parents due to incarceration were far more likely to be delinquent and to be classified as having antisocial personalities throughout their lives than were children separated from their parents for other reasons (Murray and Farrington 2005).

5. Studies from other countries, such as England (Shaw 1987), Ireland (Dublin Institute of Technology Centre for Social and Educational Research 2002), Israel (Lowenstein 1986), and South Africa (Skinner and Swartz 1989), have documented reactions to parental incarceration similar to those reported among children in the United States.

6. Early research reporting various emotional, behavioral, and academic difficulties among children includes the work of Baunach (1985); Bloom and Steinhardt (1993); Friedman and Esselstyn (1965); Fritsch and Burkhead (1981); Hunter (1984); Lowenstein (1986); Sack, Seidler, and Thomas (1976); and Skinner and Swartz (1989). More recent research includes that of Arditti, Lambert-Shute, and Joest (2003);

Hanlon et al. (2005); D. Johnston (n.d.); Phillips et al. (2002); Trice and Brewster (2004); and Wilbur et al. (2007).

7. See, for instance, Farrington et al. (2001); Lipsey and Derzon (1998); Loeber and Dishion (1983); and Robins, West, and Herjanic (1975).

8. Many of the researchers who report that children experience psychological and behavioral difficulties (see note 6) also document reports of aggressive behavior. In addition, see Gabel and Shindledecker (1992, 1993a); Sack (1977).

9. Studies examining the criminal histories of children of incarcerated parents include Huebner and Gustafson (2007); Phillips et al. (2002); and Trice and Brewster (2004).

10. Exceptions in the research literature include the work of Boswell and Wedge (2002) in England and the recent work of Nesmith and Ruhland (2008). See also Bernstein (2005) and the report entitled "No-one's Ever Asked Me" issued by the Federation of Prisoners' Families Support Groups in London.

11. Also, for reasons of personal safety, I felt more comfortable at the prospect of going into women's homes alone than into men's.

12. The sample comprised more mothers than children because, in some cases, the child was unavailable for interviewing after the mother was interviewed, despite both individuals' initial agreement to participate. For instance, on the date of one scheduled interview, I arrived at a child's house only to learn that the child's father had been released from prison the day before and the child had gone to his grandmother's for the homecoming festivities. I interviewed the mother that day, with assurances that the child would be available the next day. However, despite my repeated attempts to schedule an interview with the child, the mother finally informed me that she believed the child simply would never schedule an interview. On another occasion, I interviewed the mother in prison and her daughter had agreed to be interviewed at home. When I arrived at the child's home, no one was home, although I had spoken to the child just minutes before by phone to verify the address. Despite repeated calls and letters, I was never able to reach the child again.

13. Two of the mothers whom I interviewed at home were in jail when first recruited but subsequently released before the interviews.

14. For instance, nearly 30 percent of female but only 8 percent of male prisoners were receiving welfare before incarceration, according to the most recent national survey of prisoners available (Greenfeld and Snell 1999). Female prisoners with children are even more likely to receive assistance, with 42 percent reporting that they received some form of transfer payment from the government (Bloom and Steinhart 1993), a rate that is more than three times that for men (Glaze and Maruschak 2008). According to a national survey of prisoners in 2004, 53 percent of mothers in state prison had incomes under $1,000 in the month before their arrest, compared to 33.3 percent of men in state prison (Glaze and Maruschak 2008). If that monthly income was typical of their earnings, then they were earning less than $12,000 annually, an income level that places them well below the poverty threshold of $15,219 for a family of three (i.e., an adult and two children) in 2004 (DeNavas-Walt, Proctor, and Lee 2005). Furthermore, just over half (51.9 percent) of mothers in state prison said that they provided the primary financial support for their children before they were incarcerated, and nearly one in three of them had incomes under $600 the month before they were imprisoned (Glaze and Maruschak 2008). Children in such low-income families would be considered to be living in extreme poverty, which would leave them more vulnerable to any ill effects of economic hardship. A significant minority

(16.7 percent) of prisoners' children are under age five (Glaze and Maruschak 2008), which places them among those for whom poverty exerts the most direct influence on cognitive ability and achievement.

15. For information on women and drug offenses, see Green et al. (2005); Greene, Haney, and Hurtado (2000); McClellan, Farabee, and Crouch (1997); Mumola and Karberg (2006); Owen and Bloom (1995); and Schafer and Dellinger (1999).

16. For instance, the most recent national surveys of prisoners available found that 57.2 percent of women in state prisons report having been victims of violence at some point before their incarceration, with 45 percent reporting they were victimized as adults (Harlow 1999). Smaller-scale studies using other methods of questioning respondents and measuring victimization report even higher rates of adult sexual and physical victimization, some as high as 93 percent (Browne, Miller, and Maguin 1999; DeHart 2004; Girshick 1999; Islam-Zwart and Vik 2004; Richie 1996; Sheridan 1996; Singer et al. 1995). By contrast, nationally representative surveys of nonprison populations find that about 25 percent of women report having been raped and/or physically assaulted (Tjaden and Thoennes 2000).

Given these extremely high victimization rates, we can expect that children of prisoners will be much more likely to witness violence at home than will other children. When Susan Greene and her colleagues (2000) interviewed 102 inmate mothers in California, 70 percent of them reported that their children had witnessed violence at home, much of it involving instances where the mother herself was abused. Other researchers investigating women prisoners' histories of victimization have found that many expressed concerns about their children witnessing the violence perpetrated against them and the potential effect this has on the children (DeHart 2004).

17. For example, 79 percent of mothers in prison in Wisconsin scored in the clinical range for depression, a rate four times higher than that for the general population (Poehlmann 2005b). Sheridan (1996) found that the majority of female inmates in his study had scores at or above the clinical cutoff for nine of thirteen symptoms measured, including depression, aggression, problems with family members, and problems with friends. Such high rates are consistent with findings from a national survey of prison and jail inmates conducted by the U. S. Department of Justice (James and Glaze 2006), which found that approximately three-quarters of incarcerated women had mental health problems, a rate more than six times that of women in the general population. Furthermore, mental health problems were associated with several other indicators of social ills.

18. Evidence indicates that children who live in poverty over the long term are those most affected by low income. Furthermore, extreme poverty seems to have more detrimental effects than more moderate levels of poverty. In addition, the timing of exposure to poverty matters, with the long-term effects most pronounced for children who experience poverty before the age of six (Duncan et al. 1998). However, the impact of family income appears to lessen as children age because the importance of extrafamilial factors, such as peer influences and the quality of schooling, increases. In poor neighborhoods, these factors can contribute to outcomes like school dropout and delinquency.

19. For instance, about half the effect that income exerts on young children's cognitive ability is explained by their home environment through factors such as the quality of parent-child interactions and the physical condition of the home environment (J. R. Smith, Brooks-Gunn, and Klebanov 1997).

20. High school dropouts and individuals whose highest degree is a high school diploma earn significantly less than people with more education (Day and Newburger 2002). A 1997 survey of state prisoners found that 44 percent of women in state prison had not graduated from high school and the highest level of education for another 39 percent was high school or a GED (Greenfeld and Snell 1999). These rates are similar to those of an earlier report which found that 55 percent of imprisoned mothers had less than a high school degree (Bloom and Steinhart 1993).

21. There is even some evidence of the effect that a mother's educational level can exert on prisoners' children from a study of the children of 36 mothers in a Virginia prison. The high dropout rate (36 percent) among their children was significantly related to the mother's level of education, with 52 percent of children whose mothers were dropouts dropping out, compared to only 15 percent of those whose mothers had completed high school (Trice and Brewster 2004).

22. In addition to being at risk of alcoholism themselves, alcoholics' children have an increased chance of delinquency, truancy and academic problems, child abuse victimization, anxiety, and depression (Chassin et al. 1999; Dube et al. 2001; J. L. Johnson and Leff 1999; M. O. West and Prinz 1987). Less is known about the effects of parental drug abuse on children, but available research indicates that children of drug abusers are at risk of similar negative consequences, including aggression (Dunlap, Johnson, and Rath 1996; Gabel and Shindledecker 1993b); delinquent and antisocial behavior and substance abuse (Kandel, Simcha-Fagan, and Davies 1986; Kumpfer 1987; Nurco et al. 1999); achievement and behavioral problems at school (Kolar et al. 1994; Sowder and Burt 1980); family breakup, running away, and foster-care placement (Kolar et al. 1994; McKeganey, Barnard, and McIntosh 2002; Sowder and Burt 1980); psychological problems (Merikangas, Dierker, and Szatmari 1998; VanDeMark et al. 2005); and being subjected to physical abuse and harsh discipline (Kolar et al. 1994; McKeganey, Barnard, and McIntosh 2002).

23. See Dunlap, Johnson, and Julia Ruth 1996; Johnson, Dunlap, and Maher 1998; Nurco et al. 1998; and Straus, Gelles, and Steinmetz 1980.

24. As Eloise Dunlap, Bruce Johnson, and Rath (1996) pointed out in their ethnographic studies of crack abusers' households: "Drugs come first; other responsibilities come later—if they are thought about at all" (literature review section, para. 7).

25. Compared to children who are not exposed to community or domestic violence, youths who witness violence in their homes and neighborhoods are more likely to engage in aggressive behavior, experience academic difficulties, and develop psychological problems like post-traumatic stress disorder and depression (Buka et al. 2001; Edleson 1999; Fitzpatrick and Boldiza, 1993; Fox 2000; Heyman and Slep 2002; Hurt et al. 2001; Kitzmann et al. 2003). The environment of children raised in families where a parent has mental health problems also may increase the likelihood of poor outcomes for them (Beardslee, Versage, and Giadstone 1998; VanDeMark et al. 2005).

26. Denise Johnston (1995) of the Center for Children of Incarcerated Parents has theorized about the ways in which a parent's incarceration is likely to affect the development of children of various ages. For an infant, for instance, separation from a parent can interfere with the bonding that normally occurs between a parent and child in the years immediately after birth. Children whose parents are imprisoned during the early childhood years, ages two to six, may be more susceptible to long-term negative effects than any other age group. Johnston theorizes that the

trauma these children experience as a result of their parent's criminal behavior, arrest, and imprisonment may interfere with their development of autonomy and initiative. During middle childhood and early adolescence, children may have difficulty learning to work with others and may develop maladaptive behaviors, including aggression. By the time children reach their late teenage years, they may have had significant experience with parental incarceration, and Johnston suggests that many will themselves be engaging in delinquent behavior and at risk of incarceration.

CHAPTER 1   LIVING WITH MOM–MOST OF THE TIME

1. Shaquilla's interview was recorded by hand, so there is some paraphrasing in this quote. However, it accurately reflects the substance of what was said.

2. For instance, the state penal code stipulates that statutory sexual assault occurs when someone who is four or more years older than a complainant engages in sexual intercourse with a complainant who is under the age of sixteen and the two are not married to each other. The offense is classified as a felony of the second degree.

3. Although Jeremiah lived with just one sibling, he was the youngest of four children. His two oldest siblings were being raised by relatives in another state because Tiffany, a teenager at the time, had been unable to care for them when they were babies.

4. At the time Tiffany was arrested for her current offense, they had been staying at the home of Tiffany's girlfriend's mother, who was herself in jail.

5. The less than private conditions at this facility initially raised concerns that our conversation might be overheard. When we entered the room, two or three prisoners were meeting with their lawyers at tables at the front of the space, near where the correctional officers were sitting. However, we were permitted to seat ourselves at the far corner of the room, diagonally opposite the others, making it extremely unlikely that our conversation could be overheard. However, everyone surely heard Lucinda's loud sobs when her son entered the room. Ultimately, I prevailed upon the guards to permit her to cross the room to embrace her son. Information about Lucinda and her family is based not only on this interview but also on several conversations we had in a private room at the jail in the city sample, as well as interviews with another son, Ian, and his grandmother.

6. This proportion is less than might have been expected based on estimates of the prevalence of mental disorders among incarcerated populations. I did not explicitly ask the women about a history of mental illness, so only those who spontaneously mentioned it were counted as having a mental illness. However, given the extent of substance abuse among the mothers and the high rates of co-occurrence of substance abuse and mental disorder, it is likely that other women in the study in fact had mental disorders.

7. This episode might have warranted a report to the child protective services agency, but the family was already under their supervision, with a court hearing already scheduled.

CHAPTER 2   OUTSIDE THE CURTAINED WINDOWS

1. Some evidence suggests racial variation in the connection between adult-child relationships and a child's development, with white children benefiting the most from involvement of nonrelated adults (Marshall et al. 2001).

2. The schools themselves report on the number of low-income children among their students. They generally define as low-income those students who are eligible for free or reduced-price lunches.

3. Information on city schools was obtained from the state's department of education and extensive data published by one of the city's major newspapers. References to these sources, however, would reveal the identity of the city and thus have been omitted.

4. Individuals under the age of eighteen are permitted to drive only if a licensed driver aged eighteen or older is in the car. They are not permitted to drive at all between the hours of 11:00 PM and 5:00 AM.

5. Actually, he had not beaten his case; it had been postponed while some assessment was done. Eventually, Peter was adjudicated delinquent on this charge and placed on probation.

CHAPTER 3   THE UBIQUITY OF VIOLENCE

1. When Lucinda was released from jail after several weeks, she came back to her family's house with a firm resolve not to use drugs again. Six days later, her brother's girlfriend invited her to smoke some crack with her and Lucinda was lost to the streets again—until her next arrest.

2. Nicole was not the only youth who saw a benefit to arrest. One ten-year-old boy described his neighborhood as "cool" because "everybody locked up like, ain't nothin' goin' on around here. You know, like all the people that used to be out in the street locked up now." Apparently, the shooting that used to occur in his neighborhood had stopped, although fights in the streets continued, including one in which his mother was involved, resulting in her arrest.

3. Researchers have examined the effects of various forms of violence exposure on children. For recent reviews of studies that investigate the impact of domestic violence on child witnesses, see Edleson (1999); Onyskiw (2003); Wolak and Finkelhor (1998). Several others assess how children are affected by exposure to extrafamilial violence in the community (for reviews, see Buka et al. 2001; Lynch 2003; Overstreet 2000). Hundreds of studies have examined the consequences of the various forms of child abuse and neglect (for reviews of the consequences of physical abuse, see Malinosky-Rummell and Hansen 1993; Runyon et al. 2004; Trickett and McBride-Chang 1995). A considerable body of evidence shows that even nonabusive forms of corporal punishment, such as spanking, have serious detrimental consequences for children (Gershoff 2002; Straus 2001), although this is not a settled question (Benjet and Kazdin 2003). Furthermore, evidence suggests that the form of victimization matters less than the fact of it: the effects of witnessing violence are remarkably like those associated with the experience of being victimized directly (Kitzmann et al. 2003).

CHAPTER 4   WHEN THE CRIMINAL JUSTICE
SYSTEM COMES CALLING

1. One of the earliest books to draw attention to the plight of children of prisoners, *Why Punish the Children?* reports the results of the work undertaken in 1978 by the National Council on Crime and Delinquency (McGowan and Blumenthal 1978). The authors also discuss aspects of a parent's arrest experience that affected children in ways that had received scant attention previously. The book provided much needed recognition that a parent's arrest can be a traumatic event for children.

2. Four days after I first visited with Peter at his mother's house, the police returned and broke down the too-small door. According to Peter, this time they had a warrant to search the premises because they were trying to find one of his older friends who occasionally stayed there with him.

3. Relatively little information exists about police policy with respect to arrestees' children, but a national survey conducted by the American Bar Association published in 1994 found that although a majority of police departments that responded had written policies for dealing with children when a parent is arrested, more than four in ten rarely inquired whether a person being arrested had children (Smith and Elstein 1994). However, the sample size for the ABA survey was too small for the results to be generalizable to departments nationwide. More recently, a larger study in California found that nearly two-thirds of police departments in that state had no written policy about whether or how to assume responsibility for a child when a parent is arrested. Furthermore, officers in only 13 percent of California law enforcement agencies regularly inquire about whether an arrestee has children when an arrest is made (Nieto 2002). A recent report by the Council of State Governments Justice Center concluded that "most law enforcement agencies have no policies to guide officers responding when children are present at the scene of an arrest not involving abuse or neglect" (Nickel, Garland, and Kane 2009, 9). Thus, explicit policies that provide guidance to officers are the exception, not the rule, in this country.

4. Well-publicized but rare cases like that of Faheem Williams in New Jersey in 2003 illustrate the possible perils of leaving the parent to choose a caretaker, particularly when the parent has mental health issues. Faheem's mother left him and her two other children with her cousin when she left to serve a sentence for child endangerment. During the months the children were under the cousin's care, Faheem was killed by the cousin's son, his body dumped in a storage bin in the basement where the other two sons were eventually found, emaciated and burned (Purdy, Jacobs, and Jones 2003).

5. For a summary of case law on the issue of police responsibility for children when a parent is arrested, see Moses and Girouard (2005).

CHAPTER 5   THEY ALL DO THE TIME

1. Belinda's interview was recorded by hand, so there is some paraphrasing in this quote. However, it accurately reflects the substance of what was said.

2. Marilyn, Valenica's mother, in fact was trying her best to be a good mother to her children under the circumstances. She had been arrested and incarcerated in a state quite distant from where Valencia and her grandmother lived, which made it all but impossible for her children to see her. Through amazing perseverance and determination, Marilyn managed to persuade the correctional authorities in the state where she was imprisoned to send her to a state whose women's prison was closest to Valencia's grandmother's residence. As a result, Valencia and her family could visit Marilyn much more easily than was the case during her first three years in prison hundreds of miles from her children.

3. Although not the case in this study, some children are never told that their parent is in prison; bringing them there for a visit would reveal the truth. As a result, the children never see their parent during the parent's incarceration. Interestingly, however, I have spoken with women who have taken their children to visit their father in prison for years and maintain that their children do not know that they are visiting a prison.

4. The angry grandmother's son, who was the father of all the children, did not live with her and contributed almost nothing to the children's care. Nevertheless, the grandmother clearly blamed the children's mother, not her son, for the situation in which she found herself.

CHAPTER 6   WHAT LIES AHEAD

1. A meta-analysis of sixteen studies found that children of incarcerated parents have approximately a twofold risk of antisocial behavior and delinquency. However, the authors concluded that the quality of the studies analyzed was such that parental incarceration still cannot be deemed a causal risk factor for these outcomes (Murray et al. 2009).

2. This phenomenon is not new. In her study of women in prison published in 1964, Serapio Zalba discussed caretakers who were angry with or hostile toward the woman in prison or disapproved of her behavior and who therefore failed to facilitate visits between the children and the mothers.

3. John's memories of the places he had lived with his mother did not correspond to his or his mother's description of the place they were living at the time of her arrest. She described it as an "abandominium," the "absolute pits." John was living there on his own after his mother's arrest, and he would not allow me to come there to conduct an interview, claiming the place was in too great a state of disrepair.

4. Vanessa's interview was recorded by hand, so some quotes by her are not exact. However, the quotes accurately reflect the substance of what she said.

5. Transportation to men's facilities was similarly scarce: only 18 percent had subsidized transportation available for visiting family members and 16 percent reported that public transit was available (Hoffmann, Byrd, and Adams 2007).

APPENDIX B   A PORTRAIT OF THE CHILDREN
AND THEIR MOTHERS

1. One incident that involved an African American family did make clear that at least that family was afraid that I was not who I said I was. I had interviewed the mother in jail after she assured me that her child would participate. When I arrived at the house where the child was staying with his mother's sister, his aunt denied that he was there, going so far as to claim that her sister had no school-age children. When I returned to the jail and talked with the mother again, she told me that her sister had been afraid that I was from the state foster-care agency and was there to take the child. Despite the mother's reassurances to her sister, I was never able to interview the child.

BIBLIOGRAPHY

Ackerman, B. P., Brown, E. D., D'Eramo, K. S., & Izard, C. E. (2002). Maternal relationship instability and the school behavior of children from disadvantaged families. *Developmental Psychology, 38*(5), 694–704.

Agnew, R. (1992). Foundation for a general strain theory of crime and delinquency. *Criminology, 30*(1), 47–87.

Agnew, R. (2001). Building on the foundation of general strain theory: Specifying the types of strain most likely to lead to crime and delinquency. *Journal of Research in Crime & Delinquency, 38*(4), 319–361.

Aisenberg, E., & Herrenkohl, T. (2008). Community violence in context: Risk and resilience in children and families. *Journal of Interpersonal Violence, 23*(3), 296–315.

Akers, R. L., Krohn, M. D., Lanza-Kaduce, L., & Radosevich, M. (1979). Social learning and deviant behavior: A specific test of a general theory. *American Sociological Review, 44*(4), 636–655.

American Correctional Association. (1990). *The Female Offender: What Does the Future Hold?* Laurel, MD: American Correctional Association.

Anderson, E. (1999). *Code of the Street: Decency, Violence, and the Moral Life of the Inner City.* New York: W. W. Norton.

Annie E. Casey Foundation and Women's Prison Association. (2001). *Partnerships between corrections and child welfare: Collaboration for change, part two.* (22 pp.). Baltimore: Annie E. Casey Foundation.

Arditti, J. A., & Few, A. L. (2006). Mothers' reentry into family life following incarceration. *Criminal Justice Policy Review, 17*(1), 103–123.

Arditti, J. A., Lambert-Shute, J., & Joest, K. (2003). Saturday morning at the jail: Implications of incarceration for families and children. *Family Relations: Journal of Applied Family & Child Studies, 52*(3), 195–204.

Bandura, A. (1973). *Aggression: A Social Learning Analysis.* Englewood Cliffs, NJ: Prentice-Hall.

Baunach, P. J. (1985). *Mothers in Prison.* New Brunswick, NJ: Transaction Books, Rutgers University Press.

Beardslee, W. R., Versage, E. M., & Gladstone, T.R.G. (1998). Children of affectively ill parents: A review of the past 10 years. *Journal of the American Academy of Child & Adolescent Psychiatry 37*(11), 1134–1141.

Belknap, J. (2001). *The Invisible Woman: Gender, Crime, and Justice* (2nd ed.). New York: Wadsworth.

Benjet, C., & Kazdin, A. E. (2003). Spanking children: The controversies, findings and new directions. *Clinical Psychology Review, 23*(2), 197–224.

Bernstein, N. (2005). *All Alone in the World: Children of the Incarcerated.* New York: New Press.

Biblarz, T. J., & Raftery, A. E. (1993). The effects of family disruption on social mobility. *American Sociological Review, 58*(1), 97–109.

Block, K. J., & Potthast, M. J. (1998). Girl scouts beyond bars: Facilitating parent-child contact in correctional settings. *Child Welfare, 77*(5), 561–578.

Bloom, B., Owen, B., & Covington, S. (2003). *Gender-responsive strategies: Research, practice, and guiding principles for women offenders.* (142 pp.). Washington, D. C.: U. S. Department of Justice, National Institute of Corrections.

Bloom, B., & Steinhart, D. (1993). *Why Punish the Children? A Reappraisal of the Children of Incarcerated Mothers in America.* Newark, NJ: National Council on Crime and Delinquency.

Bonczar, T. P. (2003). *Prevalence of imprisonment in the U.S. population, 1974–2001.* Washington, DC: U.S. Department of Justice, Bureau of Justice Statistics.

Boswell, G., & Wedge, P. (2002). *Imprisoned Fathers and Their Children.* London: Jessica Kingsley.

Bowlby, J. (1979). *The Making and Breaking of Affectional Bonds.* London: Tavistock.

Bowles, S., Gintis, H., & Groves, M. O. (Eds.). (2005). *Unequal Chances: Family Background and Economic Success.* Princeton, NJ: Princeton University Press.

Bradley, R. H., & Corwyn, R. F. (2002). Socioeconomic status and child development. *Annual Review of Psychology, 53,* 371–399.

Bronfenbrenner, U. (1979). *The Ecology of Human Development: Experiments by Nature and Design.* Cambridge, MA: Harvard University Press.

Brooks-Gunn, J., & Duncan, G. J. (1997). The effects of poverty on children. *The Future of Children, 7*(2), 55–71.

Brown, K., Dibb, L., Shenton, F., & Elson, N. (2001). *No-one's ever asked me: Young people with a prisoner in the family.* London: Federation of Prisoners' Families Support Groups.

Browne, A., Miller, B., & Maguin, E. (1999). Prevalence and severity of lifetime physical and sexual victimization among incarcerated women. *International Journal of Law and Psychiatry, 22*(3–4), 301–322.

Buka, S. L., Stichick, T. L., Birdthistle, I., & Earls, F. J. (2001). Youth exposure to violence: Prevalence, risks, and consequences. *American Journal of Orthopsychiatry, 71*(3), 298–310.

Bureau of Justice Statistics. (2005). *Sourcebook of Criminal Justice Statistics,* http://www.albany.edu/sourcebook/ (Table 3.60).

Bureau of Justice Statistics. (2009). *Sourcebook of Criminal Justice Statistics,* http://www.albany.edu/sourcebook/ (Table 6.1.2006).

Campbell, C., & Schwarz, D. F. (1996). Prevalence and impact of exposure to interpersonal violence among suburban and urban middle school students. *Pediatrics, 98*(3), 396–402.

Carothers, S. S., Borkowski, J. G., & Whitman, T. L. (2006). Children of adolescent mothers: Exposure to negative life events and the role of social supports on their socioemotional adjustment. *Journal of Youth and Adolescence, 35*(5), 827–837.

Center for Children of Incarcerated Parents. (2006). *How many children of incarcerated parents are there?* CCIP Data Sheet 3a. Retrieved July 28, 2006, from http://www.e-ccip.org/publication.html#cciptop.

Chassin, L., Pitts, S. C., DeLucia, C., & Todd, M. (1999). A longitudinal study of children of alcoholics: Predicting young adult substance use disorders, anxiety, and depression. *Journal of Abnormal Psychology, 108*(1), 106–119.

Chesney-Lind, M. (1997). *The Female Offender: Girls, Women, and Crime.* Thousand Oaks, CA: Sage Publications.

Cochran, M. M., & Brassard, J. A. (1979). Child development and personal social networks. *Child Development, 50*(3), 601–616.

Confessore, N. (2007, January 9). Spitzer orders sharp cuts in cost of prisoner phone calls. *New York Times*, p. 2.

Corcoran, M. (1995). Rags to rags: Poverty and mobility in the United States. *Annual Review of Sociology, 21*, 237–267.

Coulton, C. J., Crampton, D. S., Irwin, M., Spilsbury, J. C., & Korbin, J. E. (2007). How neighborhoods influence child maltreatment: A review of the literature and alternative pathways. *Child Abuse & Neglect, 31*(11–12), 1117–1142.

Dallaire, D. H. (2007). Incarcerated mothers and fathers: A comparison of risks for children and families. *Family Relations, 56*(5), 440–453.

Davies, E., Brazzell, D., La Vigne, N. G., & Shollenberger, T. (2008). *Understanding the experiences and needs of children of incarcerated parents: Views from mentors.* Baltimore: Urban Institute.

Day, J. C., & Newburger, E. C. (2002). *The big payoff: Educational attainment and synthetic estimates of work-life earnings.* Washington, DC: U. S. Census Bureau.

DeHart, D. (2004). *Pathways to prison: Impact of victimization in the lives of incarcerated women.* Columbia: University of South Carolina College of Social Work, Center for Child & Family Studies.

DeNavas-Walt, C., Proctor, B. D., & Lee, C. H. (2005). *Income, Poverty, and Health Insurance Coverage in the United States: 2004.* Washington, DC: U.S. Government Printing Office. Retrieved from http://www.census.gov/prod/2005pubs/p60–229.pdf.

Dube, S. R., Anda, R. F., Felitti, V. J., Croft, J. B., Edwards, V. J., & Giles, W. H. (2001). Growing up with parental alcohol abuse: Exposure to childhood abuse, neglect, and household dysfunction. *Child Abuse & Neglect, 25*(12), 1627–1640.

Dublin Institute of Technology Centre for Social and Educational Research. (2002). *Parents, children, and prison: Effects of parental imprisonment on children.* Dublin, Ireland: Centre for Social & Educational Research, Dublin Institute of Technology.

DuBois, D. L., Holloway, B. E., Valentine, J. C., & Cooper, H. (2002). Effectiveness of mentoring programs for youth: A meta-analytic review. *American Journal of Community Psychology, 30*(2), 157–197.

DuBois, D. L., & Rhodes, J. E. (2006). Introduction to the special issue: Youth mentoring: Bridging science with practice. *Journal of Community Psychology, 34*(6), 647–655.

DuBois, D. L., & Silverthorn, N. (2005). Natural mentoring relationships and adolescent health: Evidence from a national study. *American Journal of Public Health, 95*(3), 518–524.

Dugdale, R. L. (1910). *The Jukes: A Study in Crime, Pauperism, Diseases, and Heredity* (4th ed.). New York: G. P. Putnam's Sons.

Duncan, G. J., & Brooks-Gunn, J. (1997). *Consequences of Growing Up Poor.* New York: Russell Sage Foundation.

Duncan, G. J., Yeung, W. J., Brooks-Gunn, J., & Smith, J. R. (1998). How much does childhood poverty affect the life chances of children? *American Sociological Review, 63*(3), 406–423.

Dunlap, E., Johnson, B. D., & Rath, J. W. (1996). Aggression and violence in households of crack seller/abusers [electronic version]. *Applied Behavioral Science Review, 4*(2), 191–217.

DuRant, R. H., Cadenhead, C., Pendergrast, R. A., Slavens, G., & Linder, C. W. (1994). Factors associated with the use of violence among urban black adolescents. *American Journal of Public Health, 84*(4), 612–617.

Eccles, J. S., Barber, B. L., Stone, M., & Hunt, J. (2003). Extracurricular activities and adolescent development. *Journal of Social Issues, 59*(4), 865–889.

Edleson, J. L. (1999). Children's witnessing of adult domestic violence. *Journal of Interpersonal Violence, 14*(8), 839–870.

Elder, G. H., Jr. (1994). Time, human agency, and social change: Perspectives on the life course. *Social Psychology Quarterly, 57*(1), 4–15.

Elder, G. H., Jr. (1998). The life course as developmental theory. *Child Development, 69*(1), 1–12.

Farley, R. (1996). *The New American Reality: Who We Are, How We Got Here, Where We Are Going.* New York: Russell Sage Foundation.

Farrington, D. P., Jolliffe, D., Loeber, R., Stouthamer-Loeber, M., & Kalb, L. M. (2001). The concentration of offenders in families, and family criminality in the prediction of boys' delinquency. *Journal of Adolescence, 24*(5), 579–596.

Fitzpatrick, K. M. (1997). Aggression and environmental risk among low-income African-American youth. *Journal of Adolescent Health, 21*(3), 172–178.

Fitzpatrick, K. M., & Boldizar, J. P. (1993). The prevalence and consequences of exposure to violence among African-American youth. *Journal of the American Academy of Child and Adolescent Psychiatry, 32*(2), 424–430.

Ford, F. M. (1955). *The Good Soldier: A Tale of Passion.* New York: Vintage Books.

Fox, G. L. (2000). No time for innocence, no place for innocents: Children's exposure to extreme violence. In G. L. Fox & M. L. Benson (Eds.), *Families, Crime, and Criminal Justice* (Vol. 2, pp. 163–181). New York: JAI.

Friedman, S., & Esselstyn, T. C. (1965). The adjustment of children of jail inmates. *Federal Probation, 29*, 55–59.

Fritsch, T. A., & Burkhead, J. D. (1981). Behavioral reactions of children to parental absence due to imprisonment. *Family Relations, 30*(1), 83–88.

Gabel, S. (1992). Behavioral problems in sons of incarcerated or otherwise absent fathers: The issue of separation. *Family Process, 31*(3), 303–314.

Gabel, S. (1993). Paternal incarceration and family dysfunction: Relationships to antisocial behavior in male youth. *Child and Adolescent Mental Health Care, 3*(3), 229–239.

Gabel, S., & Shindledecker, R. (1992). Incarceration in parents of day hospital youth: Relationship to parental substance abuse and suspected child abuse/maltreatment. *International Journal of Partial Hospitalization, 8*(1), 77–87.

Gabel, S., & Shindledecker, R. (1993a). Characteristics of children whose parents have been incarcerated. *Hospital & Community Psychiatry, 44*(7), 656–660.

Gabel, S., & Shindledecker, R. (1993b). Parental substance abuse and its relationship to severe aggression and antisocial behavior in youth. *American Journal on Addictions, 2*(1), 48–58.

Garmezy, N. (1983). Stressors of childhood. In M. Rutter & N. Garmezy (Eds.), *Stress, Coping, and Development in Children* (pp. 43–84). New York: McGraw Hill.

Garmezy, N. (1991). Resiliency and vulnerability to adverse developmental outcomes associated with poverty. *American Behavioral Scientist, 34*(4), 416–430.

Gershoff, E. T. (2002). Corporal punishment by parents and associated child behaviors and experiences: A meta-analytic and theoretical review. *Psychological Bulletin, 128*(4), 539–579.

Girshick, L. B. (1999). *No Safe Haven: Stories of Women in Prison.* Boston: Northeastern University Press.

Glaze, L. E., & Maruschak, L. M. (2008). *Parents in prison and their minor children.* Washington, DC: U.S. Department of Justice, Bureau of Justice Statistics.

Graue, M. E., & Walsh, D. J. (1998). *Studying Children in Context: Theories, Methods, and Ethics.* Thousand Oaks, CA: Sage Publications.

Green, B. L., Miranda, J., Daroowalla, A., & Siddique, J. (2005). Trauma exposure, mental health functioning, and program needs of women in jail. *Crime and Delinquency, 51*(1), 133–151. doi: 10.1177/0011128704267477.

Greenberger, E., Chen, C., & Beam, M. R. (1998). The role of "very important" nonparental adults in adolescent development. *Journal of Youth and Adolescence, 27*(3), 321–343.

Greene, S., Haney, C., & Hurtado, A. (2000). Cycles of pain: Risk factors in the lives of incarcerated mothers and their children. *Prison Journal, 80*(1), 3–23.

Greenfeld, L. A., & Snell, T. L. (1999). *Women offenders.* Washington, DC: U. S. Department of Justice, Bureau of Justice Statistics.

Groves, B. M., & Zuckerman, B. (1997). Interventions with parents and caregivers of children who are exposed to violence. In J. D. Osofsky (Ed.), *Children in a Violent Society* (pp. 183–201). New York: Guilford Press.

Hagen, K. A., Myers, B. J., & Mackintosh, V. H. (2005). Hope, social support, and behavioral problems in at-risk children. *American Journal of Orthopsychiatry, 75*(2), 211–219.

Hairston, C. F. (1988). Family ties during imprisonment: Do they influence future criminal activity? *Federal Probation, 52*(1), 48–52.

Hairston, C. F. (2007). *Focus on children with incarcerated parents: An overview of the research literature.* Baltimore, MD: Annie E. Casey Foundation.

Haney, C. (2003). The psychological impact of incarceration: Implications for postprison adjustment. In J. Travis, M. Waul, & C. Haney (Eds.), *Prisoners Once Removed: The Impact of Incarceration and Reentry on Children, Families, and Communities* (pp. 33–66). Washington, DC: Urban Institute Press.

Hanlon, T. E., Blatchley, R. J., Bennett-Sears, T., O'Grady, K. E., Rose, M., & Callaman, J. M. (2005). Vulnerability of children of incarcerated addict mothers: Implications for preventive intervention. *Children and Youth Services Review, 27*(1), 67–84.

Harlow, C. W. (1999). *Prior abuse reported by inmates and probationers.* Washington, DC: U. S. Department of Justice, Bureau of Justice Statistics.

Hawkins, J. D., Herrenkohl, T., Farrington, D. P., Brewer, D., Catalano, R. F., & Harachi, T. W. (1998). A review of predictors of youth violence. In R. Loeber & D. P. Farrington (Eds.), *Serious and Violent Juvenile Offenders: Risk Factors and Successful Interventions* (pp. 106–146). Thousand Oaks, CA: Sage Publications.

Hawkins, W. E., & Duncan, D. F. (1985). Perpetrator and family characteristics related to child abuse and neglect: Comparison of substantiated and unsubstantiated reports. *Psychological Reports, 56*(2), 407–410.

Heinz, W. R., & Marshall, V. W. (Eds.). (2003). *Social Dynamics of the Life Course: Transitions, Institutions, and Interrelations.* Hawthorne, NY: Aldine de Gruyter.

Heyman, R. E., & Slep, A.M.S. (2002). Do child abuse and interparental violence lead to adulthood family violence? *Journal of Marriage and the Family, 64*(4), 864–870.

Hoffmann, H. C., Byrd, A., & Adams, A. (2007, November 15). *The Prevalence and Nature of Prison Programs and Services for Prisoners with Underage Children.* Paper presented at the American Society of Criminology, Atlanta.

Homer, E. L. (1979). Inmate-family ties: Desirable but difficult. *Federal Probation, 43*(1), 47–52.

Hotaling, G. T., & Sugarman, D. B. (1986). An analysis of risk markers in husband to wife violence: The current state of knowledge. *Violence and Victims, 1*(2), 101–124.

Huebner, B. M., & Gustafson, R. (2007). The effect of maternal incarceration on adult off-spring involvement in the criminal justice system. *Journal of Criminal Justice, 35*(3), 283–296.

Hunter, S. M. (1984). *The Relationship between Women Offenders and Their Children.* Doctoral dissertation, Michigan State University, East Lansing.

Hurt, H., Malmud, E., Brodsky, N. L., & Giannetta, J. (2001). Exposure to violence: Psychological and academic correlates in child witnesses. *Archives of Pediatrics & Adolescent Medicine, 155*(12), 1351–1356.

Islam-Zwart, K. A., & Vik, P. W. (2004). Female adjustment to incarceration as influenced by sexual assault history. *Criminal Justice and Behavior, 31*(5), 521–541.

James, D. J. (2004). *Profile of jail inmates, 2002.* Washington, DC: U. S. Department of Justice, Bureau of Justice Statistics.

James, D. J., & Glaze, L. E. (2006). *Mental health problems of prison and jail inmates.* Washington, DC: U. S. Department of Justice, Bureau of Justice Statistics.

Johnson, B. D., Dunlap, E., & Maher, L. (1998). Nurturing for careers in drug use and crime: Conduct norms for children and juveniles in crack-using households. *Substance Use and Misuse, 33*(7), 1511–1546.

Johnson, J. L., & Leff, M. (1999). Children of substance abusers: Overview of research findings. *Pediatrics, 103*(5 Pt 2), 1085–1099.

Johnston, D. (1995). Effects of parental incarceration. In K. Gabel & D. Johnston (Eds.), *Children of Incarcerated Parents* (pp. 59–88). New York: Lexington Books.

Johnston, D. (2006). The wrong road: Efforts to understand the effects of parental crime and incarceration. *Criminology & Public Policy, 5*(4), 703–719.

Johnston, D. (N. D.). *Children of offenders.* Pasadena, CA: Center for Children of Incarcerated Parents.

Johnston, L. D., O'Malley, P. M., Bachman, J. G., & Schulenberg, J. E. (2007). *Monitoring the Future National Survey Results on Drug Use, 1975–2006:* Vol. I, *Secondary School Students.* Bethesda, MD: National Institute on Drug Abuse.

Jose-Kampfner, C. (1995). Post-traumatic stress reactions in children of incarcerated mothers. In K. Gabel & D. Johnston (Eds.), *Children of Incarcerated Parents* (pp. 89–100). New York: Lexington Books.

Kandel, D., Simcha-Fagan, O., & Davies, M. (1986). Risk factors for delinquency and illicit drug use from adolescence to young adulthood. *Journal of Drug Issues, 16*(1), 67–90.

Kaufman, P., Alt, M. N., & Chapman, C. D. (2004). *Dropout rates in the United States: 2001.* Washington, DC: U.S. Department of Education: National Center for Education Statistics.

Kitzmann, K. M., Gaylord, N. K., Holt, A. R., & Kenny, E. D. (2003). Child witnesses to domestic violence: A meta-analytic review. *Journal of Consulting & Clinical Psychology, 71*(2), 339–352.

Koban, L. A. (1983). Parents in prison: A comparative analysis of the effects of incarceration on the families of men and women. In S. Spitzer (Ed.), *Research in Law, Deviance, and Social Control: A Research Annual* (Vol. 5, pp. 171–183). Greenwich, CT: JAI Press.

Kolar, A. F., Brown, B. S., Haertzen, C. A., & Michaelson, B. S. (1994). Children of substance abusers: Experiences of children of opiate addicts in methadone maintenance. *American Journal of Drug & Alcohol Abuse, 20*(2), 159–171.

Krueger, R. F., Moffitt, T. E., Caspi, A., Bleske, A., & Silva, P. A. (1998). Assortative mating for antisocial behavior: Developmental and methodological implications. *Behavior Genetics, 28*(3), 173–186. doi: http://dx.doi.org/10.1023/A:1021419013124.

Kumpfer, K. L. (1987). Special populations: Etiology and prevention of vulnerability to chemical dependency in children of substance abusers. In B. S. Brown & A. R. Mills (Eds.), *Youth at High Risk for Substance Abuse* (pp. 1–72). Rockville, MD: National Institute on Drug Abuse.

Lareau, A. (2003). *Unequal Childhoods: Class, Race, and Family Life.* Berkeley: University of California Press.

Lipsey, M. W., & Derzon, J. H. (1998). Predictors of violent or serious delinquency in adolescence and early adulthood: A synthesis of longitudinal research. In R. Loeber &

D. P. Farrington (Eds.), *Serious and Violent Juvenile Offenders: Risk Factors and Successful Interventions* (pp. 86–105). Thousand Oaks, CA: Sage Publications.

Loeber, R., & Dishion, T. J. (1983). Early predictors of male delinquency: A review. *Psychological Bulletin, 94*(1), 68–99.

Lowenstein, A. (1986). Temporary single parenthood: The case of prisoners' families. *Family Relations, 36*(1), 79–85.

Lynch, M. (2003). Consequences of children's exposure to community violence. *Clinical Child and Family Psychology Review, 6*(4), 265–274.

Mahoney, J. L. (2000). School extracurricular activity participation as a moderator in the development of antisocial patterns. *Child Development, 71*(2), 502–516.

Mahoney, J. L., & Magnusson, D. (2001). Parent participation in community activities and the persistence of criminality. *Development and Psychopathology, 13*(1), 125–141.

Malinosky-Rummell, R., & Hansen, D. J. (1993). Long-term consequences of childhood physical abuse. *Psychological Bulletin, 114*, 68–79.

Margolin, G., & Gordis, E. B. (2000). The effects of family and community violence on children. *Annual Review of Psychology, 51*(1), 445–479.

Marshall, N. L., Noonan, A. E., McCartney, K., Marx, F., & Keefe, N. (2001). It takes an urban village: Parenting networks of urban families. *Journal of Family Issues, 22*(2), 163–182.

Martin, M. (1997). Connected mothers: A follow-up study of incarcerated women and their children. *Women & Criminal Justice, 8*(4), 1–23.

Mauer, M., Potler, C., & Wolf, R. (1999). *Gender and justice: Women, drugs, and sentencing policy.* Washington, DC: Sentencing Project.

McClellan, D. S., Farabee, D., & Crouch, B. M. (1997). Early victimization, drug use, and criminality: A comparison of male and female prisoners. *Criminal Justice and Behavior, 24*(4), 455–476.

McGowan, B. G., & Blumenthal, K. L. (1978). *Why Punish the Children? A Study of Children of Women Prisoners.* Hackensack, NJ: National Council on Crime and Delinquency.

McKeganey, N., Barnard, M., & McIntosh, J. (2002). Paying the price for their parents' addiction: Meeting the needs of the children of drug-abusing parents. *Drugs: Education, Prevention, & Policy, 9*(3), 233–246.

McLanahan, S. (2009). Fragile families and the reproduction of poverty. *Annals of the American Academy of Political and Social Science, 621*(1), 111–131. doi: 10.1177/0002716208324862.

McMahon, S. D., Grant, K. E., Compas, B. E., Thurm, A. E., & Ey, S. (2003). Stress and psychopathology in children and adolescents: Is there evidence of specificity? *Journal of Child Psychology and Psychiatry and Allied Disciplines, 44*(1), 107–133.

Merikangas, K. R., Dierker, L. C., & Szatmari, P. (1998). Psychopathology among offspring of parents with substance abuse and/or anxiety disorders: A high-risk study. *Journal of Child Psychology and Psychiatry, 39*(5), 711–720.

Mills, C. W. (1959). *The Sociological Imagination.* New York: Oxford University Press.

Moerk, E. L. (1973). Like father like son: Imprisonment of fathers and the psychological adjustment of sons. *Journal of Youth and Adolescence, 2*(4), 303–312.

Moffitt, T. E. (1993). Adolescence-limited and life-course-persistent antisocial behavior: A developmental taxonomy. *Psychological Review, 100*(4), 674–701.

Moore, K. A., Hatcher, J. L., Vandivere, S., & Brown, B. V. (2000). *Children's behavior and well-being: Findings from the national survey of America's families.* Retrieved September 21, 2007, from http://urban.org/UploadedPDF/900845_1999Snapshots.pdf.

Morash, M., & Schram, P. J. (2002). *The Prison Experience: Special Issues of Women in Prison.* Prospect Heights, IL: Waveland Press.

Moses, M. C., & Girouard, C. (2005). Written policies for responding to children after a parent or caretaker is arrested. *Police Chief, 72*(9). Retrieved from http://policechiefmagazine.org/.

Mumola, C. J. (1999). *Substance abuse and treatment, state and federal prisoners, 1997.* Washington, DC: U.S. Department of Justice, Bureau of Justice Statistics.

Mumola, C. J. (2000). *Incarcerated parents and their children.* Washington, DC: U.S. Department of Justice: Office of Justice Programs.

Mumola , C. J., & Karberg, J. C. (2006). *Drug use and dependence, state and federal prisoners, 2004.* Washington, DC: U. S. Department of Justice, Office of Justice Programs, Bureau of Justice Statistics.

Murray, J., & Farrington, D. (2005). Parental imprisonment: Effects on boys' antisocial behaviour and delinquency through the life-course. *Journal of Child Psychology and Psychiatry, 46*(12), 1269–1278.

Murray, J., Farrington, D., Sekol, I., & Olsen, R. F. (2009). Effects of parental imprisonment on child antisocial behaviour and mental health: A systematic review. *Campbell Systematic Reviews,* 4. Retrieved from http://campbellcollaboration.org/lib/.

Najman, J. M., Behrebs, B. C., Andersen, M., Bor, W., O'Callaghan, M., & Willams, G. M. (1997). Impact of family type and family quality on child behavior problems: A longitudinal study. *Journal of the American Academy of Child and Adolescent Psychiatry, 36*(10), 1357–1365.

Nesmith, A., & Ruhland, E. (2008). Children of incarcerated parents: Challenges and resiliency, in their own words. *Children and Youth Services Review, 30*(10), 1119–1130. doi: 10.1016/j.childyouth.2008.02.006.

Nickel, J., Garland, C., & Kane, L. (2009). *Children of incarcerated parents: An action plan for federal policymakers.* New York: Council of State Governments Justice Center.

Nieto, M. (2002). *In Danger of Falling through the Cracks: Children of Arrested Parents.* (CRB 02–009). Sacramento: California Research Bureau. Retrieved from http://www.library.ca.gov/crb/02/09/02–009.pdf.

Nolan, C. M. (2003). *Children of Arrested Parents.* (CRB 03–011). Sacramento: California Research Bureau. Retrieved from http://www.library.ca.gov/crb/03/11/03–011.pdf.

Nurco, D. N., Blatchley, R. J., Hanlon, T. E., & O'Grady, K. E. (1999). Early deviance and related risk factors in the children of narcotic addicts. *American Journal of Drug and Alcohol Abuse, 25*(1), 25–45.

Nurco, D. N., Blatchley, R. J., Hanlon, T. E., O'Grady, K. E., & McCarren, M. (1998). The family experiences of narcotic addicts and their subsequent parenting practices. *American Journal of Drug and Alcohol Abuse, 24*(1), 37–59.

Onyskiw, J. E. (2003). Domestic violence and children's adjustment: A review of research. In R. A. Geffner, R. S. Igelman, & J. Zellner (Eds.), *The Effects of Intimate Partner Violence on Children* (pp. 11–45). New York: Haworth Maltreatment & Trauma Press.

Osborn, S. G., & West, D. J. (1979). Conviction records of fathers and sons compared. *British Journal of Criminology, 19*(2), 120–133.

Osborne, C., & McLanahan, S. (2007). Partnership instability and child well-being. *Journal of Marriage and Family, 69*(4), 1065–1083. doi: 10.1111/j.1741–3737.2007.00431.x.

Osofsky, J. D. (1999). The impact of violence on children. *Future of Children, 9*(3), 33–49.

Overstreet, S. (2000). Exposure to community violence: Defining the problem and understanding the consequences. *Journal of Child & Family Studies, 9*(1), 7–25.

Owen, B., & Bloom, B. (1995). Profiling women prisoners: Findings from national surveys and a California sample. *Prison Journal, 75*(2), 165.

Pearson, J., Muller, C., & Frisco, M. L. (2006). Parental involvement, family structure, and adolescent sexual decision making. *Sociological Perspectives, 49*(1), 67–90.

Petersilia, J. (2003). *When Prisoners Come Home: Parole and Prisoner Reentry.* New York: Oxford University Press.

Pettit, B., & Western, B. (2004). Mass imprisonment and the life course: Race and class inequality in U.S. incarceration. *American Sociological Review, 69,* 151–169.

Peugh, J., & Belenko, S. (1999). Substance-involved women inmates: Challenges to providing effective treatment. *Prison Journal, 79*(1), 23–44.

Phillips, S. D., Burns, B. J., Wagner, H. R., Kramer, T. L., & Robbins, J. M. (2002). Parental incarceration among adolescents receiving mental health services. *Journal of Child and Family Studies, 11*(4), 385–399.

Poehlmann, J. (2005a). Children's family environments and intellectual outcomes during maternal incarceration. *Journal of Marriage and Family, 67*(5), 1275–1285. doi: 10.1111/j.1741–3737.2005.00216.x.

Poehlmann, J. (2005b). Incarcerated mothers' contact with children, perceived family relationships, and depressive symptoms. *Journal of Family Psychology, 19*(3), 350–357.

Pratt, T. C., & Cullen, F. T. (2005). Assessing macro-level predictors and theories of crime: A meta-analysis. In M. Tonry (Ed.), *Crime and Justice: A Review of Research* (Vol. 32, pp. 373–450). Chicago: University of Chicago Press.

Puddefoot, G., & Foster, L. K. (2007). Keeping children safe when their parents are arrested: Local approaches that work. Sacramento: California Research Bureau.

Purdy, M., Jacobs, A., & Jones, R. L. (2003, January 12). Life behind basement doors: Family and system fail boys. *New York Times,* pp. L1, L30. Retrieved from http://proquest.umi.com/pqdweb?did=866786152&sid=4&Fmt=2&clientId=16246&RQT=309&VName=HNP.

Rank, M. A. (2001). The effect of poverty on America's families: Assessing our research knowledge. *Journal of Family Issues, 22*(7), 882–903.

Reiss, A. J., Jr., & Roth, J. A. (1993). *Understanding and Preventing Violence: Panel on the Understanding and Control of Violent Behavior.* Washington, DC: National Academy Press.

Rennison, C. M. (2000). *Intimate partner violence.* Washington, DC: U.S. Department of Justice, Bureau of Justice Statistics.

Rennison, C. M. (2003). *Intimate partner violence, 1993–2001.* Washington, DC: U.S. Department of Justice, Bureau of Justice Statistics.

Richie, B. E. (1996). *Compelled to Crime: The Gender Entrapment of Battered Black Women.* New York: Routledge.

Richters, J. E., & Martinez, P. (1993). The NIMH Community Violence Project: I. Children as victims of and witnesses to violence. *Psychiatry, 56*(1), 7–21.

Rishel, C., Sales, E., & Koeske, G. F. (2005). Relationships with non-parental adults and child behavior. *Child & Adolescent Social Work Journal, 22*(1), 19–34.

Robins, L. N., West, P. A., & Herjanic, B. L. (1975). Arrest and delinquency in two generations: A study of black urban families and their children. *Journal of Child Psychology and Psychiatry, 16*(2), 125–140.

Roman, C. G., & Travis, J. (2006). Where will I sleep tomorrow? Housing, homelessness, and the returning prisoner. *Housing Policy Debate, 17*(2), 389–418.

Rose-Krasnor, L., Busseri, M. A., Willoughby, T., & Chalmers, H. (2006). Breadth and intensity of youth activity involvement as contexts for positive development. *Journal of Youth and Adolescence, 35*(3), 385–399.

Runyon, M. K., Deblinger, E., Ryan, E. E., & Thakkar-Kolar, R. (2004). An overview of child physical abuse. *Trauma, Violence, & Abuse, 5*(1), 65–85. doi: 10.1177/1524838003259323.

Sabol, W. J., & Minton, T. D. (2008). *Jail inmates at midyear 2007.* Washington, DC: U.S. Department of Justice, Bureau of Justice Statistics.

Sack, W. H. (1977). Children of imprisoned fathers. *Psychiatry, 40*(2), 163–174.

Sack, W. H., Seidler, J., & Thomas, S. (1976). The children of imprisoned parents: A psychosocial exploration. *American Journal of Orthopsychiatry, 46*(4), 618–628.

Sampson, R. J., & Laub, J. H. (1993). *Crime in the Making: Pathways and Turning Points through Life.* Cambridge, MA: Harvard University Press.

Saunders, B. E. (2003). Understanding children exposed to violence: Toward an integration of overlapping fields. *Journal of Interpersonal Violence, 18*(4), 356–376.

Schafer, N. E., & Dellinger, A. B. (1999). Jailed parents: An assessment. *Women & Criminal Justice, 10*(4), 73–91.

Seccombe, K. (2000). Families in poverty in the 1990s: Trends, causes, consequences, and lessons learned. *Journal of Marriage & the Family, 62*(4), 1094–1113.

Sen, B. (2010). The relationship between frequency of family dinner and adolescent problem behaviors after adjusting for other family characteristics. *Journal of Adolescence, 33*(1), 187–196. doi: 10.1016/j.adolescence.2009.03.011.

Sharp, S. F., & Marcus-Mendoza, S. T. (2001). It's a family affair: Incarcerated women and their families. *Women & Criminal Justice, 12*(4), 21–49.

Shaw, R. (1987). *Children of Imprisoned Fathers.* London: Hodder and Stoughton.

Sheridan, M. J. (1996). Comparison of the life experiences and personal functioning of men and women in prison. *Families in Society, 77*(7), 423–434.

Singer, M. I., Bussey, J., Song, L.-Y., & Lunghofer, L. (1995). The psychosocial issues of women serving time in jail. *Social Work, 40*(1), 103–113.

Skinner, D., & Swartz, L. (1989). The consequences for preschool children of a parent's detention: A preliminary South African clinical study of caregivers' reports. *Journal of Child Psychology and Psychiatry, 30*(2), 243–259.

Smith, A., Krisman, K., Strozier, A. L., & Marley, M. A. (2004). Breaking through the bars: Exploring the experiences of addicted incarcerated parents whose children are cared for by relatives. *Families in Society, 85*(2), 187–195.

Smith, B. E., & Elstein, S. G. (1994). *Children on hold: Improving the response to children whose parents are arrested and incarcerated.* Washington, DC: ABA Center on Children and the Law.

Smith, J. R., Brooks-Gunn, J., & Klebanov, P. K. (1997). Consequences of living in poverty for young children's cognitive and verbal ability and early school achievement. In G. J. Duncan & J. Brooks-Gunn (Eds.), *Consequences of Growing Up Poor* (pp. 132–189). New York: Russell Sage Foundation.

Snyder, H. N., Espiritu, R., Huizinga, D., Loeber, R., & Petechuk, D. (2003). *Prevalence and development of child delinquency.* Washington, DC: U.S. Department of Justice, Office of Juvenile Justice and Delinquency Prevention.

Solomon, A. L., Johnson, K. D., Travis, J., & McBride, E. C. (2004). *From prison to work: The employment dimensions of prisoner reentry.* Washington, DC: Urban Institute.

Sowder, B. J., & Burt, M. R. (1980). *Children of Heroin Addicts: An Assessment of Health, Learning, Behavioral, and Adjustment Problems.* New York: Praeger.

Stack, C. B. (1974). *All Our Kin: Strategies for Survival in a Black Community.* New York: Harper & Row.

Stanton, A. M. (1980). *When Mothers Go to Jail.* Lexington, MA: Lexington Books.

Stein, B. D., Jaycox, L. H., Kataoka, S., Rhodes, H. J., & Vestal, K. D. (2003). Prevalence of child and adolescent exposure to community violence. *Clinical Child and Family Psychology Review, 6*(4), 247–264.

Straus, M. A. (2001). *Beating the Devil out of Them: Corporal Punishment in American Families and Its Effects on Children*. New Brunswick, NJ: Transaction Publishers.

Straus, M. A., & Gelles, R. J. (1990). How violent are American families? Estimates from the National Family Violence Resurvey and other studies. In M. A. Straus & R. J. Gelles (Eds.), *Physical Violence in American Families: Risk Factors and Adaptations to Violence in 8,145 Families* (pp. 95–112). New Brunswick, NJ: Transaction Publishers.

Straus, M. A., Gelles, R. J., & Steinmetz, S. K. (1980). *Behind Closed Doors: Violence in the American Family*. New York: Doubleday.

Sutherland, E. H., Cressey, D. R., & Luckenbill, D. F. (1992). *Principles of Criminology*. Dix Hills, NY: General Hall.

Tjaden, P., & Thoennes, N. (2000). *Extent, nature, and consequences of intimate partner violence: Findings from the National Violence Against Women Survey*. Washington, DC: National Institute of Justice and Centers for Disease Control and Prevention.

Trice, A. D., & Brewster, J. (2004). The effects of maternal incarceration on adolescent children. *Journal of Police and Criminal Psychology, 19*(1), 27–35.

Trickett, P. K., & McBride-Chang, C. (1995). The developmental impact of different forms of child abuse and neglect. *Developmental Review, 15*(3), 311–337.

Tubbs, C. Y., Roy, K. M., & Burton, L. M. (2005). Family ties: Constructing family time in low-income families. *Family Process, 44*(1), 77–91.

U. S. Census Bureau. (2004). *Educational attainment in the United States: 2003*. Detailed tables for Current Population Report, 20-550. Retrieved July 24, 2007, from http://www.census.gov/population/www/socdemo/education/cps2003.html.

VanDeMark, N. R., Russell, L. A., O'Keefe, M., Finkelstein, N., Noether, C. D., & Gampel, J. C. (2005). Children of mothers with histories of substance abuse, mental illness, and trauma. *Journal of Community Psychology, 33*(4), 445–459.

Visher, C. A., & Travis, J. (2003). Transitions from prison to community: Understanding individual pathways. *Annual Review of Sociology, 29*, 89–113.

Waller, M. A. (2001). Resilience in ecosystemic context: Evolution of the concept. *American Journal of Orthopsychiatry, 71*(3), 290–297.

Walmsley, R. (2009). *World prison population list* (8th ed.) London: International Centre for Prison Studies, Kings College.

Walters, G. D. (1992). A meta-analysis of the gene-crime relationship. *Criminology, 30*(4), 595–613.

Werner, E. E., & Smith, R. S. (1982). *Vulnerable but Invincible: A Longitudinal Study of Resilient Children and Youth*. New York: McGraw-Hill.

Werner, E. E., & Smith, R. S. (1992). *Overcoming the Odds: High Risk Children from Birth to Adulthood*. Ithaca, NY: Cornell University Press.

West, H. C., & Sabol, W. J. (2008). *Prisoners in 2007*. Washington, DC: U.S. Department of Justice, Bureau of Justice Statistics.

West, M. O., & Prinz, R. J. (1987). Parental alcoholism and childhood psychopathology. *Psychological Bulletin, 102*(2), 204–218.

Wilbur, M. B., Marani, J. E., Appugliese, D., Woods, R., Siegel, J. A., Cabral, H. J., & Frank, D. A. (2007). Socioemotional effects of fathers' incarceration on low-income, urban, school-aged children. *Pediatrics, 120*(3), e678–685.

Wildeman, C. (2009). Parental imprisonment, the prison boom, and the concentration of childhood disadvantage. *Demography, 46*(2), 265–280. doi: 10.1353/dem.0.0052.

Wilson, G. (2007). Racialized life-chance opportunities across the class structure: The case of African Americans. *Annals of the American Academy of Political and Social Science, 609*(1), 215–232.

Wolak, J., & Finkelhor, D. (1998). Children exposed to partner violence. In J. L. Jasinski &
    L. M. Williams (Eds.), *Partner Violence: A Comprehensive Review of 20 Years of Research*
    (pp. 73–112). Thousand Oaks, CA: Sage Publications.

Woolley, M. E., & Bowen, G. L. (2007). In the context of risk: Supportive adults and the
    school engagement of middle school students. *Family Relations, 56*(1), 92–104.

Yllo, K., & Straus, M. A. (1981). Interpersonal violence among married and cohabiting
    couples. *Family Relations, 30*(3), 339–347.

Zalba, S. R. (1964). *Women Prisoners and Their Families.* Los Angeles: Delmar.

INDEX

225

ABOUT THE AUTHOR

JANE A. SIEGEL, Ph.D., is associate professor of criminal justice and chair of the Department of Sociology, Anthropology, and Criminal Justice at Rutgers University in Camden, New Jersey. She is also an associate at the Rutgers University Center for Children and Childhood Studies in Camden and an affiliate of the Center for Behavioral Health Services and Criminal Justice Research at Rutgers in New Brunswick. She received her M.S. and Ph.D. degrees in criminology from the University of Pennsylvania, and her B.A. at Drew University. She has been principal investigator and coprincipal investigator on several federally funded studies focused on topics such as child abuse, the effect of parental incarceration on children, and risk factors for victimization, and has published numerous articles on these topics. In addition to her academic work, the author is actively involved in community organizations that reflect her research interests, serving as a board member for an alternative-to-incarceration program for female offenders, as an advisory committee member for a program for female jail inmates who are pregnant or mothers of young children, and as a member of a multiagency working group to enhance services to incarcerated women.